HISTORY
OF RUSSIA

Sergei Mikhailovich Soloviev

The
Academic International Press
Edition
of
Sergei M. Soloviev

History of Russia From Earliest Times

G. EDWARD ORCHARD
General Editor

Contributing Editors

HUGH F. GRAHAM

JOHN D. WINDHAUSEN

ALEXANDER V. MULLER

K.A. PAPMEHL

RICHARD HANTULA

WALTER J. GLEASON, JR.

WILLIAM H. HILL

G. EDWARD ORCHARD

LINDSEY A.J. HUGHES

NICKOLAS LUPININ

GEORGE E. MUNRO

DANIEL L. SCHLAFLY, JR.

ANTHONY L.H. RHINELANDER

PATRICK J. O'MEARA

SERGEI M. SOLOVIEV

History of Russia

Volume 37
Empress Elizabeth's Reign
1741–1744

Edited, Translated and With an
Introduction by

Patrick J. O'Meara

Academic International Press
1996

The Academic International Press Edition of S.M. Soloviev's
History of Russia From Earliest Times in fifty volumes.

Volume 37. *Empress Elizabeth's Reign, 1741–1744*
Unabridged translation of the text of Chapters II-IV of Volume 21
of S.M. Soloviev's *Istoriia Rossii s drevneishikh vremen* as found
in Volume XI of this work published in Moscow in 1965, with
added annotation by Patrick J. O'Meara.

ISBN: 0-87569-175-7

Composition by Peggy Pope

Printed in the United States of America

ACADEMIC INTERNATIONAL PRESS
Box 1111 • Gulf Breeze FL 32562-1111 • USA

CONTENTS

Problems—Foreign Affairs—Congress and Treaty of
Åbo—A Popular View

WEIGHTS AND MEASURES

Linear and Surface Measures

Arshin: 16 vershoks, 28 in (diuims) 72.12 cm

Chetvert (quarter): 1/4 arshin, 1/2 desiatine, 1.35 acre (sometimes 1.5 desiatinas or ca 4.1 acres)

Desiatina: 2,400 square sazhens, 2.7 acres, 1.025 hectares

Diuim: 1 inch, 2.54 cm

Fut: 12 diuims, 1 foot, 30.48 cm

Obza (areal): c. 10 chetverts, 13–15 acres

Osmina: 1/4 desiatina, 600 sq. sazhens, .256 hectare

Sazhen: 3 arshins, 7 feet, 2.133 m

Vershok: 1.75 in, 4.445 cm, 1/16 arshin

Verst: 500 sazhens, 1,166 yards and 2 feet, .663 miles, 1.0668 km

Voloka (plowland): 19 desiatinas, 20 hectares, 49 acres

Liquid Measures

Bochka (barrel): 40 vedros, 121 gallons, 492 liters

Chetvert (quarter): 1.4 bochkas, 32.5 gallons

Kufa: 30 stofy

Stof: Kruzhka (cup), 1/10 vedro, c. 1.3 quarts, 1.23 liters

Vedro (pail): 3.25 gallons, 12.3 liters, 10 stofy

Weights

Berkovets: 361 lbs, 10 puds

Bezmen: c. 1 kg., 2.2 lbs

Chetverik (grain measure dating from 16th century): 1/8 chetvert, 15.8 lbs

Chetvert (grain measure): 1/4 rad, 3.5 puds, 126.39 lbs, c. 8 bushels

Funt: 96 zolotniks, .903 lbs, 14.4 ozs, 408.24 kg

Grivenka: 205 grams

Kad: 4 chetverts, 14 puds, 505.56 lbs

Kamen (stone): 32 funt

Korob (basket): 7 puds, 252 lbs

Osmina (eighth): 2 osmina to a chetvert (dry measure)

Polbezmen: c. 500 g, 1 lb

Polosmina (sixteenth): 1/2 osmina

Pud: 40 funts, 36.113 lbs (US), 40 lbs (Russian), 16.38 kg

Rad: 14 puds, 505.58 lb

Zolotnik: 1/96 lbs, 4.26 grams

Money

Altyn: 6 Muscovite dengas, 3 copecks

Chervonets (chervonny): gold coin of first half of 18th century worth c. 3 rubles

Chetvertak: silver coin equal to 25 copecks or 1/4 ruble (18–19th centuries)

Copeck: two Muscovite dengas

Denga: 1/2 copeck

Grivna: 20 Muscovite dengas, 100 grivnas equals 1 ruble, 10 copecks

Grosh: 10 peniaz

Grosh litovsky (Lithuanian grosh): 5 silver copecks

Kopa grosh: 60 groshas, one Muscovite poltina, 1/2 ruble

Moskovka: 1/2 copeck

Muscovite Denga: 200 equals 1 ruble

Novgorod Denga: 100 equals 1 ruble

Novgorodka: 1 copeck

Peniaz: 10 equals one grosh (Lithuania)

Poltina (poltinnik): 50 copecks, 100 dengas, 1 ruble

Poltora: 1 1/2 rubles

Polupoltina (-nik): 25 copecks, 50 dengas

Ruble: 100 copecks, 200 dengas

Shiroky grosh (large silver coin): 20 Muscovite copecks.

Foreign Denominations

Chervonnyi: c. 3 rubles

Ducat: c. 3 rubles

Efimok: c. 1 ruble, 1 chervonets or chervonnyi

Levok: Dutch silver lion dollar

Thaler (Joachimsthaler): c. 1 ruble, 1 chervonets or chervonnyi

Note: Weights and measures often changed values over time and sometimes held more than one value at the same time. For details consult Sergei G. Pushkarev, *Dictionary of Russian Historical Terms from the Eleventh Century to 1917* (Yale, 1970).

PREFACE

This book is an unabridged translation of Volume 21, Chapters 2-4, which are pages 129-301 in Volume XI of Soloviev's *Istoriia Rossii s drevneishikh vremen* (History of Russia from the Earliest times, 29 vols., St. Petersburg, 1851-1879), published from 1962 through 1966 in Moscow.

For the sake of convenience I have subdivided the lengthy chapters of Soloviev's text. Chapter I of the translation corresponds to pages 129-142 of the 1962-1966 edition, Chapter II to pages 142-157. Chapter III corresponds to pages 157-181, and Chapter IV to pages 181-199, which is the end of Soloviev's Chapter II. Soloviev's third chapter, pages 200-248, corresponds to Chapters V-VI of this translation, the division occurring at page 226. Similarly, Soloviev's fourth chapter corresponds to our Chapters VII-VIII, pages 249-275 and 275-301 respectively.

The present translation endeavors to render the text and Soloviev's thought as accurately as possible. No attempt has been made to reproduce his style and text word for word for this would have yielded a bizarre Russianized text. The main consideration has been to make his history as readable as possible consistent with accuracy, while retaining at least something of the flavor of the language of the era. An effort has been made to find English-language equivalents for all technical terms Soloviev employs (ranks, offices, titles, legal, administrative and so forth) in the belief that English is no less rich in such terms than other languages. This is intended to smooth the flow of the narrative for the reader and to avoid marring the pages with annoying untranslated words. The exception involves Russian words which have become common in English— boyar, tsar, cossack. In all of this the translator remains painfully aware of the inevitable shortcomings that may remain.

Soloviev's pages are featureless and interminable, one long and complex sentence marching after the last. To make the text easier to follow for today's readers, long paragraphs and sentences have been broken into shorter ones. Most of the subtitles are based on the descriptive topic headings clustered at the beginnings of the chapters in the Russian edition. These headings have been moved into the body of the text as subtitles to mark and ease for the reader the transition from one subject to another. In some cases, to even the frequency of breaks in the text or to show topics not listed by Soloviev at the beginning of chapters, new subtitles have been added. Soloviev's arrangement of the material has been followed strictly.

Brief explanatory or interpretive materials have been inserted into the text enclosed in brackets, or added as footnotes to each chapter at the end of the book. All material enclosed in brackets has been added by the present editor and all materials in parenthesis are the author's. Emphasized words or phrases in italics are the author's.

The general policy followed in annotating has been to identify prominent personalities at first mention, and to give explanation and elucidations of less common or obscure terms and passages, assuming the typical reader to have relatively little familiarity with Russian history. If brief, these have been included in the text in brackets; otherwise they appear as numbered footnotes at the back of the book by chapters. Most of the author's own notes are not included because their highly specialized archival, documentary and bibliographic nature is of value solely to specialists who, in any case, will prefer to consult the original Russian text. In addition, most of the notes added by the editors of the edition published in the Soviet Union, which also are technical in nature—fuller bibliographic citations than those in Soloviev's notes—have not been included. When the author's notes and those of the Soviet editors are included, they are so designated. All other notes are those of the present editor.

Russian personal names are preserved in their Russian form except for Alexander, Alexis, Michael, Nicholas, Catherine and Peter, which English usage has made familiar with respect to Russian historical figures, and important ecclesiastics whose names have been recast into Latin or Greek equivalents, especially for the earlier period of Russian history. This applies to prominent individuals; Russian forms usually are used for the less prominent. Certain other names and terms have been anglicized for the sake of clarity and because they are used widely—Casimir, Sophia, Danzig, boyar, rubles, versts, Dnieper river, and others.

The editors of the edition published in the USSR frequently have added patronymics and other names, and these have been retained without brackets; patronymics appearing in the original edition also have been included. Plural forms for names and terms which might be confusing have been anglicized—Vologdians rather than Vologzhane, Voguls and not Vogulichi, the Dolgorukys not Dolgorukie, and so forth. Even so, in a few cases the Russian plural form is used when this form is common. Most Slavic surnames show gender, and this has been preserved. Since an "a" at the word end usually signifies a female, Golovkin would have a wife or daughter Golovkina. The final transliterated "iia" in feminine personal names has been shortened to "ia"—"Maria" and "Evdokia" instead of "Mariia" and "Evdokiia."

Non-Russian names, locations, terms, ranks and so on are spelled according to the language native to the person or particular to the city, region or culture when this can be determined. Confusion arises at times because the text is not clear about nationalities. An excruciating example is Lithuania where at least three languages intermingle. In such cases the context is the guide used and as a last resort the Russian spelling in the text is accepted. Individuals whose names were once non-Russian but had been in Russian service for generations are named by the original spelling of the family name. Turkish, Tatar, Persian and other names and terms are spelled in the original according to accepted forms in scholarly books. In some instances, if not otherwise ascertainable they are translated from the Russian as given by Soloviev. The names of geographical locations conform to commonly accepted English usage—Podolia, Moscow, Copenhagen, Saxony and so forth.

With respect to transliteration, this translation follows a modified version of the Library of Congress system, omitting diacritical marks and ligatures, and rendering an initial "Ia-" and "Iu-" as "Ya" and "Yu" ("Yasnaia" and "Yury") and occasionally the initial "E-" as "ye" (Yermak, Yevlev); the suffix "-yi" or "-ii" as "y" ("Dmitry Poliansky," instead of "Dmitrii Polianskii"); and the form "-oi" has been replaced by "-oy" ("Donskoy" instead of "Donskoi"). The soft sign, indicated by an apostrophe in some transliteration systems, is usually dropped altogether ("tsar" instead of "tsar'"), although in some cases "i" has been inserted in place of a hard or a soft sign: "Soloviev" instead of "Solov'ev."

All dates, as in the original, except where otherwise specified, are according to the Julian calendar ("Old Style"); that is for the eighteenth century eleven days behind the Gregorian used in the West. A table of weights and measures is included at the front of this volume for the convenience of the reader.

A number of people have helped at various stages over the years that this volume of Soloviev's *History* has been in preparation. The original typescript was produced very efficiently before any of us ever had heard of word-processors by Mrs. Marlene Finch of the School of Modern Languages in Trinity College, Dublin. Dr. Lindsey Hughes, School of Slavonic and East European Studies, University of London, herself a Soloviev contributing editor, helped elucidate a number of problems of translation. My main debt is to Professor Edward Orchard, University of Lethbridge, Canada, for his invaluable criticisms and corrections of the typescript. While he is largely responsible for ensuring the publication of this section of the Soloviev project, any errors or defects to be found in it are entirely of my own making.

Patrick J. O'Meara

INTRODUCTION

Sergei Mikhailovich Soloviev (1820-1879) is the author of an unprecedentedly comprehensive history of Russia, of which the present volume is only a modest segment. It is on this m*agnum opus* that his formidable reputation as historian and scholar is based and most certainly will endure.[1]

Soloviev was born in Moscow, the son of a priest. In 1838 he became a student in the faculty of history at Moscow University, at a time when severe constraints were imposed on Russian intellectual and political life by the notoriously reactionary regime of Tsar Nicholas I. Indeed, the faculty of history was headed by one of its foremost apologists, M. P. Pogodin.[2] In spite of the rigors of censorship and the nefarious activities of the ubiquitous Third Section, the secret police, intellectual life did go on. Soloviev witnessed the intense discussions in Russia which were being conducted concerning Russia's relationship to its own past and to Europe in the debate between the home-based Slavophile camp and the more European-oriented Westerners.

After graduation he spent two years abroad (1842-1844) as tutor in the family of Count Stroganov and took advantage of his stays in Paris, Berlin and Prague to hear lectures given by the leading scholars of the day. In this way he became familiar with contemporary European trends in the study of history. Soloviev himself always considered that European and Russian historical development ran along parallel lines. For him Russia always was placed firmly in the European context. This particular volume is an illustration of the paramount importance Soloviev attached to considering Russia's development in the light of its relationship with Western Europe as a whole.

On his return to Russia his continued studies brought him into close contact with a group of liberal historians headed by T. N. Granovsky. In 1845 he completed his master's thesis, "Novgorod's Relations with the Grand Princes," and two years later successfully defended his doctoral thesis, "A History of the Relations among the

Russian Princes of the Riurik Dynasty." The brilliant young historian's reputation was established quickly, and in 1847 he replaced his erstwhile teacher Pogodin as professor of Russian history at the university. In 1851 he embarked upon his *History of Russia From Earliest Times*, proceeding at the astonishing rate of one volume every year until his death. He had planned to bring his account up to the nineteenth century, but on his death the last volume had reached 1774. The first complete edition of the History was published between 1893 and 1895. It is a work which has never been matched, either in size or in the enormous wealth of documentary material it incorporates. It can be said to have superseded the work of the early nineteenth-century historian N. M. Karamzin, although the latter's *History of the Russian State* was quite different, both in scope and character. The latter was above all a history of Russian absolutism rather than of the Russian people; its author, more properly an imaginative writer than a historian, was certainly as concerned with style as with content. Soloviev now set new standards of objectivity in the writing of history, demonstrably not a major concern for Karamzin.

He resisted any scheme of periodization of Russian history, an art since highly developed, arguing that "in history nothing suddenly comes to an end, and nothing suddenly begins; the new begins simultaneously with the continuation of the old." In this, as in many other views, Soloviev was influenced by Hegel, whose *Philosophy of History* he had read and studied very closely. He was primarily concerned with offering his own interpretations. As a result he has been considered a rather dry historian. It is true that his style does not scintillate like that of his celebrated pupil and successor, V. O. Kliuchevsky, to give just one example, but it is no less true that his monumental labor puts historians in his debt to this day. An historian of today has aptly said of him, "He is truly an historian's historian."[3]

This judgment is particularly applicable to the period of Russian history presented here. In providing a detailed account of the reign of Elizabeth, Soloviev broke new ground, since the period was not studied previously. Hitherto historians of the eighteenth century traditionally focussed on the reigns of Peter I and Catherine II. Consequently there were very few published sources available to him at the time of writing. He therefore was obliged to rely largely on archival material drawn from the papers of the Senate, the Secret Chancellery, the Ministry of Foreign Affairs and other official and unofficial collections. For this reason his study of Russia in the 1740s remains a valuable source of primary material for today's student of the period. Against this some reservations perhaps should be made. It will be noticed that Soloviev, while of necessity selective, did not avail himself of Senate documentation which might have provided a much fuller treatment of social and economic conditions in the 1740s. And while he tends to quote from source at considerable length, he often tantalizingly refrains from evaluating or commenting on the sources used. It may be felt also that his presentation of sources is somewhat unsystematic.

As suggested, the twenty-year reign of Elizabeth (1741-1762) by and large has been overshadowed by those of her illustrious father, Peter the Great (1682-1725), and her celebrated successor Catherine the Great (1762-1796). It was only during the first half of the eighteenth century that Russia emerged as a modern power in the European diplomatic system. Not fifty years before Elizabeth's accession Russia possessed no Baltic coastline, nor did it enjoy a southern outlet on the Black Sea. And less than a century before Russia was so little known to the West that in 1657 Louis XIV addressed an official letter, not to the reigning tsar Alexis, but to his predecessor Michael, who died twelve years earlier. Above all, Russia was insulated and isolated from Europe by the influence of the Orthodox church, which was almost pathologically wary of foreigners and conservative in the extreme.[4]

Yet the Russia inherited by Elizabeth had undergone far-reaching changes as a result of the reforms of Peter the Great. In particular this remarkable figure placed Russia for the first time in its history firmly on the map of Europe. On her accession, Elizabeth declared her intention to reign according to her father's tenets. This book is concerned with the first three years of her reign, and in particular with the development of her foreign policy. The circumstances of her accession require some amplification. Generally, the period from Peter's death to Catherine II's accession in 1762 is known as "the age of the palace revolutions" since the throne characteristically was won or lost with the active participation of the Guards regiments. It was as a result of one such conspiracy at the end of 1740 that power passed from one group of foreigners (mostly Germans) headed by Biron, to another headed by Münnich.[5] After Biron's arrest by Münnich in November 1740, Anna Leopoldovna was declared regent. She was the mother of the infant emperor, Ivan Antonovich, of the house of Brunswick (or Braunschweig). Münnich received the rank of "prime minister" and his supporter A. I. Ostermann that of "general-admiral."[6] Several Russian courtiers, abettors of Münnich, including G. I. Golovkin and A. M. Cherkassky, also were promoted. But Germans such as Ostermann and Mengden remained the most powerful figures in government.

Anna Leopoldovna was, as Soloviev pointed out, a nonentity. "She could not rule, she was bored by affairs of state, but at the same time she neither could nor would find a more experienced and capable person to take up the burden of government." It was therefore not difficult for Elizabeth, prompted by dissatisfied Russian Guards officers under their hated German overlords, to lead a palace coup on November 25, 1741 and proclaim herself empress. It is at this point that Soloviev takes up the story in this volume. Clearly Soloviev views Elizabeth's accession as a return to the legality of succession from which the reign of Anna Ivanovna (1730-1740) represented a deviation. Anna was the widow of the duke of Courland and the daughter of Ivan V, whereas Elizabeth was the daughter of Peter the Great. This explains the book's frequent reference to Elizabeth's avowed intent to return and hold fast to the government principles laid down by her father. Soloviev notes with approval the consequent fall from power of the Germans and their replacement by Russians. This again was in accord with the spirit of Peter's administration.

Soloviev makes little attempt to analyze the positions of such contemporary social groups as the peasantry, the nobility and the emergent middle class. Nevertheless he indicates the hard lot of the peasantry by mention of their frequent flight and use of troops to quell disturbances, which were generally on the increase at this time.[7] Industry was perhaps stronger than Soloviev suggests. For example, Russia had thirty-one blast furnaces on Peter's death in 1725, while ten years into Elizabeth's reign there were seventy-four. Light industry saw similar expansion. But coercive measures often were employed to secure an adequate labor force, a problem discussed by Soloviev. This in turn led to violent outbreaks of unrest.

The bulk of this book is given over to a study of Russian foreign policy. The extensive factual material presented here relating to this subject ensures the consultative value of the book to this day. Once again, Elizabeth's adherence to the policy of Peter the Great is emphasized. This period saw the increasing importance of Russia's role in the international arena. The weakening of the Habsburg empire and of Sweden, the strengthening of Prussia, and the increasing tension between England and France all contributed to threaten Europe's balance of power. Its continued stability depended largely on Russia. It was for this reason "understandable that Petersburg or Moscow, depending on the location of the imperial court, now should become the center of European diplomatic activity," as Soloviev writes. Of all the varied and complex problems confronting the foreign ministry at Petersburg, it is the issue of Russia's relations with Sweden, the Swedish war of 1741-1743 and the congress and Treaty of Åbo to which Soloviev devotes most attention. As concerns the personalities behind the intricate diplomatic maneuvers of Russian and European foreign policy, Soloviev focuses in particular on the brilliant, if at times precarious, career of Elizabeth's vice-chancellor, Alexis Bestuzhev-Riumin.

At this point, a few words should be said about Empress Elizabeth herself. In characterizing Elizabeth biographers inevitably refer to her unfailing courtesy and kindness, to her indolence, quick temper, piety and profligacy and, above all, to her gross extravagance. The British ambassador to Russia described her court in 1742 as the most expensive in Europe, and complained that he found it impossible to meet current expenses on his allowance. Similarly biographers like to recall that she reputedly changed her clothes up to six times a day, that she had an estimated fifteen thousand dresses on her death, most of which worn only once, and that at least one of her exasperated Paris suppliers refused her further credit.

One of Elizabeth's most striking characteristics was her remarkable lack of ambition. To effect her coup in 1741 she required persistent encouragement and coaxing from her supporters. She had missed a similar opportunity on Peter II's death in 1730, but subsequently never regretted it. "I am very glad that I did not assert my right to the throne earlier. I was too young, and my people would never have borne with me," she once declared later in her reign.[8] On that occasion she failed to respond to the entreaties of her followers to make her bid, and while she slept the Supreme Privy Council elected as empress her cousin, Duchess Anna of Courland, whose claim to the throne was inferior to her own.

During Anna Ivanovna's reign Elizabeth, who with her natural vitality and striking good looks easily might have eclipsed her cousin, took care to keep out of the political limelight, and contented herself with her favorite and essentially frivolous pastimes, among them hunting, gossiping and dancing. She was a most sociable young lady, and befriended many a guardsman, standing godmother for their children. While it is doubtful that there was any ulterior motive in forming such friendships, they were certainly to stand her in good stead in the years to come. The popularity which attended young Elizabeth wherever she went, and her obvious reluctance to abandon her several liaisons for the monogamy and monotony of marriage, served to increase Anna Ivanovna's unease. But Elizabeth appeared in no more of a hurry to take the throne from her than she had from Peter II before her, or from the regent, Anna Leopoldovna, after her.

For suggestions of Elizabeth's presence and appearance it is worth recording the first impressions of her successor, Catherine the Great (1725-1796). "Certainly it was quite impossible on seeing her for the first time not to be struck by her beauty and the majesty of her bearing. She was a large woman who, in spite of being very stout, was not in the least disfigured by her size, nor was she embarrassed in her movements; her head, too, was very beautiful."[9]

Soloviev's most famous pupil, V. O. Kliuchevsky, concluded his celebrated character sketch of Elizabeth by saying that she "was a clever and kind, but a disorganized and capricious eighteenth-century Russian lady who, according to Russian custom, was cursed by many while she lived, and was mourned by all when she died."[10]

The first chapter of the present work describes the aftermath and immediate consequences of the successful coup of November 25, 1741. These were the banishment of the Brunswick family to Riga, Elizabeth's invitation to her nephew, the duke of Holstein, to come to Russia, the reinstatement of those disgraced in the previous reign, notably A. Bestuzhev, and the fall of the German party led by Ostermann and Münnich. Soloviev notes with approval that their trials proceeded with due process of law, without torture or capital punishment, in stark contrast to those of the reign of Anna Ivanovna.

Soloviev stresses in the following chapter that the main feature of the domestic policy of Elizabeth's new administration was its intention to return to the principles of government established by Peter the Great. These are outlined in his review of finance, industry and attitudes to foreigners. It is clear that the lot of the peasantry saw no improvement under the new "all Russian" government, for numerous instances of flight are recorded. Those peasants who had supposed that, in accordance with Elizabeth's stated Petrine policy, once again they would be able to join the army, were punished severely for such presumption. Soloviev quotes at great length from church sermons in eulogistic support of Elizabeth and her declared policy. On the other hand, he notes the first indications of a markedly less ecstatic European reaction to the new policy. The chapter also contains a very detailed account of certain criminal cases dealt with by the Senate.

In connection with Elizabeth's coronation Soloviev quotes extensively from a sermon delivered to mark the approval of the church. Its main theme once more is fulsome endorsement of Elizabeth's deliverance of Russia from foreign hands, and her promised return to the Petrine ideas. To avoid any future confusion about the issue of succession, Elizabeth was quick to appoint an heir. Her choice fell on her nephew, the unprepossessing duke of Holstein, who was to reign briefly in 1762 as Peter III. Another sermon yields Soloviev source material relating to a conspiracy aimed at restoring the infant Ivan and his mother Anna.

This third chapter introduces what for this volume is a central theme, Russia's foreign policy. Soloviev demonstrates Russia's significance in European affairs, and shows why it was bound to support Austria against France and Prussia. In describing the petty jealousies and enmities at court which frustrated the immediate and wholehearted implementation of this policy, Soloviev defends Elizabeth against charges of inconsistency and vacillation by pointing out that she lacked natural brilliance and the advantages of a good education.[11] "It is worth noting," he writes, "that complaints that Elizabeth was lazy and pleasure-seeking came from irritated and impatient people." All the same, he acknowledges that "the pursuit of this policy was hindered by Elizabeth's personal attitude to Europe's courts and by her own like or dislike of their representatives in Russia."

Initial exchanges between the new empress and King Fredrik of Sweden in 1742 seemed to promise rapid settlement of the war between their two countries. But French intrigues against Russia served only, as France intended, to complicate matters, and led to a hardening of Russian attitudes. France insisted that it had encouraged Sweden to go to war against Russia only to help Elizabeth gain the throne, and now demanded as right the role of mediator between Stockholm and Petersburg. Elizabeth roundly rejected both these claims and made it clear that she would not yield an inch of the territory which, as she very well knew, Sweden intended to gain by declaring war. Preliminary negotiations broke down in May over the question of French mediation, then resumed in July as Sweden was collapsing in the face of Russia's advance. The following month saw the Swedish army's complete capitulation and the Russian occupation of Helsingfors (Helsinki). By the end of 1742 Russia was in a position to demand the appointment, as heir to the Swedish throne, of a candidate of its own choosing, and to declare its intention to retain all territory it now occupied in Finland. The complex series of moves underlying these events Soloviev traces by means of extensive quotation from the correspondence of those involved in the negotiations on behalf of Russia, Sweden and France.

Still on the theme of foreign policy, the fourth chapter is devoted entirely to a review of Russia's international relations. Typically, it is based on lengthy citation of official communiqués, dispatches and personal correspondence. A strong division of opinion existed between Elizabeth's most influential advisers, Bestuzhev and Lestocq, over the latter's espousal of French interests. Bestuzhev also deeply resented the intimacy Lestocq enjoyed with Elizabeth as her doctor. In the event, French stock fell considerably after Elizabeth's firm rejection of French mediation in the Swedish question, and the French ambassador, Marquis de la Chétardie, was obliged to leave Petersburg as a consequence. Elizabeth was warned constantly of the growing danger from France, both by Bestuzhev and by her ambassador to Paris, the writer and poet Prince Antioch Cantemir.

England's overtures to the new Russian government were based on the naval alliance with Peter and expectations of lucrative expansion in Anglo-Russian trade. London hoped to secure the services of the notoriously opportunistic and avaricious Lestocq to conclude an Anglo-Russian treaty of alliance. This was duly signed in December 1742. English and Russian ministers agreed on the need to maintain the balance of power in Europe by coming to the support of the beleaguered Maria Theresa, but Elizabeth was not so easily persuaded. She personally had no great liking for Austria, knowing that its attitude towards her candidacy for the Russian throne during the previous reign at best had been lukewarm. Meanwhile Austria's greatest antagonist, Prussia, was supporting actively French attempts to keep Russia and Sweden at war. In this way Prussia hoped to prevent their involvement in European affairs in general, and Russia's interference with Prussian designs on Austrian territory in particular.

Nearer home Russia was watchful of any change in the feeble *status quo* in Poland, since it represented in the words of one commentator "the threshold over which Russia stepped into Europe." King August III, the elector of Saxony, had been placed on the Polish throne with Russian backing. But Polish political life was dominated by the internecine strife of a few ancient noble families.[12] In any case Poland's fear of an increasingly powerful Prussia obliged it to look to St. Petersburg for support. To the south France attempted to rouse Turkey against Russia but shrewdly suspicious of French and Swedish blandishments, and more immediately concerned with Persia, Turkey refused to be drawn into any such conflict.

In marked contrast to the frenetic activity of Europe's diplomats was the laxity and inefficiency of Russia's government institutions. The fifth chapter gives an account of attempts made to remedy this state of affairs. The rigorous policy of russification applied to such national minorities as the Mordvinians apparently meets with Soloviev's approval. Nevertheless the Senate urged a cautious approach in dealing with the Old Believers. Soloviev illustrates the friction between the Senate and the Holy Synod, especially over matters of criminal jurisdiction, with a number of graphic examples. The Holy Synod at this time called for a complete ban on Western books and on their translation into Russian.

Viewing the growing struggle at court to sway Russia's foreign policy, Soloviev's own sympathies are clearly with the "Russian" group headed by Bestuzhev, and against Lestocq and his associates whose prime concern he viewed as personal advancement rather than Russia's best interests. Considering the peace negotiations with

Sweden resumed at Åbo, he finds the Swedes hard bargainers in the face of Russia's demands. By agreeing to accept Russia's candidate as heir to the throne, the Swedes maneuvered to retain as much of Finland as possible. But bickering and discord among the delegates on both sides compounded the problem of reaching a satisfactory conclusion. Sweden pointed to the potential threat from Denmark, were it to comply with the terms demanded by Russia. Ultimately the Treaty of Åbo (1743) allowed Russia to secure acceptance of its chosen heir, and gain a small part of Finnish territory.

An immediate consequence of the Treaty of Åbo was, as Sweden had foreseen, mobilization in Denmark. In Chapter VI Soloviev describes the joint countermeasures taken by Russia and Sweden, and the arrival in Sweden of the newly-elected crown prince, Bishop Adolf Friedrich of Lübeck.

Russia's ambassador to France rightly judged French interests in the outcome of Åbo to be at odds with Russia's, and warned his government against any rapprochement with France. Bestuzhev welcomed Cantemir's caveat, but determined opponents in Russia, with active French support, were bent on overthrowing the vice-chancellor at any price. An unsuccessful attempt was made to implicate Bestuzhev in a somewhat nebulous conspiracy, which Soloviev describes at length. Far from establishing Bestuzhev's guilt, it served merely to strengthen Elizabeth's confidence in him. The fate of those whose guilt was established showed, incidentally, just how vindictive Elizabeth could be. The affair did have one serious consequence. The proven complicity of Marquis Botta, Maria Theresa's envoy to Petersburg, very nearly wrecked the already fragile accord between her and Elizabeth. Just such an estrangement between the two sovereigns was sought ardently by the French, together with supporters at the court of Petersburg, to prevent the restoration of political equilibrium in Europe which, they felt, would militate against French interests. The documented exchange on the Botta affair between the two monarchs, which Soloviev reproduces, represents some of the most remarkable pages of this section of his history, and shows Elizabeth to be capable of surprisingly cogent argument.

In spite of setbacks encountered by Bestuzhev's enemies, attempts to unseat him and his brother, the marshal of the court, continued unabated. But Bestuzhev unexpectedly stole a march on his adversaries in exposing the true nature of their aims by having their correspondence intercepted and deciphered. The most incriminating passages he passed on to Elizabeth with his own acerbic comments appended. Soloviev includes several examples. Upon the surprise return from France of Elizabeth's old friend, Marquis de la Chétardie, the intrigues against Bestuzhev acquired a new momentum, and his fate, together with that of his foreign policy, hung in the balance.

At this point Soloviev interrupts his account of foreign affairs and returns, at the beginning of Chapter VII, to domestic themes already touched on in Chapter V. The inefficiency in administration noted in 1742 persisted through 1744. Absenteeism occurred on a quite extraordinary scale. Typical of the apparent inability of the machinery of government to respond to a crisis was the salt shortage of 1744. In February of that year the producers of salt, a privately owned monopoly, petitioned the Senate for state assistance. Eventually, in September, the Senate responded with threats and bluster; beyond making similar threats two months later, it left the matter unsatisfactorily resolved. Industry was not flourishing as it might because of an acute shortage of labor, while smoldering discontent among the peasantry flared up in places in the form of armed rebellion.

Church life, too, was marked by unrest at this time. Dissent from Orthodoxy was fairly widespread, and took various forms, one of which, the *khlysty* or flagellants, Soloviev describes in some detail.

In 1744 Elizabeth was preoccupied by a domestic matter which "in view of the current tension in Europe inevitably was bound up with political intrigue." This was the choice of a bride for the heir to the throne. Bestuzhev favored a Saxon match, but in the event a princess from the lowly house of Anhalt-Zerbst was chosen. This was the future Catherine II, and her selection, which seemed to represent a defeat for Bestuzhev, strengthened the resolve of his opponents to overthrow him. Their efforts were supported by the envoys of Prussia and France. Bestuzhev again hit back with the only weapon available to him: his enemies' intercepted and decoded letters. Interestingly, one of these which Soloviev quotes contains the only character sketch of Elizabeth in these pages. It is on the whole a profoundly shattering one, and has provided Elizabeth's subsequent biographers with some piquant material. Equally interesting, perhaps, is the fact that Soloviev himself refrains from commenting on it. It was its author, Marquis de la Chétardie, who finally brought down the wrath of Elizabeth on the anti-Bestuzhev faction. It further caused the veteran French intriguer's ignominious expulsion from the court of Petersburg, which in turn heralded the vindication of Bestuzhev, and his promotion from the office of vice-chancellor to that of chancellor. All this of course provides some remarkable insight into the extent to which Russia's foreign policy at this time was decided by the outcome of personal intriguing and machination.

In the final chapter Soloviev shows that, with France clearly embarrassed by Chétardie's expulsion, the way was open for Bestuzhev to intensify his warnings against Prussia. He was supported in this by representations made by England, urgently drawing Elizabeth's attention to the threat posed by Prussia. The Bestuzhevs' overwhelming anti-Prussian case is presented by Soloviev in lengthy quotations from their correspondence. Vice-chancellor Vorontsov similarly expressed his grave misgivings about growing Prussian influence in Poland and Sweden. Indeed, Russian diplomatic efforts were engaged actively in bolstering the power of the Swedish monarchy threatened by Prussian intrigue. Russia's main preoccupation in Poland at this point was to ensure that Russian Orthodox believers encountered no Catholic-inspired discrimination. Prussian efforts to woo Poland by suborning leading nobles were to Russia's relief unavailing, while the need to support Austria against Prussia, in spite of Elizabeth's antipathy for Maria Theresa as a result of the Botta affair, was eloquently demonstrated by Elizabeth's advisers, and by the Bestuzhevs in particular. Pressure was exerted on the Austrian government to ensure that the outcome of the Botta affair provided Elizabeth with the satisfaction she so adamantly demanded.

Soloviev's account of the reign of Elizabeth in 1744 concludes with the presentation of further proof submitted by Bestuzhev from intercepted letters testifying to the pro-Prussian intriguing at Elizabeth's court engaged in by the princess of Zerbst, mother of the young Catherine. This is followed by a plea from the character last mentioned in the book's opening pages, the disgraced Biron. In the most pathetic terms he begs Bestuzhev to secure for him some improvement of his wretched condition. It is on this note that the present volume of Soloviev's history comes to an end.

History of Russia

Volume 37

Empress Elizabeth's Reign

1741–1744

I

THE REIGN OF EMPRESS ELIZABETH PETROVNA
1741-1742

ELIZABETH'S RIGHT TO THE THRONE

The manifesto of November 25 promised, as noted, a second providing a "circumstantial and thorough elucidation."[1] This was published on November 26. It sought above all to explain the procedure of succession ordained by the will of Catherine I and affirmed by the loyal oath of all the nation. It provided that in the event of Peter II dying without issue the throne was to pass to Anna, daughter of Peter the Great, and to her heirs. Next in line were Princess Elizabeth and Grand Duchess Natalia Alekseevna.[2] The male gender took precedence over the female, but it also was stipulated that nobody could be a successor who did not belong to the Orthodox church or held any other crown.

On this basis, the only legitimate heir on the death of Peter II was Elizabeth. But Catherine's will was concealed by the evil and treacherous designs of Andrei Ostermann, in whose hands power was concentrated at that time. It was through his machinations, too, that Anna Ivanovna was elected to the throne. He supported her candidature and sought to remove Elizabeth because he knew that Elizabeth was aware of the many perfidious activities he had undertaken against the interests of the realm.

When in 1740 Anna was on her deathbed Ostermann drafted the decree on succession whereby the throne passed to the son of Prince Anton of Brunswick by Princess Anna of Mecklenburg.[3] Elizabeth thus suffered the insult of having the Brunswick family appointed heirs to the throne over her head. Anna, now at her last breath, duly signed the decree. All were obliged to swear allegiance to Ivan Antonovich, since the Guards and field regiments were under the command of Count Münnich and Prince Anton. Prince Anton and his wife also swore to observe the late empress's decree concerning the regency. But later, abetted by Ostermann, Münnich and Golovkin, disregarding their oath, annulled the decree and seized the government of the empire.[4] Princess Anna of Mecklenburg unashamedly styled herself Grand Princess of All-Russia, which brought about general disorder, and her rule was accompanied by extreme oppression. The situation was aggravated by Princess Anna's confirmation as empress of Russia in spite of the fact that she had a son.

BANISHMENT OF THE BRUNSWICK FAMILY

At this point Elizabeth sought to gain her parents' throne by appealing to all loyal subjects and "in particular and especially to the regiments of our Life Guards." The manifesto concluded with these words "Whereas Princess Anna and her son Prince Ivan and their daughter Princess Catherine have no rightful claim whatsoever to the Russian throne, nevertheless in consideration of the kinship by marriage of the princess and of Prince Ulrich of Brunswick to Emperor Peter II, and by virtue of our especial and innate imperial favor towards them we, not desiring to cause them any hurt and with all due honor and respect to them, graciously overlooking their aforementioned and divers crimes against us, hereby command that they all be amicably dispatched home."

At the time this manifesto was published Elizabeth really did want to send the Brunswick family out of Russia as quickly as possible. She told Chétardie[5] that "the departure of the prince and princess of Brunswick and their children is settled. In order to repay evil with good they are to be given funds to cover the expense of the journey and to be treated with the respect appropriate to their rank." Depending on their behavior towards her, Elizabeth wanted to settle a fairly substantial allowance on them. The princess was allowed to keep the Order of St. Catherine and Prince Anton, his son and his brother the Order of St. Andrew.

THE DUKE OF HOLSTEIN ARRIVES IN RUSSIA

At the same time the empress sent to Kiel for her nephew, the young duke of Holstein.[6] She was very anxious about whether he would be permitted to come to Russia at all, and in her anxiety hit upon the idea of detaining the now departing Brunswick family at Riga until the duke of Holstein reached the Russian border.

Accordingly Vasily Fedorovich Saltykov, who was accompanying the Brunswick family with instructions not to enter any towns, received an edict indicating that special circumstances demanded an immediate change of plan. He was instructed to continue the journey with as little fuss as possible and to halt a day or two at a certain place.

Major Baron Nicholas Friedrich Korf was sent to fetch the duke of Holstein, whom he brought back safely to Petersburg on February 5, 1742, together with his lord marshal of the court Brümmer and his lord chamberlain Bergholz.[7] The empress immediately bestowed on her nephew the St. Andrew ribbon with diamond star, while the duke awarded Razumovsky and Vorontsov[8] the order of St. Anne, which was instituted by his father. The duke's fourteenth birthday was celebrated on February 10.

It has been noted that the second manifesto contained Catherine's provision that, after Peter II, the throne should pass to the duke of Holstein. The only reason Elizabeth inherited the throne was that her nephew's candidature was precluded on grounds that he was not of Orthodox confession. But the empress had declined marriage and intended to pronounce her nephew heir to the throne. To do this it was essential that the duke adopt the Orthodox faith and until this condition could be fulfilled the grandson of Peter the Great was styled his royal highness, sovereign duke of Holstein.

PROMOTION OF BESTUZHEV-RIUMIN AND CHERKASOV

From the very first days of the new reign it was apparent that with the changes in government personnel immediate changes in government institutions were bound to follow. No trace was to be found of the cabinet's guiding light, Ostermann, nor for that matter of the cabinet itself, in the composition of the executive committee for domestic and foreign affairs, the so-called "assembly of ministers and generals constituted at court." Neither Ostermann, Münnich nor Golovkin were members of this assembly. Yet there were no new appointments made to replace those excluded, particularly Ostermann. Who was to conduct foreign affairs at such a difficult moment, when all Europe was in flames and when every attempt was being made to plunge Russia into them? There was nobody but the leading figure of the cabinet, Ostermann, whom the chancellor Prince Cherkassky[9] was not considered capable of replacing.

The fallen government found itself compelled, in order to counteract Ostermann, to recall Alexis Petrovich Bestuzhev-Riumin from exile.[10] The new government naturally had to retain this very Bestuzhev to effect the complete overthrow of Ostermann. It is said that Lestocq in particular disposed Elizabeth in favor of Bestuzhev, and further, that the empress predicted to Lestocq that Bestuzhev would be a rod for his own back,[11] though perhaps this prediction was thought up after the event.

Be that as it may, Lestocq's espousal of Bestuzhev's cause is readily understood, for it will be recalled that during his time of misfortune the old man established links with the court of Tsarevna Elizabeth, and with Lestocq in particular. This same circumstance, of course, compelled Elizabeth herself to regard the Bestuzhevs favorably. Bestuzhev was promoted and made a cabinet minister at the end of Anna's reign when Biron, Bestuzhev's patron, quarrelled with the Brunswick family and hence sided with Elizabeth, with whom he had never quarreled.[12] Their intimacy increased during the regency. It is understandable that Bestuzhev, whose interests were identical with those of Biron, should have become an intimate of the tsarevna and her court. Nor, of course, did he shrink from doing so. Biron's regency awoke in the new empress very agreeable memories, and Bestuzhev obviously figured prominently in what she recalled. Elizabeth's fondness for Bestuzhev therefore, even without Lestocq's intercession, is easily explained, as are Lestocq's own sympathies. An edict signed by the empress was presented to the Senate on November 29 requiring that Alexis Petrovich Bestuzhev-Riumin's seniority be deemed valid as from the time of his initial promotion by Empress Anna Ivanovna on March 25, 1740, "on account of his well-known and unjust suffering."

The same day a decree was published concerning the promotion of a man who from the outset was one of the leading members of the Bestuzhev party, Ivan Cherkasov. Formerly privy cabinet secretary, he was now promoted to senior state councillor and was given an appointment at her majesty's court in charge of dispatching the sovereign's personal correspondence. It was easy for Bestuzhev to intercede with Elizabeth for Cherkasov, a loyal servant of her father and mother who was persecuted after their deaths, at the same time as her own difficulties started.

The first ceremony in the new reign took place on November 30. In the present circumstances it was a very important one for it was a reminder of the empress's great father—the festival of the order of St. Andrew the First-Called. After liturgy in the court church the empress bestowed the Andrew ribbon upon the three generals-in-chief, Rumiantsev, Chernyshev[13] and Levashov, and upon Senior Privy Councillor A. P. Bestuzhev-Riumin. Count Golovin and Prince Kurakin,[14] who were already holders of the decoration, received the golden chains of the order. In addition, Peter and Alexander Shuvalov,[15] Vorontsov and Razumovsky,[16] all holders of decorations from the princess's former court, were made high chamberlains.

Then on various dates in 1741 and early in 1742 the following awards were made. Hermann Lestocq was promoted to senior privy councillor in recognition of his long and outstanding service and his extraordinary skill in the office of high crown surgeon. He also was appointed director of the Medical Chancellery and of the whole medical faculty with a salary of seven thousand rubles. Bestuzhev and Cherkasov did not forget their associates. Collegial Assessor Isaac Veselovsky was made senior state councillor and assigned to the College of Foreign Affairs; Abraham Petrov Hannibal, lieutenant colonel of the artillery, was promoted to major general, made chief commandant at Reval and received 569 serfs; Mikhail Petrovich Bestuzhev-Riumin was made lord high marshal of the court.[17]

EXILES RETURN

Together with the edicts concerning these conferments the Senate received directions ordering the return of those who had suffered in the previous reign. On December 4 Princes Vasily and Mikhail Vladimirovich Dolgoruky were returned from exile and restored to their former ranks.[18] In view of their advanced years, they were retired from service. But on December 23 Prince Vasily Vladimirovich was made president of the War College. Prince Sergei Mikhailovich Dolgoruky and Count Platon Musin-Pushkin were permitted to leave their estates, the former to reside in Petersburg and the latter in Moscow. Fedor Soimonov similarly was granted permission to reside wherever he wished. Suda, a former official, was permitted to leave Moscow for Petersburg.

Menshikov's celebrated sister-in-law, Varvara Arseneva, was not forgotten.[19] She was released from the convent to which she was banished in 1728 and permitted to reside in Moscow at a convent of her choosing. On January 8 all of Volynsky's confiscated estates were restored to his children.[20] Ten days later there followed an edict commanding Biron's return from exile, together with his brothers and Bismarck, and their retirement from service. Biron's Silesian estate, Bartenburg, which was given to Münnich, was restored to him. The sailor Maxim Tolstoy who was tortured and mutilated for refusing to swear the oath of allegiance to Ivan Antonovich in 1740 was promoted to captain in the army, granted retirement for his mutilation and given five hundred rubles.

Obviously denunciations relating to those disgraced during Anna's reign no longer were considered valid. The man who had informed on the Dolgorukys, the secretary of the Chancellery of Siberia, Osip Tishin, was relieved of his duties for disorderly conduct, disobeying orders, incompetence and drunkenness, and banned from service anywhere else.

THE IMPERIAL LIFE GUARDS

We noted that Elizabeth acceded to the request of the Grenadier Company of the Preobrazhensky Regiment to become its captain. In this connection a edict with the empress's own signature appeared on the last day of 1741. "Whereas at the time of our accession to the throne of All Russia, which we received by inheritance from our parents, the regiments of our Life Guards, and especially the Grenadier Company of the Preobrazhensky Regiment, so manifested their zealous loyalty to us that, aided by the Lord God Almighty, they secured for us without reservation and without bloodshed our accession to the throne, which was the earnest desire of the whole country. Wherefore we are grateful to the Lord God, bestower of all blessings, for His ineffable goodness to us and to all our nation, and, having in our gracious consideration the aforementioned loyal service, we are sensible of our bounden duty to display our especial imperial favor to them." The favor consisted of the award to the officers of the Guards and of the Ingermanland and Astrakhan regiments of a sum of money equivalent to one third of their salary. Twelve thousand rubles were to be distributed among the soldiers of the Preobrazhensky Regiment, nine thousand rubles among the men of the Semenovsky and Izmailovsky regiments, six thousand among the cavalry and three thousand to the Ingermanland and Astrakhan regiments.

The Grenadier Company of the Preobrazhensky Regiment received the honorary title of Imperial Life Guards, with the empress herself as honorary captain. All ranks were promoted as follows: captain-lieutenant to major general, ensign to colonel, sergeant to lieutenant colonel, and corporal to captain. Non-commissioned officers, corporals and common soldiers received hereditary ennoblement, their insignia bearing the inscription "for zeal and loyalty."

The officers, non-commissioned officers and common soldiers of the Imperial Life Guards received estates, some of them with numerous serfs. Adjutant Grünstein, for example, received 927, while 258 common soldiers each received 29. Grünstein's generous award is explained by the fact that he was consistently foremost among those guards who supported Elizabeth. The son of a Saxon Jewish convert, Grünstein came to Russia eighteen years earlier to seek his fortune. He began a business and made a considerable sum of money, then went off to Persia, where he spent eleven years. But while returning with his sizeable fortune he was robbed in the steppes by two Astrakhan merchants, beaten and left for dead. After regaining his senses he was taken prisoner by Tatars, somehow escaped from them and, once in Russia, filed a suit against the merchants who robbed him. But he petitioned in vain, for his opponents bribed the judges. In despair Grünstein joined the Preobrazhensky Regiment and abandoned Lutheranism for Orthodoxy.

On the last day of 1741 all grants earlier awarded by any but crowned monarchs, meaning those received during the reign of Ivan VI,[21] were annulled, with the exception of those who received promotion at the recommendation of their commanding officers.

OSTERMANN ON TRIAL

The officers and men of the Imperial Life Guards received their estates from the confiscated property of those arrested on the night of November 25. Chief among them was Ostermann, the "oracle" of three reigns.[22] As mentioned, an unjust judgement was pronounced on him in Elizabeth's second succession manifesto, in which he stood accused of concealing Catherine I's instructions and thereby keeping Peter the Great's daughter from the throne. Consequently no one could expect that forgiveness be shown the celebrated minister, against whom much hatred mounted.

Elizabeth's succession to the throne was accompanied by resentment at the state of affairs which prevailed during the two previous reigns, when foreigners occupied the highest posts and wielded greatest influence in military and civil matters. Most recently Ostermann, the most outstanding and influential, was the personification of this state of affairs. In Russia it was said of him that he was a German and had therefore placed a seal on *The Rock of Faith*,[23] while abroad his name was a byword for German domination of Russia.

After the coup of November 25 those who gained the upper hand and sought office were hostile to Ostermann and all had old scores to settle with him. He had no friends, for the celebrated diplomat's character tended to repel rather than attract, and such characteristics condemn people to isolation. Thus there were few to mediate with the new empress on Ostermann's behalf. All others hastened to outdo one another in turning her against him, justifying her dislike for him by reference to the general hatred he had incurred. And, as we have noted, this dislike was intense.

Elizabeth disliked Ostermann because she saw in him not the slightest trace of the sympathy she felt she was entitled to as the daughter of Peter the Great, the man who had launched Ostermann on his career. From the time of Peter II there were inevitably clashes between Ostermann and Elizabeth as they jostled for power. During Anna's reign there could be no reconciliation between them and, in recent times, fear had become an added ingredient in their mutual dislike. Elizabeth feared Ostermann more than anyone else, and fear is an emotion not conducive to affection. It has been observed that Elizabeth was unable to refrain from ridiculing Ostermann, who repaid her in kind. For all his caution and secretiveness, he could not refrain from mocking Elizabeth when they came to arrest him, which of course did nothing to mollify the rage of the new empress.

The commission charged to investigate Ostermann and his associates consisted of Generals Ushakov[24] and Levashov, Privy Councillor Naryshkin, Procurator General Prince Trubetskoy and Prince Mikhail Golitsyn. Ostermann was asked why he had not implemented Catherine I's directions concerning the succession and had participated in the election of Anna Ivanovna. He answered that he was with Peter II constantly in his illness and was in such a state that he forgot himself. He was sent for and informed of Anna's election. He countered by proposing Princess Elizabeth, but his suggestion found no agreement. During Anna's reign the empress frequently suggested in his presence and in Biron's that Elizabeth should be married off and sent abroad, and he personally submitted written proposals about this. To please Empress Anna he had written proposals barring Elizabeth and the duke of Holstein.

When accused of having patronized foreigners to the detriment of Russians, Ostermann conceded that more and more foreigners were being accepted into the Russian service, decorated and promoted to high posts, but stressed that there was no attempt to deprive Russians of promotion or of any other favor. In this regard he referred to the memorandum on government administration requested from him by the former regent and ruler, in which he recommended that Russians indeed have priority over foreigners in matters of promotion and decoration.

He was asked why he persuaded Princess Anna to imprison and interrogate Lestocq. Ostermann replied that it was because Lestocq was mentioned in a letter and in a warning sent from abroad. Ostermann claimed that he expressed the view that Anna, in order to show confidence in Elizabeth, should inform her of this. Should she not wish to do this alone, he felt she ought to do so in the presence of the cabinet ministers. When the princess informed him about her conversation with Princess Elizabeth he answered that in his opinion the princess really did not know about the Lestocq affair. He was ordered to try to secure the recall from Petersburg of the suspect French minister, Chétardie.

There then followed a question for which the "oracle" could find no answer. "Among papers found at your house were several of the commission's original minutes and rough notes relating to the Volynsky affair.[25] These contained insulting accusations against Volynsky. They include a note of your own views on the matter and a plan to reprimand him in the name of Empress Anna. They indicate the manner in which Volynsky was to be dealt with and arrested, the identity of those who were to be appointed to the commission, which included among others Privy Councillor Nepliuev, how this commission was to be set up, the indictments against Volynsky, the names of those who were to be arrested along with him, and the questions drawn up for Volynsky to answer. Why did you strive to eliminate Volynsky?"

"I am guilty and at fault," answered Ostermann, "Nepliuev was involved in this matter on my instructions because he was a friend of mine. Through him I counted on being informed about everything that was going on, since Volynsky turned against me." He added to his testimony that he planned the succession of the daughters of Princess Anna be accomplished by means of an appeal to the nation, and that he asked Löwenwolde to suggest this to the princess.[26]

The second state criminal was Field Marshal Münnich, who now found himself in the same unhappy position as his enemy Ostermann. The latter, as we have suggested, had won himself no friends and many enemies, thanks to his suspiciousness, his secretiveness, his peculiar way of speaking which nobody understood, his fearful ambition which caused him to tolerate neither superiors nor equals unless they were his intellectual inferiors, and finally his striving to place everything under his personal control, leaving others merely to sign what he put before them.

Münnich evidently was the direct opposite of Ostermann, with his lively nature and his constant readiness to speak frankly. But if today he acted so warmly and sincerely towards you that you could not find words enough to praise him and declared your readiness to go through fire and water for him, tomorrow he would treat you so unpleasantly as to repel you for good. This combination of good and bad qualities and, consequently, of good and bad actions, gave nobody confidence in the stability of their relations with the field marshal and caused people to treat him with caution, all the more so because he had no idea how to go about things and would hack his way to a desired goal, cutting down anyone who got in his way. Consequently, in his hour of need, Münnich was similarly unable to find anyone to defend him. Elizabeth herself could accuse him, apart from lack of respect, of outright hostile actions. During Anna's reign, for example, he kept her under constant surveillance.

There was in addition a curious accusation brought against him. The Grenadier Guards testified that when Münnich called on them to arrest Biron he also mentioned the names of Elizabeth and her nephew, the duke of Holstein. There were two conflicting depositions made on this issue, one of which stated "The grenadiers on watch who participated in Biron's arrest declared that the field marshal came and told them, 'If you wish to serve the sovereign, you should know that there is a regent who is oppressing the sovereign princess, her nephew Prince Ivan and his parents. This regent must be arrested.' He asked them 'Are your weapons loaded?' To this they replied 'We are ready and glad to serve the sovereign.' So they went off and arrested him but the next day, seeing that the matter was going nowhere, they gave up. Nine of these grenadiers, at this time serving in the Imperial Life Guards, were brought before Münnich. They confirmed that it was he who spoke to them about Empress Elizabeth and the duke of Holstein while they were standing at their posts on guard duty. Count Münnich replied that he never made any such mention of them. At first, each side held its position when brought face to face. But when his guilt was established by an ensign, by the sergeant-majors and men of the Imperial Life Guards, Münnich capitulated. He claimed that he asked to be relieved of his duties. He now remembered saying what was alleged, and only denied it before because he simply had forgotten ever having said it. He now admitted his guilt and begged for mercy. He doubtless uttered those words, he added, to give encouragement to the grenadiers in the execution of Princess Anna's will."

In this testimony Münnich lied about Biron's oppression of the crown princess and her nephew, but at least he was not guilty of deceit, since his main concern was to find out whether the soldiers were willing to serve the sovereign and, after all, the soldiers gladly indicated their readiness to do so. No other sovereign, apart from the one to whom they had sworn allegiance could have been meant. Other testimony speaks more clearly. "Münnich went up to the men on guard duty saying that if they wanted to serve Princess Elizabeth and her nephew they should go with him and arrest Biron 'for you can either have the duke of Holstein or Prince Ivan as sovereign, whichever you like.' When they heard all this, they declared that they were united in their ardent desire to serve her majesty (Elizabeth)."

Along with such notables as Ostermann and Münnich the relatively obscure Marshal of the Court Löwenwolde also fell into disgrace. Himself indebted to Catherine I for his advancement, he secured the promotion of Ostermann, who otherwise hardly would have been dubbed by Bestuzhev and his associates "the creature of Löwenwolde." Now Löwenwolde fell along with his "creature," hated by the Russians as a strong member of the German party by virtue of his position at court, but also unlamented in the German camp, which could find nothing positive about him at all. The Germans could not fairly claim that in Löwenwolde Russia suffered a great loss, as was maintained concerning Ostermann and Münnich. Finally Löwenwolde had aroused Elizabeth's personal displeasure, although he tried to justify himself by saying that he acted according to the ruler's command. Such justifications in such situations are not acceptable.

"I always had due respect," Löwenwolde said, "for the present sovereign. It is true that at the birthday celebrations for Prince Ivan a place was set for her at the common table with the other ladies. But this was done at the princess's orders, not mine. I did, in fact, put it to the princess that this might be insulting to the crown princess, but she nevertheless instructed that the princess's place be so set, adding that she herself would do what was necessary."

Golovkin, Mengden, Temiriazev and Yakovlev were obliged to give account of themselves for having been too enthusiastic in their service to the fallen government. At the end of the inquiry, on January 13, the Senate received a decree "to judge them according to the laws and edicts of the state." Apart from the senators themselves, the presidents of the colleges were invited to constitute this court. They discussed at length extracts from the inquiry's proceedings, then began to collect votes from the most junior upwards. Ostermann was sentenced to death. Prince Vasily Vladimirovich Dolgoruky went so far as to demand that he be broken on the wheel. Münnich was sentenced to be quartered; Golovkin, Mengden, Löwenwolde and Temiriazev, to be beheaded.

Bestuzhev, either because he was still feeling the effects of his own recent trial and sentence, or because he wanted to show the foreigners how magnanimous he was, told Pezold, secretary of the Saxon embassy, that he thought the sentences passed by the court on Ostermann and his associates were frightful. Chancellor Prince Cherkassky and Procurator General Prince Trubetskoy insisted, he said, that Ostermann be broken on the wheel, and Münnich quartered. Bestuzhev, on the other hand, hoped for the empress's mercy and, together with Lestocq, was making every effort to see that leniency was applied in this case.

On the morning of January 17 drum beats resounded through all the streets of Petersburg. Proclamations informed the people that on the following day at ten in the morning the public execution of the enemies of the empress and the violators of public order would take place. Early in the morning of the eighteenth crowds began to gather on the square in front of the colleges' building on Vasilevsky Island. Here the Astrakhan Regiment was drawn up round the scaffold, on which the fateful block could be seen.

That same morning the prisoners were brought from the fortress to the colleges' building. On the stroke of ten they were led out onto the square. The way was led by Ostermann, who because of lameness rode in a drayman's sledge pulled by a single horse. He wore a short wig, a black velvet cap and an old, short fox-fur coat, the one he usually wore at home. Ostermann was followed by Münnich, Golovkin, Mengden, Löwenwolde and Temiriazev. When all were formed up in a little circle, one beside the other, four soldiers lifted Ostermann, carried him to the scaffold and sat him on a chair.

The secretary of the Senate began to read the sentence, which Ostermann had to listen to with bared head. The former grand admiral heard himself accused of having concealed the will of Catherine I, drawn up projects which purported to show that Elizabeth and her cousin had no right to the throne and proposed, as a safeguard, to marry Elizabeth off to some beggarly foreign prince. "Worst of all," he had dared to draft plans whereby the daughters of Princess Anna of Mecklenburg were to succeed to the Russian throne.

There were several other offenses to be taken into consideration. He had neglected the defense of the realm; in important matters he did not consult formally with others in positions of responsibility, and instead usually acted according to his own will; he employed foreigners rather than Russians in several important posts, a slight against the entire Russian people. While in office he concentrated the administration of the realm into his own hands and excluded from government members of many venerable and illustrious Russian families. He aroused the animosity of the monarchs. He expelled numerous individuals from court and unleashed cruel and unprecedented tortures and executions on both nobles and non-nobles. Not even the clergy was exempted. He sought to stir discord among the Russian people, and so forth.

After the sentence was read, the soldiers placed Ostermann face down on the floor. The executioners bared his neck and placed his head on the block. One held his head by the hair while the other took the axe from the bag. At this point the secretary approached the condemned man, took out another scroll and read "God and the empress have spared your life." The soldiers and executioners lifted him up, took him from the scaffold, and sat him in the sledge where he remained while his accomplices had their sentences read out to them.

Münnich was told that he failed to uphold Catherine I's will, and took more trouble than most to see Biron made regent, only to overthrow him later for his own personal gain. He deceived the soldiers by telling them that the regent had Princess Elizabeth and her nephew under his absolute control, and that they might have as sovereign either Prince Ivan or the duke of Holstein. He wronged the present empress in many ways and spied upon her. As commander of the army he neglected the men, shamefully punished officers without trial, and squandered state money.

Golovkin, Löwenwolde and Mengden were accused of aiding and abetting the cause of Princess Anna. In addition Löwenwolde was accused of having squandered large sums accrued from sale by the state of salt, and Mengden of abusing his post as president of the College of Commerce. Temiriazev stood charged of supporting the cause of the former ruler. All three of them had their sentences commuted, without first having to ascend the scaffold.

No change was observed in Ostermann after his pardon apart from a slight trembling of the hands. Münnich conducted himself throughout courageously and proudly, Löwenwolde calmly and decently, while in Golovkin and Mengden the onlookers noticed abject fear. When the crowd realized it would be deprived of the beheadings promised them the evening before, riots began which troops had to break up. Some of the crowd were perhaps annoyed at being denied the spectacle of heads rolling, while others were irritated by the memory of the recent executions of the Dolgorukys and Volynsky a fate which they now saw Ostermann, Mengden and Löwenwolde spared. But the historian is bound to observe that in contrast to the bloody precedents of Anna's reign, none of these dangerous enemies of the realm were executed, neither were any tortured during interrogation.

Siberia was to be the place of exile for the reprieved. Ostermann was destined for Berezov, Münnich for Pelym, but Löwenwolde was only sent as far as Solikamsk. The task of dispatching these men from the fortresses to their places of exile fell to Prince Yakov Shakhovskoy, who was struck off the list of senators because of his friendship with Golovkin, and appointed chief procurator of the Holy Synod.[27] Shakhovskoy has left an account of how he carried out his dismal mission. When he went into Ostermann's cell he found him lying down and complaining bitterly about his gout. On seeing Shakhovskoy, he expressed regret for his crime and for having aroused the wrath of the sovereign. He requested that his children be received into the patronage of the empress. His wife was sent into exile with him. "I am unable to say anything about her, except that she wept and lamented bitterly," Shakhovskoy wrote.

Having sent Ostermann on his way, Shakhovskoy entered Löwenwolde's cell. "Hardly had I got into his cell," Shakhovskoy wrote, "which was large and dark, when I perceived a man shyly embracing my knees. In his confusion he spoke so quietly that I could not make out what he was saying. The sight of the unkempt head of hair and ragged, grey beard, the pale face and sunken cheeks, the worn and dirty clothing was not at all what I was expecting, and I assumed this was some prisoner from the artisan class who was arrested for some crime or other. Consequently, I turned to the officer and asked him to take the man away and to lead me to the cell of the former Count Löwenwolde. But the officer retorted that this was indeed Count Löwenwolde. At that moment I vividly recalled his customary behavior which I observed over many years, the exceptional favor and confidence he enjoyed at court, decorated with orders of chivalry, foppishly dressed and held in exclusive esteem above all others.

"With my head in a whirl, I came next to the cell which housed the former hero, Münnich, now a most wretched creature, expecting to find in him the bitterness and bewilderment of a defeated man. As soon as the doors to his cell were opened for me, I saw him standing with his back to the door, at the window of the wall opposite. He turned round immediately, with an air of confidence, his eyes quick and alert, an expression in his face which I saw frequently in the heat and smoke of dangerous battles. He came up to me, staring unflinchingly and waiting for me to begin. Maintaining as impassive an expression as I could, I informed him, in an appropriately official manner, as I had the other two, of the fate that lay in store for him.

"I noticed that his face betrayed annoyance rather than grief or fear. When I finished speaking he raised his arms in a pious attitude, and looking to heaven, said loudly 'God bless her majesty and her reign!' Then, lowering his eyes, he said after a pause 'Now that there remains nothing more for me to want or expect, I make so bold as to request that a pastor be sent with me save my soul from eternal damnation.' Everything was prepared for his departure. His wife was ready too. She looked as though she were about to leave on some pleasant outing. Dressed in her travelling coat and bonnet, and holding a tea set in her hands, she steadfastly concealed her inner turmoil."

For Shakhovskoy the hardest part of his duty was to arrange the departure of his "benefactor" Count Golovkin, whom he found in his cell in a very miserable state. "He was groaning bitterly because of the pain his gout and arthritis were giving him, causing him to sit motionless, able to move only his left arm. I went up to him and had to steel myself so that the pity I felt deep in my heart, and which was written on my face, would not cause me to shed tears, which in the circumstances might have had very unfortunate consequences for me. I pronounced the imperial judgment on him.

"Looking at me pitifully, he said that he felt particularly unhappy because he was brought up in plenty, and that his prosperity grew over the years to attain great heights, giving him no foretaste of the awful burden which he could not now find the strength to bear."

Apart from the five mentioned, the following received lighter sentences: the son of the field marshal, Marshal of the Court Münnich; a relative of Ostermann's wife, Privy Councillor Vasily Streshnev, for spying at court on Ostermann's orders; General Khrushchov, for his services to Ostermann; Senior State Councillor Andrei Yakovlev, for sharing the "extreme and close confidence" of Ostermann; Peter Gramatin, director of Prince Anton's chancellery; Secretary Semenov, for "constantly being in the company and personal service of Count Ostermann;" Major Vasily Chicherin, for spying on Elizabeth; and Secretary Pozdniakov, for having accepted payment for services rendered to Temiriazev in drawing up manifestos.

II

DOMESTIC AFFAIRS
1741-1742

REFORM OF GOVERNMENT INSTITUTIONS

The most influential members of the previous administration were
dismissed and sent into exile. But who would now replace them?
On December 12, 1741 an imperial edict was published stating that
the empress had examined the extent to which the system of government established by her father was undermined. By means of
intrigue several men re-established the Supreme Privy Council.[1]
Then a cabinet was formed equal in strength to the supreme council,
and differing from it only in name. This body was exceedingly
negligent in domestic affairs of state of every kind, while the administration of justice was greatly enfeebled.

To correct former irregularities the empress decreed that the
Governing Senate be restored to the position of strength and authority it commanded during the reign of Peter the Great. She further
ordered that all edicts and laws of Peter the Great strictly be observed and future laws enacted in full accordance with them. All
edicts subsequent to those of Peter were not to be suspended unless deemed inappropriate and disadvantageous to the realm in the
present circumstances.

The following were appointed to the Senate: Field Marshal
General Prince Ivan Trubetskoy, Grand Chancellor Prince Cher-
kassky, Lord High Steward of the Court Count Semen Saltykov,[2]
General Grigory Chernyshev, General Ushakov, Admiral Count
Golovin, Grand Master of the Horse Prince Kurakin, Senior Privy
Councillors Alexis Bestuzhev-Riumin and Alexander Naryshkin,
Lieutenant Generals Prince Mikhail Golitsyn, Prince Urusov and
Prince Bakhmetev, Privy Councillor Novosiltsev, and Senior State
Councillor Prince Alexis Golitsyn.[3] The procurator general, Prince
Nikita Trubetskoy, and the deputy procurator, Brylkin, had their
appointments confirmed.[4] The procurators in the colleges, chancel-
leries, government offices, in embassies abroad and in provincial
government were to be restored to their former duties.

The direction of foreign affairs was entrusted to Chancellor Prince Alexis Cherkassky and Senior Privy Councillor Alexis Bestuzhev-Riumin, who was promoted to vice-chancellor, and to Privy Councillor Brevern, who was restored to his former post in foreign affairs.[5] When any important matter arose they were to be joined in their deliberations by Admiral Count Golovin and Grand Master of the Horse Prince Kurakin. Like the Senate, the foreign affairs officials were to hold their meetings in the imperial quarters at the palace, in special apartments. When necessary the empress personally would attend them. The cabinet was abolished, and its place taken by a cabinet at court with the status it enjoyed in Peter the Great's day. Senior State Councillor Ivan Cherkasov was to be its chairman.

Subsequent to this edict, at the end of December 1741 and during 1742, Elizabeth attended the Senate seven times. Sometimes she arrived at eleven in the morning or a little earlier, sometimes at nine and remained for about three hours. The procurator general suggested to the reconvened Senate that one day a week be set aside for the most pressing affairs of state. On Fridays, therefore, the senators were to assemble earlier, at seven.

THE SENATE'S ACTIVITY

At the end of 1741 and during the following year the Senate adopted several resolutions revealing certain trends. An awful incident occurred in Siberia when a fourteen-year-old girl murdered two other little girls. Yet in the legal code and in subsequent edicts there was no definition about the age at which children were liable to torture and capital punishment. Clearly it was essential to give a ruling. The procurator general found an edict of Peter the Great which required the Senate to convene all the colleges to consider and discuss such cases. Accordingly, the presidents and several members of each college assembled. The procurator general put the issue to the meeting and then placed an hourglass on the table, allowing for two hours' discussion. The ensuing deliberations resulted in the decision that a child attained majority at seventeen years of age. Until that age children convicted of criminal offences no longer were liable to banishment, the knout or capital punishment. They could be flogged only and sentenced up to fifteen years penitence in a monastery.

At one of the meetings where the empress was present the procurator general asserted that in many matters of imperial decree simple slips of the pen were occurring. As a result the accused were sent to the Secret Chancellery and made to suffer while other cases were held up. The empress instructed that those thus wrongfully accused were not to be prosecuted further; mistakes were to be put right and care taken to see that the writing was accurate in future. On another occasion when she attended the Senate the empress decreed that those convicted of bearing false witness must not be knouted. If they were peasants, they were to be handed back to their landlords, while townsmen must be returned to their homes.

In another case the Senate directed that a priest from Moscow, one Mikhail Stepanov, of the church of St. Sergius in Rogozhskaia, was not to be executed for manslaughter of a woman worker. Instead he was to be exiled by the Holy Synod to a remote monastery and there to serve penitence. In two interrogations at the ecclesiastical court the priest admitted to stabbing the woman, provoked by her insolent words and behavior. At the Chancellery for Investigations he maintained under torture at three inquiries that he had knifed her in the heat of the moment, and that it was not a premeditated action. He claimed that his testimony to the ecclesiastical court was forced from him by the judges and secretary, who promised they would not send him to the Chancellery for Investigations if he confessed his guilt, but would place him in the care of a monastery. Forty-nine witnesses testified that at various times he was in a state of drunken frenzy and as a result there sometimes were no church services for two or three weeks at a time. Apart from this, they asserted, he was a good man and there were no other charges against him.

ATTITUDES TO FOREIGNERS

Elizabeth's accession to the throne coincided with popular discontent at the preponderance of foreigners in government service during the two previous reigns. The exile of Ostermann, Münnich, Löwenwolde and Mengden showed that this domination was to cease under the new administration. The foreign diplomatic community, because of its inexperience and ignorance of the course of Russian history and, indeed, of history in general, did not understand what was happening. Each interpreted this his own way, according to the interests he was sent to the Russian court to pursue.

The Germans bemoaned the fall of their countrymen, whom they considered their own representatives at court, looking askance at the new government in which they foresaw no good, maintaining that without Ostermann and Münnich Russia would be unable to extricate itself from its difficulties, and anticipated their return from exile. The Frenchman Chétardie took a different view. From the time of Russia's entry into the European family of nations France sensed a dangerous rival. France feared Russian support for Europe's weakest members, especially France's traditional enemy Austria, and the resultant frustration of French attempts at hegemony in Europe. For France, Russia was an uninvited guest in Europe, and its return to the Asiatic fold together with the transfer of its capital from Petersburg back to Moscow became the cherished aim of French foreign policy.

In pursuit of this policy Chétardie sought the overthrow of the Brunswick family through Elizabeth. He was therefore delighted by her hostility towards Ostermann and encouraged this trend by urging the empress to replace with Russians all Germans occupying diplomatic posts at foreign courts. The brilliant marquis did not understand that it was much more difficult for the daughter of Peter the Great to abandon the domestic policies instituted by her father than the lands he conquered, yet he realized that the latter course would be quite impossible for her. Nor did he foresee that Russians, clearly aware of purely Russian interests as a result of Peter's policies, would preserve Russia's new significance in Europe more jealously than would Germans.

From the very first days of Elizabeth's reign it was evident that national feeling was to manifest itself in a return to the precepts of Peter the Great. Consequently it was in accordance with these precepts that the question of Russian attitudes to foreigners was to be decided. Peter's view on this was known to everyone: while foreign experts should be recruited and their services utilized, they were not to be given preference over Russians who indeed exclusively were to occupy the most important administrative posts. Elizabeth made a clear pronouncement on this question at a meeting of the Senate on February 15, 1742 when she was informed of the recruitment of a military engineer, Lieutenant Colonel Hamberger, and of his posting to the engineer corps. "The quartermaster general of the engineer corps is to ascertain whether there is an eligible Russian lieutenant colonel. If not, Hamberger's qualifications are to be scrutinized and the findings presented to her majesty."

XENOPHOBIA

Disturbances among the common people might have been expected since it was here especially that the expulsion of all foreigners from Russia long was associated with Elizabeth's succession. There were rumors during Anna's reign to the effect that "Her highness Tsarevna Elizabeth Petrovna is vexed with her imperial majesty concerning the foreigners, whom Empress Anna pays in gold, while Elizabeth receives only bronze. The empress requested Elizabeth be summoned to her side so that the Russian state might be entrusted to her rule. But Elizabeth is said to have replied that if only her imperial majesty improved the lot of the common people over the next three years by expelling all foreigners from Russia would she be pleased to accept the burden of state."

But now that the tsarevna was ruler she did not expel foreigners, although they lived in a constant state of anxiety, alternating between fear and hope, the object of threats from the soldiery.

The foreign envoys sent back reports that soldiers were using violence, especially against the Germans, although they cited not one example to substantiate their claims. Details of only one clash have come down to us. The incident occurred in Petersburg on April 18, 1742. On Admiralty square, on the promenade near the swing bridge, men of the Semenovsky Regiment were fighting with a hawker who had sold them rotten eggs, and then turned on each other. Officers von Ros, Geikin, Sitmann and Müller, who were in a nearby billiard room, came out to break up the fight. One of the soldiers swore at them, and was struck by an officer.

This was the signal for a general attack on the officers, who retreated hastily to the billiard room pursued by the soldiers. Fighting renewed on the porch. One officer drew his sword, wounding a soldier in the hand. Seeing blood, the soldiers' mood grew even uglier and they surged against the porch. Two more were wounded in the process. The officers retreated inside and locked the doors, but the soldiers broke them down. Then the officers ran up into the attic and barricaded its entrance with benches and chairs. Medical

Officer Fousadie, who was in the billiard room at the time, hid with the owner of the house in a box room. The soldiers climbed to the attic where, apart from the officers already mentioned, there were several others who were in the billiard room, all of them foreigners. The soldiers swarmed up, hurling oaths and obscenities at the officers, calling them scoundrels, dogs and wretched foreigners.

The officers fled through the skylight out onto the roof and climbed down into the neighboring courtyard, leaving behind Captain Braun, Aide-de-Camp Sotreau, and Braun's servant Kampf. These men stood with drawn swords and held the soldiers back. But the soldiers, now joined by others, broke through and began to punch and kick the Germans. Sotreau was struck on the head by a sword and was thrown down from the attic. Braun also was dragged down and slain. The surgeon Fousadie and the owner of the billiard room Berlar were discovered and killed. This brawl was accompanied by the looting and wrecking of the premises.

At the ensuing enquiry the officers testified that the soldiers attacked them saying "You Swedish canaille have been told to get out of Russia. Don't think that you swine can just stay put! We are not looking for another Ochakov siege![6] We have orders to cut you to pieces. All you foreigners must be beaten to death. All you German dogs are going to be hanged today." The men downstairs shouted "All foreigners get out!" But the matter only amounted to shouting.

The brawlers were seized and court-martialed. They testified that they were drunk at the time and that their action was not premeditated. The court-martial sentenced the ringleaders to be broken on the wheel. Their accomplices were sentenced to be hanged, the less guilty knouted and made to run the gauntlet. The officers also received sentences. They were imprisoned for two to three months for dealing with the troops themselves instead of calling out the guard to arrest them, and for having failed to observe correct procedures of defense in the billiard room.

The Senate, taking into consideration lack of premeditation on the part of the convicted, petitioned the empress to commute the sentences. Elizabeth sentenced the four ringleaders to hard labor for life in the Siberian factories, and the remainder to service in remote garrisons.

CHURCH ATTITUDES TO FOREIGNERS

Understandably this change of attitude towards foreigners, and the fall of Ostermann, pleased the clergy. We have seen how the archbishop of Novgorod, Ambrose Yushkevich,[7] "complained about Ostermann," and did not confine himself to mere complaints. Temiriazev's compromising testimony, claiming that Ambrose acted on Princess Anna's behalf, might have brought serious trouble upon a layman. As it was, Novgorod's leading prelate was left unmolested for, apart from the well known piety of the new empress, it would have been too imprudent to begin the reign by persecuting such an outstanding cleric and adherent of Orthodoxy. In any case, Ambrose's activity was not actually on Anna's behalf, but directed against the heretic Ostermann.

Ambrose hastened to thank Elizabeth for her graciousness to him. To mark the empress's birthday on December 18, 1741 he preached a sermon. Anna Ivanovna's edict ordering sermons to be kept short was forgotten. In his oration he started to praise Elizabeth in his usual fashion by flattering reference to Peter the Great. He might praise Peter for the same reasons that previous orators had venerated him. "When he went to war he taught the army how to fight. When he had taught the army he arranged the tranquillity of the realm at home. When home affairs were put on secure footing he did not overlook the duties of his moral calling. He knew very well both from ancient history and from his own experience how lacking in achievement and dignity the Russian people were at that time. He saw how completely ignorant and unenlightened they were and therefore employed scholars for large sums of money. He provided them with all they needed and sent his own subjects abroad to study and to acquire new skills. He strove to erect church and state educational establishments everywhere and furnished them with wise and illustrious teachers," and so forth.

The preacher recounted the events of November 25. "Elizabeth went to her most reliable supporters and to the soldiers who long awaited her, and briefly declared her intentions, saying, 'Do you realize who I am, whose daughter I am? My parents, our dear Peter the Great and Catherine, worked hard, introduced new order and gained by their manifold labors a great treasure. But now all this is being undone. Moreover my life is threatened. Yet is not for myself that I am concerned but for our beloved fatherland which, governed by foreigners, is being brought vainly to ruin, while so many of our people perish on account of strangers. Whom do you wish to serve loyally? Me, your natural ruler, or those who have robbed me unlawfully of my inheritance?' Hearing these words they all cried with one voice, 'You, most merciful sovereign!'" and so on.

But the most remarkable aspect of this sermon was its portrayal of the foreigners ruling Russia. "Look what the cunning the devil inspired in them! First they affront the honor of our Orthodox faith. They attempt to replace it not with religion, but with obscene superstition harmful to Christianity. O, the number of religious and learned men they have destroyed, the number of monks they have unfrocked and tortured! You ask, to what end? You will hear no other answer than this: superstitious hypocrites and flatterers are good for nothing.

"All this is done with such cunning and craft that the Orthodox clergy in Russia is being completely exterminated and replaced by their newly devised priestless society. It seemed that they could talk about nothing else but scholars. 'O God!' they said, 'how unhappy is Russia in that it has no scholars and is unable to introduce learning!' Anyone ignorant of their cunning and deceit would suppose that they were speaking from love of Russia. But this is an impression they created deliberately, so that meanwhile, wherever they found a man of learning they killed him. If some talented Russian emerged, an artist, for example, or an engineer, an architect or an old soldier and, in particular, if he were a follower of Peter the Great, they immediately devised hundreds of ways of involving and implicating him in some crime. Then they arrested him and either cut off his head or else sent him to a place where unfailingly he died of starvation, just because the man was an engineer, an architect or a pupil of Peter the Great.

"Under the pretext of preserving the honor, welfare and interests of the realm thousands upon thousands of men, upright, loyal, of good conscience, innocent, loving God and Russia, were abducted and shut up in stinking cells and dark dungeons, starved to death, tormented and tortured. Rivers of innocent blood have been spilled! The unsuspecting men imagined that all this was done out of the greatest loyalty, whereas it was loyal men who were exterminated behind a veil of deceit in this godless fashion.

"In short, all good and sincere men who held the interests of the nation at heart, and whom the state greatly needed, were killed under various pretexts, rooted out and destroyed, while godless, unscrupulous marauders greatly favored the plunderers of Russia's coffers, indulged and esteemed them, promoted them to high rank, rewarded them with land and large sums of money.

"It is shameful to admit that all this actually occurred, and yet it is nothing but the truth! Some unknown foreigner appears (and I am not talking about honest and worthy men who have earned every credit for their service to Russia, but about those who have not yet been to Russia and who have yet to render it any service); such, I say, a new arrival appears, and these wretches decide that he is the man they need. Even were he completely ignorant, even were he incapable of counting up to three, as long as he was a foreigner who suited their purpose, he would be appointed to a senior position as councillor or senior officer on a salary of thousands of rubles, while deserving and worthy Russians were passed over.

"That was the way our enemies at home behaved. Such satanic ingenuity! It seemed to many that they were loyal servants and warriors of Christ's church and performed valiant deeds for the fatherland. But in fact they reduced Russia to a position of weakness, poverty and utter destruction. You need only recall the recent Turkish war.[8] How many old soldiers died of starvation without ever seeing battle! How many died of thirst on the steppes! How many hundreds of thousands of clergy and other conscripts they called up to no avail, all in pursuit of their own gain and empty greed!

"Everything they did was a sham. Everything was done under the guise of loyalty. They frequently referred to their services, speaking highly of their loyalty and benevolence to Russia, but at heart they lied unscrupulously. For if they truly wished our country well, would they deliberately have sent our men to certain death? Would they not have found in Russia a spiritual as well as a physical home? They showed themselves in their true colors when they sent out of Russia all their treasure and illegally acquired many millions to be deposited and invested in banks abroad."

In Moscow the same day Kirill Florinsky, rector of the local academy and archimandrite of the Savior (Zaikonospassk) monastery,[9] preached a sermon in much the same spirit. "Over the last decade we all have been as insensible as so much wood. We failed to appreciate the vitality and maturity of Peter's seed. We forgot that when Peter the Great embraced us, he found us to be no better than a weak, decaying, neglected tree, incapable of bearing fruit. But with his own hands he managed to make us, after his own image, something of great value. He gave us our souls. What a miraculous transformation!

"Peter's seed took root and waxed strong. Under its branches we long ago became happy and contented. But then we were most cruelly oppressed, tormented, tied and bound. We were deprived of our fatherland and our faith. No longer could we see this fragrant, leafy and shady tree, planted by Peter. It was this tree that those vultures, Ostermann, Münnich and their hateful flock, were bent on mutilating, felling and utterly destroying.

"In this torpid and blind state we were insensible, until Peter's sturdy seed asked us how long we would slumber and suffer.... And now we see that while we were slumbering Ostermann, Münnich and their ilk crawled into Russia as emissaries of the devil. God, it seemed, had granted them wealth, the glory and the honor they sought. But it was promised them by Satan in the guise of true service to the Russian realm, in return not just for the transformation of our cherished Russian faith and virtues, but for their utter destruction....

"Just as in the scriptures Jeremiah was a golden idol, so in Russia were Ostermann and Münnich. They were just as bereft of conscience and devoured without scruple any victim sacrificed to them. But now they are crushed under the firm fundament of Peter's rock. God himself will destroy Ostermann, Münnich and their ilk, these altars of sacrifice, these graven images, these high priests of Baal, as pagan idols, them and not us."

THE SYNOD

Kirill Florinsky cited as evidence of the previous government's hostility to the Orthodox church the fact that in Moscow an Armenian church was erected in the Kitay quarter.[10] The Holy Synod

shared Florinsky's view and in January 1742 petitioned the empress
for an edict closing Armenian churches in Petersburg, Moscow and
Astrakhan, apart from one stone church in the latter, and forbidding their future construction. The Holy Synod called for priests
to be exempted from street patrols, fire duty and other police obligations which interfered with their church duties. On April 7 the
synod's request was granted.

As mentioned, Yakov Shakhovskoy was appointed chief procurator of the Holy Synod.[11] He described taking up his new post as
follows. "I arrived during a meeting of the Holy Synod, which was
a pleasant experience, for I was met by a holder of the equivalent
Senate rank, who was awaiting my arrival. He met me on the stair-
way, flanked by several secretaries and other lower officials. He
introduced himself courteously and, clearing the way for me, led
me into the chamber where the Holy Synod was in session.

"Both doors were half opened and I was met there by the senior
secretary. My first glance into the chamber produced a very agreeable impression on me, for it was elegant and orderly. Seated around
the table were, as far as I remember, eight or nine ecclesiastical
dignitaries, archbishops, bishops and several archimandrites, men
who aroused respect both by their resplendent vestments and by
their dignified bearing. As soon as I approached the end of the table
they rose respectfully from their chairs, one after the other. Among
the first was Ambrose, the most reverend archbishop of Novgorod,
clearly the senior member. They began to greet me, congratulating
me on my appointment and welcoming me as a new colleague in
their midst. After I courteously introduced myself to them, they
replied most cordially. Then they sat down again and resumed their
consideration of the matter which my entry had interrupted.

"I noticed a small table prepared for me in the chamber. I went
over and sat at it. Seeing on it only an inkwell and several sheets
of blank paper, I asked the senior secretary to bring me the Ecclesiastical Statute,[12] any edicts which had passed into law subsequent
to it, the instructions of the previous chief procurators of the Synod
and the edicts relating to that post. I further asked for the usual
registers of unresolved matters lying before the Synod, of convicts
and of the treasury.

"The senior secretary took the Ecclesiastical Statute from his desk
and handed it to me. With regard to the edicts and the register of

unresolved matters, he informed me that although they were collected, it was not done very thoroughly, and asked for a few days to prepare the requested material for presentation to me in an organized fashion. He told me there was not a single line recorded concerning the manner in which the various matters hitherto within the field of competence of the chief procurators were handled. He explained to me at length that many papers were lost in fires and other mishaps in the Synod chancellery, and that as a result of various difficulties the papers now lay scattered and unclassified in boxes and trunks in several rooms, and that there was no archive."

The new chief procurator discovered edicts of Peter the Great requiring that when church services were in progress there was to be no talking and no walking around to touch the relics and icons. A fine for the church coffers was to be exacted from offenders. Shakhovskoy proposed to the Synod that as these edicts were not enforced, they should be reinstituted by means of further decrees. To ensure due observance of the edicts and imposition of fines, the Senate appointed certain retired officers to the monasteries to record the fines in bound books in the presence of priests and deacons to prevent embezzlement.

The Synod approved permission for the building and renovation of churches but would allow their consecration only after it was ascertained that they were built correctly, equipped with everything necessary and that the priest and deacon had sufficient endowment. The Synod complained to the Senate that a Siberian governor failed to observe Peter the Great's edict prohibiting the trial of church personnel in secular courts without consulting the ecclesiastical authorities. The Senate reissued this decree and had it distributed among those serving in diocesan chancelleries and in local government.

FINANCIAL MATTERS

In November 1742 the Senate received a complaint from the College of Church Landed Properties about the failure of diocesan chancelleries and various monasteries to pay quitrent revenue on property and estates sold since 1730 up to June 14 of the current year, 1742. The outstanding sum amounted to 44,324 rubles. A Corporal Starkov, who was sent to investigate this, collected 1,806 rubles at the Savior monastery in Yaroslavl. He was about to leave for Moscow but was prevented from doing so by the cellarer of this monastery, Joseph, and the superior, Feofilakt. These two wrecked the carts in which Starkov was leaving and, roundly cursing the appointed tax-collector, threatened to beat him to death if he went to Moscow to deliver the money he collected.

This was a matter of state money and state revenue. At the outset of her reign Elizabeth declared that she would rule according to the precepts of her illustrious father. A certain soldier expressed a very coarse view on Peter's rule about money and state revenue, for which he was taken off to the Secret Chancellery, which failed to appreciate that beneath his coarse expression lay great praise. The soldier said that Peter the Great would choke the last copeck out of you. The Senate, restored by Elizabeth to the significance it enjoyed under her father, was reminded that in Peter's time one of its main duties was to "collect as much money as possible." When Elizabeth came to the throne, the soul tax in 1742 and 1743 was fixed at ten copecks a head, which produced more than one million rubles, "in consideration whereof our loyal subjects have improved by degrees the payment of the soul tax for the last years."

But Elizabeth had inherited a war,[13] and in August 1742 the head commissariat reported to the Senate that regardless of any confirmation of soul tax collection either for preceding years or for the first half of the current year there was still a large amount outstanding. This meant, for example, that several regiments of the Baltic expedition had not received the more than two hundred thousand rubles arrears in pay. The Senate ruled that for such malfeasance a fine be imposed on governors and vice-governors of a hundred rubles, on provincial governors fifty rubles, on town governors and on regional and provincial secretaries twenty-five rubles, and on town officials twelve rubles.

It turned out that it was not just administration which was at fault, but "initially the landowners personally, and then in emulation of them, the governors and provincial governors, together with those appointed to make the tax collections. They gave as cause for this non-payment their own slackness." As a result it was decreed that payments be made within four months; defaulters were to be fined ten copecks per ruble, an appropriate deduction made from their salary and their estates irrevocably confiscated. Those found guilty of the slightest cheating in making collections were not to count

on leniency in view of their previous service "for anyone who breaks
the laws of the state or who acts against the national interest will,
on judgement of the court, be punishable by death."

But towards the end of the year it became clear that existing
revenue was not enough to finance the war, and so a measure used
by Peter the Great in extreme cases was reintroduced. On December
11 the empress signed an edict in the presence of the Senate decree-
ing the deduction for a one year period of the following amounts
of money from the salaries of the clergy, serving soldiers, and ci-
vilian and court officials: archbishops and generals were to forfeit
twenty copecks per ruble, staff officers and archimandrites fifteen,
senior officers and abbots ten, senior officers in garrisons, court and
civil servants, artisans without ranks and the lower echelons of the
clergy, five. At the same session Elizabeth signed a decree forbidding the wearing of gold and silver. Silk dresses were to be worn
according to social ranks and a three-inch limit was imposed on the
amount of lace to be worn. At the beginning of the year Elizabeth
decreed personally before the Senate that firework displays be re-
stricted to coronation day, New Year, the empress's birthday, her
nameday[14] and anniversary of her accession. The birthday and
nameday of the duke of Holstein were to be marked by one firework display only.

The Senate recognized that to check the financial chaos and
excessive fiscal impositions it was essential to conduct a new census.
It accordingly petitioned the empress to permit "for the satisfaction
of all landowners and the cessation of hitherto frequent irregularities
both in the rendering of service and of negligence in poll-tax payment, to take a census once more and in future to conduct it every
fifteen years, so that all irregularities, especially the harboring of
refugees and wilful flight, be checked, while poor and needy landlords, who with their wives and children are living in dire distress
and even dying, be freed from such poverty." The empress agreed.
The Senate presented information concerning the large population
decrease. According to reports from the provinces, between 1719
and 1727 there was an overall decline of 988,456. Of these, 733,158
died, 198,876 fled and 53,928 were conscripted. The number of
conscripts from 1727 to 1736 was 147,418.

INDUSTRY

The edict of December 12, 1741 directed that the administration of domestic affairs of all descriptions be based on the edicts of Peter the Great, except for those incompatible with present circumstances or contrary to the state's interests.

Under Peter Colleges of Mining and Manufacture were established for the supervision and direction of these industries. Under Anna these colleges were abolished and merged with the College of Commerce, while a General Mining Directorate was set up under Baron von Schomberg. For the supervision of private factories special directors was appointed and paid to inspect them.

The Senate found that these changes were not for the better. Schomberg owed debts to the treasury and now protested that he was not in a position to repay them. With respect to the factories, the College of Commerce could not be relied on since it had many duties of its own and was therefore unable to provide the kind of supervision offered by a specific agency. The Senate proposed that the empress re-establish a College of Mining and Manufacture.[15] Assent was granted on April 7, 1742.

On June 25 Elizabeth appeared at a meeting of the Senate to approve its decision to summon Director General of Mines von Schomberg and order him to repay the treasury the sum of 134,944 rubles 13 copecks and to give reliable sureties for bail of 99,635 rubles 73 copecks. In the event of his inability to repay the treasury or to give sureties, his estates were to be confiscated and he himself placed under arrest. As the empress left, Schomberg was summoned before the Senate. He declared he was unable to repay his debts or to provide the required sureties. Accordingly he was placed under house arrest and his property impounded. He was allowed no visitors and was refused paper and ink. The total amount of Schomberg's deficit was based on the revenue owing from the factories entrusted to him in Lapland and Goroblagodatsk.

The government dealt with two matters concerning factories. First it required that they supply the state with products of the desired quality, for example, cloth for the armed forces and paper for government institutions. Second, it sought to define the relationship between factory owners and workers, since there were instances of oppression. The Senate ruled that the skilled workers of the Kazan cloth mill be paid the same as they were when it was state owned and later when owned by Mikliaev. Under this arrangement weavers were to receive six copecks per arshin and spinners three copecks per pound, instead of the five copecks and two copecks the current owner Dreblov was paying them. It was decreed further that workers in cloth mills be paid six rubles per length of cloth. Wool was bought at that time for one ruble twenty copecks.

Peter the Great's edict concerning writing paper was reaffirmed. This ordered that tattered and unusable paper be collected at places of work for redistribution and handed to the College of Commerce by weight. In return, proportionate amounts of usable paper were to be drawn from the college. During Anna's reign printing paper was ordered from the factory of Zatrapezny. But the Synod now contended that this paper was too thick for book printing and that a finer paper was needed so that books might be "more delicate" and their covers no longer damaged by their thickness. Moreover, the Zatrapezny paper was more expensive than that produced by other factories. The empress decreed that paper be procured from other Russian factories if it was better and cheaper than that produced by Zatrapezny.

An Armenian, Nyrvanov, presented designs of various sorts of best quality silk, manufactured at his factories in Kizliar and Astrakhan. He received a warrant for the manufacture of silk and paper at his establishment in Astrakhan.

It was felt necessary, as before, to stimulate industrial production by giving the factory owners and manufacturers the incentive of rank. Rank was essential at this time to protect both the individual and his labor from the excesses of government officials. On the other hand, of course, every new rich official only added to the number of such offenders.

On the death of the celebrated factory owner Zatrapezny his factory passed to his son-in-law Captain Lakostov, who was permitted to resign his commission "lest this factory, famed throughout the Russian empire, fall into neglect, but that through his diligent supervision might be maintained in good order. For his zealous care of the factory he is awarded the rank of major."

For painstaking work and increased output of iron and brass products State Councillor Akinfy Demidov was promoted to senior state councillor. His brother, the nobleman Nikita, was appointed state councillor. Yakov Yevreinov, the owner of a silk factory, received the rank of councillor of the College of Manufacturing for his services as consul in Spain and as one of those sent abroad by Peter the Great to study commerce and manufacturing. Afanasy Goncharov, the owner of a sailmaking concern and a paper mill, was made collegiate assessor for his management of these enterprises, in particular the latter, to the benefit of the state. The silk producer Semen Mylnikov and the paper manufacturer Vasily Korotky were made directors of their factories with the rank of collegiate secretary.

Six skilled men were sent abroad to study, all members of the nobility and one of them even a prince (Narytsky). Some of them trained as locksmiths, others as joiners or carpenters and had worked at court and in various towns. They had retired to their estates prior to the edict. Now some of them requested permission to work at court once more, while others asked for an allowance. The Senate directed that they be sent to the Chancellery of Works and there assigned work for the state according to their skills. They were to be given the requested number of apprentices.

As regards the arrangements made for trade in 1742 we need only note the imperial edict of December 2 on the subject of Jews. "Although Jews are forbidden to live in our empire, nevertheless it was brought to our notice that there are still some domiciled here, particularly in Little Russia, where they are engaged in various occupations. Only extreme harm to our faithful subjects is to be expected from these haters of the name of Christ the Savior. We therefore command all Jews, both male and female, together with their belongings, immediately be expelled from our empire. On no account are they to be readmitted subsequently even if they are desirous of becoming Christians of the Greek confession."

THE PEASANTRY

Many of those who worked the land demonstrated dissatisfaction with their lot in customary fashion, by taking flight. The Senate was informed that many house serfs and peasants were fleeing their landlords, claiming that by edict of her highness men of all ranks were ordered to make for the Don, to join the cossacks and to settle in Don Cossack townships. Moreover, the Senate learned that they were fleeing not only by the household, but in entire villages. In the Don Cossack townships they received asylum and settled on cossack lands.

The Senate instructed that an official declaration be sent to the Don, that the Don Host be closely watched, that under no circumstances were fleeing peasants or servicemen to be given refuge, while fugitives must be returned to their former domicile.

Straight after this the landowners, stewards and elders of the Murom district reported the flight of numerous serfs with their wives and children. From January to July of 1742 more than a thousand took flight, in some cases entire settlements. In the village of Gorki, which belonged to the Trinity monastery, the hundredman apprehended fifty-three fugitives. They testified that they were making for the cossack townships on the Medveditsa and Don because they heard rumors that fugitives were being resettled by a cossack called Krasnoshcheky and given a grant of five rubles and other benefits for five years. The serfs were beaten with knout and rod, and a major with three hundred dragoons were dispatched to the Don to seek out the refugees.

The peasants of Mamontova, a village near Moscow, presented the empress with a petition indicting their landlord Yevlev, claiming that he led a debauched life and kept a concubine, the wife of a merchant. On her orders they were systematically ruined, beaten and tormented. Many, they claimed, were fleeing just such misery with the result that there was no one to pay the soul tax. The serfs in the hamlet of Bachurin in the Moscow district complained of ruin and murder at the hands of their landlord Ladyzhensky. The Senate ordered the cases investigated and settled by an edict barring such landlords from owning serfs.

In connection with the census the empress endorsed the Senate's findings. Peasants who fled in entire settlements, from crown, church or private lands and settled in local towns on state or church lands or on lands they had bought, were not to be returned to their original lands but be registered where they settled. If landowners' serfs fled and resettled in entire settlements they were not to be sent back either. On the other hand peasants who formed new settlements, having fled from several different landlords, were to be returned to their original lands.

In Peter's time serfs were permitted to join the army to swell the ranks of the newly formed regular army as quickly as possible. But after Peter's death this practice was strictly forbidden. On his daughter Elizabeth's accession a rumor spread among the serf population that once again they would be allowed to volunteer for the army, and they began both individually and in large groups to petition the empress to be accepted into military service. Others simply fled from their landlords to join up. But they were cruelly mistaken in their hopes. For such impudence they were subjected to harsh punishment on the public square. Those petitioning collectively were beaten with the knout and most sent to Siberia where they were put to work in state factories for life. Those who made individual petitions were whipped, others beaten with rods and handed back to their landlords.

III

RUSSIA AND EUROPE
1742

ELIZABETH'S CORONATION

The meetings in 1741 of the governing bodies, the Senate and the Synod, took place partly in Petersburg and partly in Moscow, to which Elizabeth hastened for her coronation, designed to formalize the coup of November 25.

On January 27, 1742 the Senate ruled that preparations for the coronation were to be placed in the hands of Count Semeon Andreevich Saltykov and Archbishop Ambrose of Novgorod. They were to be conducted along the lines of those made for similar ceremonies in 1724, 1728 and 1730. These two were to be assisted by State Councillor Peter Kurbatov from the College of Foreign Affairs, who was involved actively in coronation preparations in the three previous aforementioned years. Brocade, velvet, braid fringes, and so on, were to be ordered from Russian factories in Moscow or from the market stalls. If they were unavailable ready made the factories were to produce a special order. If they were unable to do so, the Senate was to be informed in writing. Thirty thousand rubles were to be allocated initially for preparations. The French expert Rochebeau was invited to Moscow to make the canopies, assisted by court craftsmen. Triumphal arches were to be erected first in the Earthen City,[1] on Tver street, under the supervision of the Moscow regional office and at the region's expense. The second set was to be constructed in the Kitay quarter, by the church of the Kazan Virgin, under the direction of the Holy Synod, and from the revenue of the College of Church Landed Properties. The third, on Miasnitsky street, was to be built by the merchants of Moscow at their own expense under the supervision of the provincial chancellery.

Elizabeth left Petersburg on February 23. At five in the morning of the twenty-sixth she reached Vsesviatskoe, a village seven versts from Moscow.[2] Here the empress rested on the twenty-seventh. Meanwhile preparations went ahead for her triumphal entry into Moscow on the day after. At five in the morning of February 28 a nine-gun salute resounded across Red Square and the huge Ivanovsk bell began to chime. At ten the empress arrived from Vsesviatskoe into the Tverskaia-Yamskaia suburb. Here the state coach was waiting to take her triumphantly into Moscow in the manner little changed since.[3]

When Elizabeth and her nephew the duke of Holstein took the place customarily reserved respectively for the emperor and his consort in the Kremlin cathedral of the Dormition, Archbishop Ambrose of Novgorod delivered the following address. "Rejoice, O Russia, before the firm and unshakable fundament of your welfare! Rejoice at the termination of your manifold and most grievous shifts in fortune! Rejoice in your tranquillity, well-being, and in the undoubted hope of all your sundry desires! The Orthodox church rejoices in this staunch defender of its faith, while the entire Governing Senate[4] rejoices that from her it will acquire both an affirmation of its honor and dignity and a living example of mercy and justice. The entire army also is ardent in its love and zeal for their empress, having the good fortune to acquire a just avenger of the abuses in the system of promotion, a courageous heroine who has freed Russia from domestic strife. The civil estates also rejoice in that henceforth they may hope for promotion in rank not through fear and bribes but through merit in service....

"Although today all Russia is celebrating and rejoicing, it is nevertheless this city, which is seemingly the heart of all Russian cities, which experiences the most profound joy, because it contains all the causes and prerogatives of this joy.... But, O Russia, look at yourself with unblinking eyes and see to it in all conscience that you do not anger and estrange the All-merciful God for all eternity. The Righteous Lord has visited your sins and lawlessness with most

dire punishment by taking from you Peter II, the first grandson of
Peter the Great.[5] Following his death Russia endured so many great
trials and changes of fortune, acts of terror, fires, terrible wars,
severe and cruel famines, untimely deaths and countless other
misfortunes.

"Henceforth be vigilant, preserve as the apple of your eye the
cherished health of her imperial majesty and his imperial highness.
Always fear God and His dreaded judgement. Fear the strong and
inescapable hands of God. Flee from sin as from the face of the
serpent. Cease forthwith your lawlessness, deception, violence,
drunkenness, fornication, larceny, insults, adultery and all your other
sins and transgressions, or else you will incur God's punishment.
Also be grateful for the divine providence which the Merciful Lord
clearly manifests to you in sending to replace Peter II, the first
grandson of Peter the Great, a second illustrious grandchild of the
same name, and blessed with the same virtues.[6] Accept him with
a joyful heart and favorable spirit, be unswervingly faithful to his
name and, in every adverse change of fortune, be not afraid, but hold
fast to Peter's name, as a firm and unshakable rock, and you will
remain forever unharmed....

"There is no more precious treasure to be found on earth than
that on which our welfare and eternal salvation depend. This treasure
is none other than sincere, universal Orthodox faith. This precious
faith from heaven itself, this treasure, our priceless piety, was
bestowed upon us by the all-merciful mother of our country. For
as soon as she ascended the throne, she deigned to inform the Synod
of her good and imperial intentions, declaring that 'we must begin
with God and from God, and as we received through Him by child-
like simple revelation truths that are concealed from the wise and
judicious, the source of our imperial power and glory, so we are
bound to preserve, defend and propagate His divine honor and
glory.' O most opportune words! Words worthy of the imperial lips.

"And what she has been pleased to say by word, she has fulfilled
in deed, for she has authorized the reappearance of *The Rock of
Faith*,[7] long locked away in the darkness of ignorance. This book
is as necessary and indispensable to us as tools to a craftsman,
weapons to a warrior, or the helm to a sailor at sea. Consider the
kind of strategy and low cunning our domestic enemies have resorted
to in devising their godless wars against us. They derived from the

first Book of Samuel,[8] a scheme resembling that employed by the
Philistines who, many times conquered by the Israelites in their
ceaseless wars, found that the only way they could in their turn
conquer and destroy them was to forbid them from making arms and
take away those they already had.

"Our enemies at home have dealt with us in the same way. They
knew very well that our faith was strong and insuperable, based as
it is not on a mere man but on a firm cornerstone, that is, on Christ,
the son of the Living God. As they could not suppress our faith, they
thought to take from us our defense, our weapon and spiritual sword,
that is, the word of God, the preserver and defender of our faith.
Thus they thought, and thus they did. Books already printed were
consigned to oblivion and the writing of others prohibited on pain
of death. They bound up, struck down and incarcerated not only the
teachers, but their teachings and their books as well. It reached the
point where it was perilous to open our mouths in our own Orthodox
homeland, and persecution lay in store for us.... O what measure-
less gratitude we owe your imperial majesty for the manifold ex-
ertions and triumphs you have brought to bear on the purification
of the faith and of the holy liturgy, and on the liberation of your
beloved motherland!"

After visiting the cathedrals of the Archangel and the Annunciation[9] the empress once more took her place in the ceremonial carriage and set off for her winter palace on the Yauza river. At the
triumphal Synod arch she was met by forty seminarists of the
Slavonic-Greek-Latin Academy,[10] all dressed in white with crowns
on their heads and laurel branches in their hands. They sang a can-
tata containing the following verses: "Draw nigh, wondrous day,
fine weather has come! Behold, heaven generously shows Russia
a long desired favor! Begone all woes! Not for one, not for two,
but for many years rain fell and there was no light. At God's command the winds fell silent and a calm prevailed. Who can withstand
Him." And so on.

The coronation was fixed for April 25. Over and above the thirty
thousand rubles already allocated to the coronation commission,
another twenty thousand were granted, together with nineteen thousand for fireworks. The illuminations were to last, as on previous
occasions, for eight days. Those on the Ivan the Great and other
belltowers were to be funded by the College of Church Landed

properties, and those at the palace, on the Red Porch[11] and round about it, by the court chancellery. The architect Jean Blanc who

Empress Elizabeth, 1741

Engraving by Piero Rotari (1707-1762)

designed the triumphal gates erected thrones in the Dormition cathedral and the Palace of Facets,[12] as well as constructing the illuminations and fountains. Medals were struck by the craftsman Reibisch.

On the day of the coronation Archbishop Ambrose of Novgorod delivered a greeting to the empress in which, among other things, he lauded the triumph of November 25. "What greater nobility of spirit could there be than to put aside the delicacy of her sex and with a small company strike a blow for the common good, not begrudging the last drop of blood for the integrity of the faith and welfare of the country; then to gather the loyal troops, draw up their ranks and lead them against the foe, those night owls and bats impudently squatting on the nest of the Russian eagle, plotting the downfall of the nation? She drove them out, bound up the perfidious destroyers of the motherland and tore the legacy of Peter the Great from alien hands. She has delivered the sons of Russia from bondage and brought every last one of them to safety. Is this not reason enough for universal admiration?

HONORS AND PROMOTIONS

In connection with the coronation a long list of honors was published, among them the following: the prince of Hesse-Homburg[13] was promoted to Field Marshal-General; the order of St. Andrew was bestowed upon Field Marshal-General Prince Vasily Vladimirovich Dolgoruky, General Vasily Saltykov, Lord Marshal of the Court Mikhail Bestuzhev-Riumin, Procurator General Prince Nikita Trubetskoy, Senator Alexander Naryshkin and, on Brümmer, the duke of Holstein's lord marshal of the court. The favorite, Razumovsky, already a senior chamberlain and a lieutenant of the Imperial Life Guards, was made grand master of the hunt and awarded the order of St. Andrew. High chamberlains and lieutenants of the Imperial Life Guards Vorontsov, and Alexander and Peter Shuvalov, received the order of Alexander Nevsky.

Apart from these, the title of count was given to certain maternal relatives of the empress: the Gendrikovs, Efimovs, General Grigory Chernyshev, and the forgotten father of two unforgettable sons, Peter Bestuzhev-Riumin. As a result the lord marshal of the court and the chancellor also became counts. An old friend and sympathizer of this family, Cherkasov, was made a baron. On March 22 Vice-Chancellor Alexis Petrovich Bestuzhev was appointed to the office vacated by Ostermann.[14]

Grand Duke Peter, age 16 (1744)

contemporary engraving

Dignitaries disgraced in previous reigns were reinstated but reminded that they now counted for less. On September 27 the following edict was published. "Her imperial majesty is aware that in

the previous administration several were exiled to various different parts of the country. Neither the Senate nor the Secret Chancellery has any record of them or their names or whereabouts.
Accordingly her imperial majesty commands that it be known
throughout the state that such are to apply in person to her imperial majesty with details of their place of exile, the date on which
it commenced, and the reasons for it." In December the former privy
cabinet secretary Eichler was made a state councillor and retired
from service. Prince Yury Dolgoruky had his estates restored to him
by way of exception "because he had suffered for her imperial
majesty."

PETER FEDOROVICH'S INVESTITURE

After the coronation the court remained in Moscow until the end
of the year. On November 7 a manifesto was published in the ancient capital appointing as successor to the throne the empress's
nephew Peter, duke of Holstein, "nearest to us in blood, whom we
command from henceforth to be named and styled 'His imperial
highness the grand duke.'" It also was announced that the successor
had adopted the devout faith of the Greek dispensation. In churches
reference was made, after the empress, to "her successor *the grandson of Peter the Great*, the noble lord Grand Duke Peter Fedorovich."

MOSCOW'S POLICE FORCE

The court's long stay in Moscow must have drawn the government's
attention to a somewhat unsatisfactory aspect of the ancient capital. The Senate observed that the police force was very feeble and
negligent in the execution of its duties, but that nevertheless considerable responsibility was entrusted to it. A very weak watch was
kept, thieving and brawling were endemic, outbreaks of shooting
were occurring, there was a virtual absence of hygiene in the town,
and the bridges were in a very bad state of repair.

The police department replied that its officers were carrying out
their duty with great care as far as was humanly possible, but faced
difficulties. First, there were many old and incompetent officers in
the police force, which resulted in a certain laxity and slowness;
second, to quell disturbances the police had at their disposal no more

than two companies of dragoons and one of infantry, which these days amounted to only about fifty men; with such a small number it was impossible to take prompt action against all the disturbances breaking out over such a large area. Third, in the discharge of police duties great confusion was caused by the guards regiments and others, who were in the habit of releasing those the police placed under arrest, and dealing with them themselves. They even took prisoners from their places of detention. Despite prohibitions, in apartments ovens were being used, from which seals were removed and not replaced. As a result complaints were being lodged by other tenants.[15] The Senate directed that improvements be made to the police force, to satisfy the police department.

THE TURCHANINOV CONSPIRACY

But just as concern was being expressed about the safety of the citizens of Moscow a rumor suddenly spread that the empress was insecure within her own palace. The rumor was confirmed when, on July 15, the day of the consecration of the church at the Moscow Academy, the rector Kirill Florinsky made a reference in his sermon to Elizabeth's enemies at home.

The sermon was on the text "Do not make the House of my father a house of trade."[16] The preacher portrayed Russia as a temple erected by Peter the Great in which, on his death, a number of men had started to conduct business. This trade did not cease even with the accession to the throne of Peter's daughter. "How terrible it is to think," the preacher said, "that not eight months have passed since the crowned Elizabeth ascended her father's throne, and already schemers are making claims on it. It is strange news indeed. Elizabeth, long yearned for, now is hated. Her name, long sweet in our hearts and on our lips, now is bitter; she brought us new life, but now her life is in danger in her own house. She was a source of joy to us, yet now she is bewailed tearfully within her own house. A mother, aye, and moreover most merciful, we now are told that she is severe and unmerciful. O the fecklessness of perfidious schemers! But woe to those of ill intent who keep silent about her majesty's good deeds because you, formerly scattered and incarcerated, forever bewailing your misfortunes, by the mercy of our mother Elizabeth are returned from exile; many are back from Siberia, Irkutsk,

Kamchatka and from numerous other lands difficult to name, restored from the bowels of the earth more dead than alive.

"Now you acknowledge with me that Elizabeth is hated by these scheming perverters of the nation, is made out to be bitter, severe and unmotherly, for no other reason than that she reassembled the country's squandered wealth, reinstituted her father's legislation and rescued you unfortunates from your misery. In a word, she restored the entire land to its original condition. She no longer tolerates these evildoers who sought to make her father's house, the house she inherited, a house of trade and a den of thieves. Your imperial majesty is long-suffering, and your measures are a wondrous thing and in accordance with God's commandment 'Leave the tares and the wheat to grow together until harvest time, for if you uproot the tares earlier, you will surely pull out the wheat with them.'"[17]

The facts of the matter were that the palace servant, Alexander Turchaninov, Ensign Peter Ivashkin of the Preobrazhensky Regiment and Sergeant Ivan Snovidov of the Izmailovsky Regiment formed a conspiracy aimed at assassinating Elizabeth and her nephew the duke of Holstein, and replacing her with the deposed Ivan Antonovich. They pointed out that Elizabeth and her sister Anna were born out of wedlock, and were therefore illegitimate daughters of Peter the Great. The trial lasted until December, when the convicted were knouted and sent to Siberia. Turchaninov had his tongue cut out and his nostrils slit. His confederates similarly lost their nostrils, but kept their tongues.

EUROPEAN AFFAIRS

In December the court returned to St. Petersburg where it was awaited impatiently by the ambassadors of the European powers demanding Russia's participation in Western affairs.

At the time of Elizabeth's accession the course of European affairs was perfectly clear. Hitherto in the opinion of educated Europeans the political equilibrium was maintained by the balance of power between the powerful Austrian and Bourbon royal houses, being the most powerful on the continent. As soon as one gained obvious supremacy over the other, thereby upsetting the balance, the other states united behind the weaker of the two and restored the equilibrium. There now arose a situation where this balance obviously was upset. Taking advantage of the extinction of the male line of the house of Habsburg,[18] France wanted to lay low once and for all its old rival Austria by partitioning its territory, so that Germany no longer should be an extensive, strong conglomeration of states, and thus a danger to France. In particular the French had their sights set on Bavaria and Saxony. In order to dismantle Austria the king of Prussia, who could make no claims on the basis of kinship, instead used the right of the strong and hastened to acquire a rich slice of the spoils.[19] In so doing he acted directly against French interests.

Frederick II's successes clearly showed that the Habsburg crown princess [Maria Theresa] could not deal with enemies threatening her on all sides without outside help. Who was there to help her? At the end of the seventeenth century and at the beginning of the eighteenth, when France similarly contrived to upset the political balance, an anti-French alliance was formed, and the balance of power restored. The initiative at that time belonged to the maritime powers, Holland and England, and William of Orange in particular. Now too England and Holland were anxious to see the political balance restored. But instead of William III, it was the untalented George II who occupied the English throne, and he was interested only in his Hanover, and for its preservation and neutrality was ready to agree to anything.[20] The maritime powers merely talked about the violation of the balance of power and about the need to assist Maria Theresa, but were unable to do anything without first forming an alliance with some strong continental power. Such a power was Russia, and it was understandable that Petersburg or Moscow, depending on the location of the imperial court, now became the center of European diplomatic activity, the arena in which the ambassadors of the various European courts vied to secure the Russian government to help Maria Theresa. They sought thereby, either to uphold the balance of power in Europe, or to compel Russia to cooperate directly, or indirectly by means of non-intervention, in the complete overthrow of this balance.

Who succeeded? It was clearly a question of whether Russia was sufficiently developed to assume the great role assigned by Peter the Great, and whether Russia's statesmen understood their country's interests in relation to those of Europe as a whole. It was also a matter of whether the government would allow itself to be guided by such a clear understanding or merely by its own narrow interests, and whether Russia intended to go to war, conclude treaties and make peace according to which party had the upper hand at court, and which foreign court could offer the most bribes.

Hitherto a foreigner [Ostermann] was the architect of Russian policy, to whom the glory of Russia's successes largely was attributable. But now that he was removed the problem was whether a Russian could be found to replace him. Now that the course of European affairs was plain, Russian policy could be determined and a decision made whether it could continue on its present course of non-intervention. In the previous reign the war with Sweden relieved Russia of the necessity of resolving this difficult question. But now that everything pointed to an early conclusion of this war, it was incumbent on Russia to define its relationship to countries presenting a greater danger than Sweden. Clearly as a member of the European family of nations Russia could not tolerate passively the upsetting of the balance of power in France's favor, since it was French intrigue that brought about the Swedish war and gave Russia no peace from Poland or Turkey. It hardly accorded with Russian interests that Austria be reduced to a minor power or that France have a free hand in Germany, and through Saxony gain influence in Poland. It was vital therefore that Russia support Maria Theresa and not abandon Saxony and Poland to the French.

But apart from France, which proved in the event not to command the means to achieve its goals, there emerged a danger much closer to home. On Russia's flank the king of Prussia, whose talent and energy far surpassed those of any other European monarch, declared he intended to strengthen his country's position, come what may. Uncertainty as to what resources he commanded made him all the more dangerous. From Peter the Great's time Russia's superiority was guaranteed by the weakness of its neighbors, Sweden, Poland and Turkey. Consequently Russia's direct interests demanded that Frederick II's ambitious schemes be kept in check. This meant that Russia was bound to support Austria and Saxony against him.

PERSONAL ALLIANCES AT COURT

Russia's program was therefore clear and simple, and the majority, including nearly all statesmen, were agreed. The policy of support for Austria and Saxony, and halting Prussia's expansionist aims for the most part was implemented, but in the early years

Count A. P. Bestuzhev-Riumin
Johann Cristoph Grooth (1716-1749)
Palace Museum of Pavlovsk

of Elizabeth's reign, for a variety of reasons desultorily and hesi-
tantly. In the first place the coup of November 25 created a new set
of relationships among statesmen. There was no longer that authoritative influence on affairs exerted by Münnich and Ostermann, while
Biron was no more. Those previously restrained by such powerful
figures now found themselves free and independent and, in hastening
to take advantage of their new situation, inevitably clashed. Most
gifted and active at this time were the Bestuzhev brothers and Procurator General Prince Nikita Trubetskoy. Alexis Bestuzhev's appointment as vice-chancellor clearly showed that he was regarded as
Ostermann's successor in foreign affairs. The office of procurator
general, restored by the Senate to its former status, gave Trubetskoy
the widest influence in domestic affairs. Clearly it would have been
possible to share responsibility, but men do not like to share power.
In Anna Leopoldovna's time, Trubetskoy gave Bestuzhev his support, but at that time wanted to use him as a foil against Ostermann
and could reckon that Bestuzhev, having no other support and therefore beholden to him, would serve as his tool.

But with Elizabeth's succession to the throne relationships
changed. Bestuzhev immediately began to canvass support, to renew old contacts now close to the new empress, and who had been
members of the former crown princess's court: Razumovsky, Lestocq
and Vorontsov. This was bound to alienate Trubetskoy from Bestuzhev, to prevent whose ascendancy he now joined forces with Senior
Chancellor Prince Cherkassky. In their eyes Bestuzhev was nothing but an upstart and an intriguer, as long as he sought to act independently, and refused to be the humble servant of their excel-
lencies. Prince Cherkassky, no longer dominated by Ostermann,
suddenly wanted to be a genuine chancellor and to control foreign
affairs himself, rather than having to rely for everything upon the
capable, experienced and energetic vice-chancellor. Such aspiration
on the part of a lazy and incompetent old man irritated Bestuzhev,
and only could affect matters adversely.

Prince Trubetskoy felt justified in regarding the Bestuzhevs from
the start as deserters to the enemy and traitors to the Russian cause
because of their alliance with Lestocq. The procurator general did
not consider the coup of November 25 complete while foreigners
still occupied important posts in the army and were close to the

empress. He attacked Field Marshal Lacy,[21] alleging that he was too old to know what he was doing and urged that General Löwendahl[22] be court-martialled for his conduct in the Swedish war. But his target was Lestocq who by virtue of his position near the throne exerted great influence. This enmity reached the stage where Trubetskoy and Lestocq complained about each other to the empress and were declaring openly their sworn enmity.

Naturally Trubetskoy's enemies gave him no quarter. They claimed that the procurator general was directing domestic affairs arbitrarily, and that his actions were nothing but a series of violent and unjust abuses. Removing all who stood in his way, especially the "Germans,"[23] he aimed to restrict the supreme power and arrange the succession to suit himself. Perhaps it was his dislike for the miniature German court of the duke of Holstein that brought matters to a head. Trubetskoy was charged with being acceptable to none save the clergy and the Guards.

Elizabeth, by nature intelligent and perceptive, could hardly miss the bickering between her court dignitaries. She was unruffled. As she was well disposed to them all, and felt they were all equally indispensable to her, she was reluctant to sacrifice one to gratify the other. But while contending for her trust and favor, they failed to appreciate, as is usual in such cases, just how much their positions depended on her goodwill. Instead they complained that she was inconsistent in apparently agreeing with one view, only to change her mind on hearing another. They claimed that she was underhand and devious. Not possessing brilliant abilities, education, preparation, experience or inclination for government, Elizabeth clearly had no independent opinions or views, except when guided by instinct. Hearing one view, she would accept it, and her lively character would prompt expressions of approval. Unwilling to settle a question on the basis of first impressions, she listened to another opinion and saw another aspect of the situation. Consequently she found it difficult to make up her mind, comparing ideas and thinking them over. This in turn irritated those who wanted to see their suggestions speedily acted upon. They protested that the empress neglected affairs of state and devoted all her time to amusements.

It cannot be denied that these complaints contained an element of truth. Perhaps Elizabeth was both lazy and pleasure-seeking, but it is worth noting that complaints to this effect arose from irritation and impatience. There were after all other reasons for slowness, above all the difficulty of reaching any decision in the face of so many conflicting opinions, of all of those whose advice she was prepared to listen.

EUROPEAN AMBASSADORS

Given the situation in Europe, the only possible course of foreign policy compatible with Russia's interests and national well-being was the preservation of the balance of power. This meant preventing France and Prussia gaining strength at the expense of Austria and Saxony. But the pursuit of this policy from the outset was hindered by Elizabeth's personal attitude to one or other of Europe's courts, and by her own like or dislike of these courts and their representatives in Russia.

We have noted that the European powers were divided into two camps, for and against the house of Austria. They had to campaign through their representatives at the court of St. Petersburg for the alliance, or at least the neutrality of Russia. Since the sympathies of the Brunswick family were with Austria, it was obvious that the representatives of the powers defending Maria Theresa enjoyed the government's special favor. For their part the representatives of these powers were bound to wish the Brunswick family well precisely because of its sympathy for Austria. Likewise they were bound to be unfriendly towards everyone hostile to Austria, including Empress Elizabeth, whose personal triumph they regarded as a triumph for France and Prussia.

The English ambassador Edward Finch[24] kept Ostermann informed of Elizabeth's moves. Maria Theresa's ambassador, Botta, had overwhelming reasons for siding with the Brunswick family against Elizabeth. From Saxony, represented by Lynar,[25] Elizabeth could expect nothing to her advantage, and consequently could not be favorably disposed. The Prussian ambassador Mardefeld acted with caution, tending to avoid Elizabeth.[26] But with the overthrow of Münnich there was some accord between Prussia and the Russian government, and consequently it was easy for Frederick II to win Elizabeth's favor.

Clearly the greatest favor of the new empress was to be enjoyed by France and its representative Chétardie. Thus it was above all those convinced that the coup of November 25 in no way should alter Russia's foreign relations, and honest enough to wish to follow a Russian national policy, even though inherited from the much-loathed Ostermann, who had to carry on the struggle with the empress's likes and dislikes.

Chétardie, who had been so anxious to secure Elizabeth's accession to the throne, was very unpleasantly surprised to learn of the coup of November 25 because it was effected without his knowledge much sooner than he anticipated, and by Russian means alone, without Swedish help. This placed France and its envoy to St. Petersburg in an extremely awkward position.

In the first days of Elizabeth's reign an unusual esteem surrounded the French ambassador, since his devotion to the new empress now was known to everybody. Finch wrote to his court that if it was the empress who was accorded the first bow, it was Chétardie who received the second. Perhaps Bestuzhev somehow realized the triumph would be short-lived and, foreseeing formidable difficulties for Chétardie, had no wish to support him. But the rest took a different view. The Guards officers, unbridled by virtue of Elizabeth's favor and not standing on ceremony, considered Chétardie a comrade in their enterprise. An eyewitness account tells how on one occasion two of them came to wish the ambassador a happy New Year, embraced him, kissed his hands, and told him that they looked upon him as their father, and upon his king as Russia's most trusted friend. They asked him to persuade the empress to go to Moscow as soon as possible, and to summon the duke of Holstein. They asked that a French princess be sent to Russia as soon as possible to be schooled in the Russian faith and given in marriage to the duke, who they guaranteed would be heir to the throne. Chétardie treated them to wine and gave them money.

THE SWEDISH QUESTION

The first and most important question confronting the new administration was the war with Sweden. The Swedes claimed that they had declared war in order to uphold the territorial rights of Peter the Great's descendants. Now that this was accomplished there was no longer any cause for war. Since the Swedes had suffered setbacks at the very outset of the war, and gave the new regime no help at all in the coup of November 25, Elizabeth felt no particular obligation towards them. To strengthen its influence in Russia, France could treat Sweden with the lack of ceremony accorded by England before the Treaty of Nystadt,[27] demonstrating that Sweden was merely a means of achieving certain ends. France should make it clear to the Swedes that because of their setbacks and their failure to help Elizabeth gain the throne they should now take advantage of her accession by bringing the war, which they were in no position to pursue successfully, to an honorable conclusion.

But instead France insisted that Russia owed Sweden reparations. This French demand only annoyed Russia by requiring concessions it felt no need to make. It produced a certain coolness in Elizabeth, dealing as it did so indelicately with what for her was such a sensitive issue, and could only lead Sweden into new difficulties, causing loss of territory rather than gain.

The first and most obvious concern of the new empress was to secure Chétardie's help in seeking an end to a war which no longer made any sense. Chétardie informed Löwenhaupt, who had commanded the [Swedish] troops on the road to Vyborg, of Elizabeth's accession, by means of which the war might be brought to an end. Löwenhaupt replied that there need be no bloodshed if he were assured that Sweden would receive favorable peace terms. Chétardie again wrote to him that assurances of a favorable peace settlement lay in the innate justice and sincerity of the Russian sovereign, and that he took upon himself the responsibility for the cessation of hostilities. His approach was based on his confidence that Sweden could not pursue the war with any success. Russia, in his opinion, was miraculously changed over the past week, its strength doubled by the coup; the confiscated estates of those arrested provided the means to continue the war without burdening the taxpayers. The Russian people, inspired by love of their country, would fight with renewed determination. The Swedes would erase Russian memories of the service they had rendered by the well-known manifesto, and perpetuate Russian hatred towards them.[28] No matter how courageously the Swedish army fought, Löwenhaupt would not lead a single man back to Sweden. Moreover, he had received information about the pitiful state of the Swedish army, and so considered himself justifiably astonished that Löwenhaupt would accept only a treaty under which Russia conceded to Sweden everything Peter the Great gained by conquest. Although at first Löwenhaupt threatened to continue the campaign unless he was given Vyborg and Kexholm, he nevertheless withdrew to Fredrikshamn.

Meanwhile a Swedish captain, Didron, was released by the Russians and sent to the king of Sweden with the news of Elizabeth's accession. Count Löwenhaupt sent Chétardie a letter dated December 30. "My master the king, having heard from Captain Didron about Princess Elizabeth (madame la princesse) commands me immediately to testify to the great joy he feels at these happy and long-desired tidings. In so doing, I request your excellency to be assured of the respect and devotion nurtured by his majesty for this great sovereign lady, and of his pleasure in seeing her on the throne which is rightfully hers by birth and which her high personal qualities warrant.

"The king is fully convinced that her majesty will respond with her good favor to his sentiments and to whatever the means which might further peace and harmony in the interests and security of both our countries. The king is very appreciative of the favor shown by her majesty to Captain Didron; he is anxious to take the first opportunity of expressing his profound gratitude, and has accordingly commanded me to free the Russian prisoners at Fredrikshamn."

In concluding the letter Löwenhaupt asked Chétardie to inform the Russian sovereign in the king's name of the death of Queen Ulrike Eleonora.[29] From the Russian court Chétardie received a note indicating the lines along which he was to reply to Löwenhaupt's letter. The empress's release of Captain Didron might serve to show the king how earnestly her majesty sought opportunities to demonstrate her profound esteem for him. Her majesty's action on this occasion should illustrate further her sincere conviction that there was nothing she desired more than to reciprocate fully the good intentions and disposition expressed in Count Löwenhaupt's letter.

This exchange of courtesies was easy, but getting down to the business of peacemaking was very much harder. How much this difficulty was felt by the instigator of the war, France, is evident from a letter of January 12, 1742 from Amelot[30] to Count Castellain, ambassador to Constantinople. "It is too early yet to draw up a plan of action in relation to Russia. Princess Elizabeth's accession is presently advantageous to us, since the 'German'[31] government was completely devoted to the Viennese court, whereas the new tsaritsa has revealed her goodwill towards France and seeks French mediation in concluding the Swedish war. But all this is only verbally apparent. His majesty the king of Sweden now, as before, desires honor and security for his people. They cannot conclude peace without in some way diminishing the security of their borders, and I foresee that Russia will only agree to a treaty for fear of hostile alliances. Therefore you should give your support to the good offices which the Porte[32] displays in favor of Sweden."

Accordingly Chétardie received a severe rebuke in a letter from Amelot. "I was very surprised that on the day after the coup you decided to write to Count Löwenhaupt about the cessation of hostilities. What astonished me even more was that you were willing to assume responsibility for all the consequences. I cannot reconcile such a course of action with the knowledge you have of the king's intentions and with your own intelligence of the enfeebled state of the Muscovite army, which is in great need of even the most basic essentials and which, in your opinion, would certainly suffer defeat on its first encounter with the Swedes.

"Your letters were full of information to the effect that the Russian government hitherto won respect abroad only on account of its outward splendor, concealing its inner weakness. How can everything have changed within twenty-four hours, and how have the Russians become so fearsome that the Swedes' only hope lies in the goodwill of the tsaritsa who is in a position to destroy them? The king thinks quite differently and more realistically. The haste with which the tsaritsa availed herself of your position to halt Count Löwenhaupt stemmed from fear caused by rumors about this general's advance, rather than from a desire to please the king and to deal cautiously with a people friendly to France.

"You were misled about news of the poor state of the Swedish army, which was terribly exaggerated if not false. But even supposing it was correct, you should never have stopped Count Löwenhaupt while the tsaritsa refused to give him the guarantees requested. It would have been better had the Swedish army been routed. Then the general's error would not have been blamed upon the ministry, which had no time to countermand its orders. Even then peace would be concluded as favorably as you feel compelled to wish at present, because you do not permit even a guess at the tsaritsa's wish to concede anything, and Sweden would not be able to reproach us. On the other hand, if Löwenhaupt were successful, the tsaritsa would feel herself fortunate if the king were able to obtain peace for her.

"I have to tell you that the Swedes are extremely annoyed and are convinced that the king of France was about to abandon them. I am sending a courier to Stockholm today in an attempt to mollify opinion there and to let them know how things stand in reality: that the change of ruler in Russia in no way alters the king's attitude nor French policy towards Sweden. Clearly the king always favored a coup in Russia only as a means to attain Swedish ends; if this coup has the contrary effect, the pains taken to bring it about must be regretted. The king's honor obliges him to support the Swedes and to afford them at least a part of the security and advantages they anticipated. His majesty cannot allow them to suffer in consequence of your word.... If the war continues the Swedes will not be without allies.... It is important that the conclusion of peace between Russia and Sweden lie in our hands. Let the tsaritsa remain assured of the king's good intentions, but she should not be too hopeful that the terms will favor her."

As a result of such views on the matter at Versailles, Chétardie was obliged to follow his instructions and inform Petersburg of the following. "Sweden took up arms both to win satisfaction for the wrongs done by the previous German government of Russia, and from a desire to regain lost provinces. The obligations which the king of France has entered into regarding Sweden cannot be conditional, and since the king made efforts on behalf of the sovereign now ruling Russia precisely to help Sweden, her majesty cannot be vexed with him for being bound to serve Swedish interests. The Swedes are hoping to receive by her majesty's goodwill that which they previously thought they could obtain only by force of arms. Count Löwenhaupt's hope is not based on chimeras, as next spring's campaigns will show if, unfortunately, the war continues."

"It was on the basis of Chétardie's plans that Löwenhaupt halted his campaign. France consequently takes responsibility for the word given by the ambassador. The king of France finds himself in a very difficult position. On the one hand from personal inclination he wishes to be of service to her majesty in furthering the glory and success of her reign, while on the other hand he is obligated to Sweden, France's oldest ally. Should he desert Sweden, he would be betraying his most formal obligation. Sweden apparently never will agree to an unfavorable peace. The king of France can moderate Sweden's demands, but he also hopes that her majesty will appreciate that she must make some sacrifice if she wishes to bring the peace negotiations to a speedy conclusion."

On January 11 Chétardie read this to the empress herself in the presence of Lestocq, who translated into Russian the passages which she did not understand. Elizabeth replied that she would use all the means indicated to her by the king of France to show her goodwill to the Swedes, provided it involved no compromise injurious to her own honor and glory. Let the king judge for himself. What would her people say when they saw that a foreign princess, little caring about Russia's interests and having by chance become ruler, nevertheless preferred war to the shame of making any concession, while the daughter of Peter the Great, for the sake of concluding the same war, showed herself ready to accept conditions contrary to the interests of Russia, contrary to her father's glorious memory, and to everything which had been bought at the cost of her subjects' blood for the achievement of his aims.

Chétardie had to repeat that as the king of France had incited the Swedes to acquire the throne for her, Elizabeth ought to help the king find a way out of the impasse into which he had stumbled on her account. Elizabeth retorted that, given the same circumstances, the king would act in exactly the same manner. Never would he tolerate any disrespect for the memory of his late father.

It was suggested to Chétardie from Versailles, among other things, that he not antagonize the Russian ministers by negotiating directly with the empress. Chétardie therefore asked Elizabeth's permission to read the same statement to Vice-Chancellor Bestuzhev. At this time Chétardie considered Bestuzhev equally as likely as Lestocq to act in France's favor, since he was at odds with Chancellor Prince Cherkassky, whose views on European affairs were very clear. He favored the Austrian cause, while Bestuzhev did not yet declare himself against France, whose good offices he probably intended to use in the Swedish question. It was on this basis that

Chétardie long wanted to see Bestuzhev promoted at the expense of the hostile Cherkassky. He put it to the empress that the foreign ambassadors were finding it difficult to establish a working relationship with Prince Cherkassky, since he did not know a single foreign language, and that they desired the appointment of a minister with whom they could communicate directly. "It is too soon," Elizabeth replied. "In any case, why do you want this? You will conduct negotiations with me directly; as for the other ambassadors, let them do as they think fit."

Bestuzhev was waiting to see what line France would take on the Swedish question. He told Chétardie frankly that he was in an awkward position because he knew neither what the French attitude would be, nor whether there would be peace or war with Sweden. Moreover the Austrian and English ambassadors, Botta and Finch, were making relentless efforts to win him over to their side. Chétardie offered him an annual pension of fifteen hundred livres as a token of the king's satisfaction with his intention to assist the French cause. Bestuzhev declined, saying that he had not yet done anything to merit the king's gratitude, and that in any case he was ready to serve the king's interests without any inducements, as long as they corresponded to those of her majesty. Lestocq, on the other hand, as a foreigner could not cultivate a strong sympathy for Russia, of whose interests he had only the vaguest understanding. He did not wait to see whether French interests corresponded with the Russian, but accepted the pension, promising to earn it.

The note which Chétardie read to Bestuzhev jolted the vice-chancellor from his state of indecision, since it showed that Russia could expect no good from France. He informed Chétardie flatly that any negotiation not based on the terms of the Treaty of Nystadt were out of the question, and rightly would he incur the death sentence were he to advise conceding an inch of land. "War will have to be waged!" Bestuzhev exclaimed. "This is what we should all demand for the glory of the sovereign and our people. We are prepared to wage war. I think, however, that without having to resort to such an extreme we will be able to guarantee Sweden's security, and even promote its interests. After all, it is not only to Russia that it has conceded land. Might it not be more advantageous to regain what it has conceded to others?"

"I take it that you are referring to Bremen and Verden,"[33] asked Chétardie, "is it not these you want to see returned to Sweden?" And he laughed.

"We can always come to an understanding," Bestuzhev replied. "We sincerely wish Sweden well and want to win its friendship. If the king of France brings about peace in the North, enters into a close alliance with us, develops trade and strengthens all this by blood ties, thus gaining Russian and Swedish goodwill, he will be in a position to give European affairs whatever direction he pleases. Assist us in our sincere intentions, and do not let us waste one more minute in ending this tense situation. Write to the king immediately, telling him that I am only too anxious to be of service."

In consequence of Chétardie's note a meeting of the three members of the council on foreign affairs convened. The procurator general and Field Marshal Lacy also were invited, and the empress herself was present. They reached the unanimous decision that any territorial concession was out of the question. Chétardie received the following reply. "We are not aware of any of the grievances brought against Russia, while Russia's actions in Sweden's favor are quite clear. Sweden's intention to take back its former provinces is most unlawful, being contrary to the Nystadt treaty and the alliance of 1735, on which Russia cannot ever compromise.[34] No matter on what Count Löwenhaupt based his hopes, were the war to continue we too should have to abide by the rules and customs of war. What right Sweden has to demand our fulfillment of promises made by France is a question we will pass over, but for the two states concerned, Sweden is not obliged to agree to a disadvantageous peace, while Russia will not agree to any violation whatsoever of the Treaty of Nystadt."

In accordance with this statement it was decided to renew and continue the war with the utmost vigor. Early in March hostilities were resumed. The Swedish army was gripped by the profoundest alarm. In Finland a manifesto from Empress Elizabeth was published, urging the local inhabitants not to take part in the unjust war. Should they wish to separate from Sweden and form an independent state, they were promised the empress's assistance. The manifesto stated that even Sweden could not find any objection to Finnish independence, since the existence of a buffer state between Russia and

Sweden could serve only to allay anxiety. Russia's decisiveness compelled the French to lower their tone.

On March 19 Chétardie asked Prince Cherkassky to authorize him to report to his sovereign that her majesty promised, as she had when heir to the throne, to find terms favorable to Sweden without violating the Nystadt treaty, taking into account that the Swedes, by undertaking this war were of considerable help to her majesty in inheriting the throne. The chancellor replied that as he had no knowledge of any such promise, he could not comment on it, but would report to the empress. He could only repeat that the empress's firm resolve was not to surrender an inch of land. The Swedes wanted it to be believed that they began the war for her highness's benefit when she was crown princess, but he could not confirm this without obvious shame to himself, since everyone knew that Sweden made preparations for war against Russia even during the reign of Empress Anna. The decision in fact was taken and Swedish troops were transported to Finland in 1739.

"I can give a genuine assurance," was Chétardie's brazen reply, "that when Sweden declared war the intention to reclaim at least some lost territories was set aside, and Sweden's sole objective was to help her majesty gain the throne. I can prove this by reference to everything that took place in strictest secrecy at the time, and can also state the promises her majesty made as early as September."

FRENCH MEDIATION

The court transferred to Moscow for the coronation. Chétardie went there too and was joined at the same lodging by the former Swedish ambassador to the Russian court, Nolcken, who came to Moscow to speed up the pace of negotiations.[35] On May 2 Nolcken was invited to a conference at the chancellor's house. Also present, apart from Prince Cherkassky, were General Rumiantsev and Marshal of the Court Mikhail Petrovich Bestuzhev, whose brother the vice-chancellor was absent through illness. When Prince Cherkassky told Nolcken that those present were ready to listen to his proposals, he replied that he was indeed empowered to conduct peace negotiations, but that since French mediation was accepted by her majesty, he could not enter any talks without the presence of Chétardie. Nolcken was told that the empress never demanded or requested

French mediation, but had simply sought their good offices; if he was empowered to conduct negotiations, no mediation was necessary.

"Good offices and mediation are one and the same thing," Nolcken said, "and I find it regrettable that I encounter difficulty on this subject. I was sent here to discuss matters in the presence and with the mediation of Chétardie, as my written instructions show. Therefore to avoid wasting time Chétardie should be sent for, so that together we can get down to business amicably. I simply cannot say anything if Chétardie is not present."

"Mediation and good offices are by no means one and the same thing," Cherkassky retorted, "and as a former ambassador you must know that. Chétardie by all means may show his good offices to you, but not during your presence here; only in the event of any deadlock between the two sides is he to make his representations to the Russian and Swedish courts alike. Apart from that French mediation is unacceptable because, as everybody knows, France and Sweden are in close alliance, and France clearly cannot abandon Sweden in its present difficulties. Consequently understand that such mediation is out of the question. Moreover it would be more honorable for Sweden to conduct negotiations without French help and bring them to the desired conclusion."

"That's as may be," Nolcken answered, "but my hands are tied, and I therefore request your help by formally excluding French mediation." He was told that Chétardie had nothing to demand. Russia never requested French mediation, but only good offices.

On May 5 a second conference took place, at which Nolcken made the following statement for transmission to the empress. "Solution of the question of French mediation is bound up with a consideration which should serve as the basis for these negotiations: the intentions and aims of Sweden as set out in the manifesto published in General Löwenhaupt's name. These intentions and aims have been endorsed by the French. Heaven has blessed them by placing the crown upon the head of her All-Russian majesty, to the great satisfaction of the allied powers, and the whole Russian people. Hopefully her majesty does not wish to challenge the validity of this basis. From the time of her successful accession to the throne the intentions of Sweden and France have not changed, and so it remains only for the matter to be formalized by treaty. On this basis there can be no good reason for prolonging the difficulties regarding French mediation, particularly in view of the peaceful declarations from both sides, which have been transmitted through the French ambassador since her majesty's accession to the throne."

The conference ministers countered that such improper observations, far from bringing peace any nearer, could only postpone it even further. They told him that they did not dare pass all this on to her majesty, for Nolcken had referred to Count Löwenhaupt's manifesto in a way which suggested, albeit implicitly, that the empress had received her rightful throne thanks to the Swedes and the French, a claim which no one in the Russian empire recognized.

"I request that this matter be reported to the empress for her to decide," Nolcken answered. "Furthermore, I go so far as to say that it was not against her majesty that my master the king and the Swedish people declared war, as is clear from the joy felt by the whole of Sweden on hearing of her majesty's accession to the throne. Everyone thought the war was now over. I came here to negotiate with friends, not enemies. I make bold to say that the causes and aims of the war are those outlined in Count Löwenhaupt's manifesto. I am not saying that it was the Swedes who put her majesty on the throne, but it is impossible to deny that this is what they wished and, since France took the same view, the necessity of her mediation in these peace talks is tangible."

The ministers replied that it was useless to refer to such a shameful manifesto. There was nobody in Russia, certainly no minister, who believed that the Swedes declared war for the sake of her majesty. Everyone knew that they long sought an opportunity to attack Russia, and everyone was aware of how many intrigues they instigated in various courts, even after her majesty's accession. As to whether French mediation could be accepted, let him decide for himself after listening to what Marquis de Chétardie had informed vice-chancellor Count Bestuzhev in his letter of January 4. This extract was read out, and Nolcken's attention was drawn in particular to the first point, which stated that Sweden began the war to regain the provinces ceded by the Treaty of Nystadt, and to the point which contended that France would violate the most solemn obligations by deserting Sweden. The ministers asked Nolcken if this statement accorded with the view he was now advancing, and whether a mediator was necessary in such straightforward relations. Even if her majesty originally requested the mediation of the king of France, now she would be perfectly justified in refusing it in view of this statement.

Nolcken was thrown into confusion by these words, and for a moment was at a loss what to say. Then he said that although previously there may have been some who shared Chétardie's view concerning war aims, he found it surprising that the marquis had expressed it to the vice-chancellor without telling him. Seeing that her majesty considered it a matter of honor not to concede anything to the Swedes, other ways would have to be found to compensate the Swedes for their losses in the war. Any concession made to Sweden would be made by friends to show her majesty's friendship to Sweden, on whose part there was a friendly demand that the security of its borders be guaranteed.

The ministers replied that Russia, as the victim of aggression, was entitled to demand compensation for the military losses inflicted by Sweden, and not contrariwise. Concessions were out of the question. Her majesty was not prepared to concede an inch of land, and in any case could not, since she was bound by the Nystadt treaty. Perhaps, in order to secure its borders, Sweden should concede to Russia the rest of Finland; if Nolcken sincerely wanted to see an end to the war, all arguments about how it started should be set aside, and they should get down to business without the interference of Chétardie, who could not be permitted to mediate. With this the conference ended.

On May 12 Nolcken informed the ministers that after careful consideration he had decided that his best course would be to leave Moscow for Sweden. There he would report the Russian government's desire for peace, and its wish to conduct negotiations directly with Sweden, without French mediation which, as he had understood, was not sought. He pointed out that in Sweden neither the king nor anybody else realized this, but were all convinced that her majesty requested French mediation and accepted it. It was on this basis that he was sent here. Nolcken informed the ministers in confidence that he would not be going to Stockholm but staying at Fredrikshamn with General Löwenhaupt.

ANTI-FOREIGN INCIDENTS

Nolcken left Moscow and actually remained in Fredrikshamn, whence on June 6 he sent a letter to Field Marshal Lacy in his encampment, by the hand of a non-commissioned officer and a drummer, informing him of his arrival, and a letter addressed to Chétardie, to be forwarded to Moscow. The non-commissioned officer and a drummer were placed under the command of the Cavalry Guards at Major General Lieven's headquarters. But on the same day a call to arms went around the Guards infantry regiments, "To arms! Swedes, Swedes!" The regular infantry regiments also were roused by the cry, but were restrained by their colonels. Then shots came from the Guards regiments, soldiers rushed to Lieven's headquarters, dragged the Swedish non-commissioned officer and drummer out, and gave them a severe beating.

Another crowd rushed to the tents of Captain Respe and Lieutenant Uexkull of the Cavalry Guards, and dragged them both out, shouting "The Germans are traitors, and are in league with the Swedes!" Meanwhile four guardsmen mounted their horses and galloped around the camp, shouting "Death to all Germans!" Hearing this, General Keith[36] rushed from of his tent with a cane, ordering the cuirassiers and Cavalry Guards to form up in battle order, and shouted to the Foot Guards that unless they laid down their weapons he would give the order to fire on them. This brought the infantry under control. Keith then placed the ringleaders under arrest. As they were pushed to the ground and tied up, they cursed their fellow soldiers. "Now look! The German traitors are tying us up, yet you are doing nothing about it. This is not what we agreed beforehand."

This was how Lieutenant Stachelberg reported the incident in Moscow, where he had been sent by Lacy. But in his report to Field Marshal Lacy, General Keith stated that "on June 6, Trinity Sunday, most of the Guards officers were dining in my quarters. Guards Major Cherntsov reported that the grenadiers were complaining that each man was allowed to take into battle only three grenades for each man. I immediately ordered that every means be taken to ensure that all available grenades be taken on campaign, and that the grenadiers be so informed, in order to pacify them. But just as I was arranging this, Guards Ensign Alekseev came in and reported that disturbances were spreading in camp, and that there was a rumor spreading among the men that most of the shot was of the wrong calibre for the cannon, and that the Cavalry Guards had no shot in their cartridges, and that there were spies in the camp at Major

General Lieven's headquarters. Next, Major of the Guards Saltykov then appeared and reported that there was great disorder in the camp. The grenadiers came to the Cavalry Guards' camp, beat up a Swedish non-commissioned officer and drummer, whom they dragged from Lieven's tent to their own camp, and were after their own officer, Uexkull.

"I myself ran immediately to their camp with the officers who were present. Arriving at the Cavalry Guards' camp, I saw a crowd of grenadiers, guardsmen and regular soldiers, without firearms, but some had swords. At the entrance to the camp I shot one grenadier and three troopers who were dragging off Captain Respe of the Cavalry Guards. I rescued the captain and ordered his captors arrested on the spot. To frighten the mutineers a little more, I ordered a Guards major to send for a priest immediately to hear the confessions of those who were to be shot summarily. I ordered the officers to check their companies and to make a note of absentees. On hearing this all the soldiers in the Cavalry Guards' camp hurried back to their units. I went myself with Major General Cherntsov to take the roll call of the Foot Guards, and came across the Swedish non-commissioned officer and the drummer in a grenadier's tent, guarded by two grenadiers with fixed bayonets. These guards had been posted on the orders of Second Lieutenant Shcherbakov to protect the Swedes from any further ill treatment. I ordered them to be taken back to the Cavalry Guards' camp. After roll call I ordered all the men back to their tents: they returned immediately. I further ordered the arrest of several men who had been identified as ringleaders."

General Alexander Ivanovich Rumiantsev was sent to conduct an enquiry into the affair, and to hold courts martial. It was found that "whereas it was stated in the decree of April 14, 1743 that all merit the sentence of death and other condign punishments, nevertheless we through our innate mercy reprieve them." The seventeen culprits were sent to work in the Siberian factories for life, or to serve as common soldiers in distant garrisons.

RENEWAL OF NEGOTIATIONS

Rumiantsev soon had another matter to attend to. On July 23 Field Marshal Lacy received a letter from Nolcken in Borga. It said he had arrived in Stockholm, where he informed his government of the

course of the negotiations in Moscow, and was now returning to
Finland as "commissary and minister plenipotentiary" to initiate
peace talks. On the Russian side these negotiations were entrusted
to Rumiantsev, later assisted by General Lübras; the Swedes' principal negotiator was Senator Baron Söderkrys, assisted by Nolcken.
Åbo was designated as the site of the conference.

All these contacts and negotiations did not halt hostilities. Many
Russians carried on fighting because they found it possible to ravage
the country unchallenged. The Don Cossacks in particular distinguished themselves under the command of their elder Krasnosh-
chekov, recently promoted to brigadier.[37] At the end of June Lacy
reached Fredrikshamn; the Swedes hastily abandoned the fortress,
having set fire to it. Löwenhaupt quickly fell back to the Kymen
in the direction of Helsingfors. As a result of the enemy's "customary faint-hearted retreat," the Russians occupied Borga without
difficulty and pursued the Swedes towards Helsingfors. On another
front Nyslott surrendered without offering resistance to the detachment under Prince Meshchersky; Tavastehus followed Nyslott's
example. In August Lacy caught up with the Swedish army near
Helsingfors and cut off its further retreat to Åbo, proceeding along
a road built by Peter the Great, and now shown to the field marshal by a Finnish peasant.[38] At the same time the Russian navy
hemmed the Swedes in from the sea.

Löwenhaupt and Buddenbrook left the field, summoned to Stockholm to account for their actions before parliament. General Bous-
quet, who assumed command of the army on their departure, capitulated to the Russians. Under the terms of surrender the entire army
was to withdraw to Sweden, leaving all its artillery behind for the
Russians. The Finnish troops were permitted to return to their
homes. On August 26 the surrender was completed, and the Russians entered Helsingfors. The capitulated Swedish army numbered
seventeen thousand, being outnumbered by the Russians by no more
than five hundred men. "The behavior of the Swedes," wrote a
contemporary who left a description, "was so strange and so contrary to what usually is expected, that it will be difficult for succeeding generations to believe accounts of this war." After the
Swedish army evacuated Finland, its capital Åbo was occupied by
the Russians.

In Stockholm the generals were put on trial and paid with their lives for their incomprehensible behavior. But this could do nothing to redeem the situation. Renewing the war to regain Finland from the Russians was unthinkable. They had come to terms with the fact that Russia would make no territorial concessions. It was now a matter of how they might secure from Russia the least severe peace conditions, and hold on to at least part of Finland. A way was found: the duke of Holstein, nephew of the Russian empress, was chosen as heir to the Swedish throne.[39] Three Swedish deputies came to Russia with this news at the end of the year. They were Count Bonde, governor of Södermanland, Conference Councillor Baron Hamilton and Chamberlain Baron Scheffer. A meeting was convened to discuss this matter at the home of Field Marshal Dolgoruky on December 25. It decided that without in any way detracting from its peaceful stance, the best means for obtaining a quick settlement consisted in a display of immutable firmness at every step, which would compel the enemy to lay aside all cunning and guile and to get down to business immediately. It further recognized that the aim of the present embassy was to get Finland back either by delusion, or by ensuring that Russia somehow be prevented from preparing for war the following spring.

At the conference of December 28 the following peace terms were put to the Swedish deputies: Russia was to keep all conquests and receive compensation for war damage. Alternatively the bishop of Lübeck,[40] uncle of the duke of Holstein, was to be designated heir to the Swedish throne. One of the deputies, Baron Hamilton, answered vehemently that Sweden never would agree to such conditions since it was bound by the Nystadt treaty. They asked to be allowed to return to Sweden, where they would report that Russia, being flushed with victory, sought to interfere in Swedish domestic affairs and violate the liberty for which every Swede was prepared to die. Baron Scheffer voiced the same sentiments, albeit more moderately.

Words were one thing, but acting on them quite another. Sweden could not continue the war. Russia's triumph over the "aggressor" was complete, and it was a triumph won by firmness of the government, which not even the personal views of the empress herself, nor of individual ministers, could hope to shake.

RUSSIA'S FOREIGN RELATIONS
1742

FRANCE

The Swedish question demonstrated clearly the parlous state of Franco-Russian relations, and led to a break between Bestuzhev and Lestocq who, in receipt of a pension from the French court, remained devoted to it and acted against Russian interests both now in regard to Sweden and later in regard to Prussia. Bestuzhev, convinced of the incompatibility of French and Prussian aims with Russian interests, had to engage in an open struggle a man who was extraordinarily dangerous because of his closeness to the empress, his position and the fact that she was accustomed to him.

This intimacy greatly annoyed Bestuzhev, since it afforded Lestocq the opportunity to speak with the sovereign at any time and undermine what the minister established during his infrequent reports on state matters. Bestuzhev complained bitterly to Pezold, the Saxon representative. "The sovereign is extraordinarily inconsistent in the way she adopts opinions, since it depends on when and how they are put to her. Lestocq, whether in jest or in earnest, can say more to her than anyone else. When she is not in the best of health as her doctor he can talk to her alone for hours at a time, whereas ministers try vainly for weeks just to have her attention for fifteen minutes. Recently the empress suffered from colic, as she frequently does. Lestocq was sent for and quickly introduced Chétardie to her majesty and held some kind of secret meeting. When the ministers arrived she informed them of new evidence why France's friendship was useful and necessary to Russia, and praised Chétardie for his devotion and impartiality.

"Even assuming Chétardie to be devoted and impartial, Prince Cantemir[1] writes from Paris for God's sake not to trust France, whose sole aim is to clip Russia's wings, and keep it out of foreign affairs. Can I therefore in all duty and conscience favor France? Do

of my plain dealing, heeds Lestocq and Chétardie, who resort to
every dishonesty and calumny in pursuit of their aims? I am aware
that there are those plotting my downfall, but I rely on the justness
of my cause."

Pezold was obliged to listen to the other side. "I am attacked for
my association with Chétardie," said Lestocq, "but I love good
company, and nowhere can I enjoy such good conversation, dine,
drink and relax so well as at this ambassador's home. Moreover I
am greatly indebted to Chétardie for the services and financial
assistance he rendered me and the sovereign. Finally, I am convinced
that France's friendship is very useful and advantageous to Russia.

"Above all we had to stop the Swedish war, and I strongly advised her majesty to turn to the king of France for mediation. The
chancellor and vice-chancellor consider this some kind of criminal
act, saying that I urged an action against the sovereign's dignity and
interests while they had to continue the winter offensive in Finland.
They have even given the sovereign to understand that I receive
money from the French court, as she told me herself.

"It would be more to the point if the chancellor and vice-chancellor paid some attention to their own shortcomings. A deputation
of Bashkirs[2] came here, and the chancellor kept them waiting for
more than two months without presenting them to the empress. The
Bashkirs eventually turned to me, and I discovered that they had
a legitimate complaint against Governor Tatishchev of Astrakhan,
who sent the chancellor a gift of thirty thousand rubles to ensure
that their pleas got nowhere. I reported this to her majesty, who
asked vehemently why the vice-chancellor did nothing even if the
chancellor kept quiet. In reply I told her what was going on in the
College of Foreign Affairs. The chancellor, out of jealousy, was in
the habit of taking all papers home, where they would remain for
weeks or even months before the vice-chancellor found out anything
about them. For his part the vice-chancellor is a very unassuming
character, and can never bring himself to report such matters.

"So it is quite evident that I never had the slightest desire to harm
Bestuzhev. On the contrary, I have always acted and petitioned on
his behalf, and secured him his position and blue ribbon in the first
place.[3] I never held a high opinion of his intelligence, but what can
you do when there is no one else more capable? I hoped he would
be dutiful, and that his brother, the lord high marshal of the court,

Dr. Lestocq, Elizabeth's Physician
Johann Cristoph Grooth (1716-1749)
Palace Museum of Pavlovsk

would be a good example to him, but I was utterly mistaken. Both brothers are limited, cowardly and lazy, and so either they do nothing or, if they do anything, they are guided by prejudices, selfishness and spite, which is especially characteristic of the vice-chancellor.

"At present they are under the influence of General Botta and, in their view, the empress should not abandon the queen of Hungary. The empress noted this long ago, and now reveals to me that she suspects the vice-chancellor of receiving twenty thousand rubles from the queen of Hungary. This suspicion is strengthened by the fact that Bestuzhev either pales or blushes every time someone says something against Botta in front of him. Consequently time will show which is more corrupt, I or the vice-chancellor, and whose advice was the more useful. Since the alliance between this cabinet and that of Vienna came into force Russia gained not the least advantage, but rather loss, as was the case in the last Turkish war.[4]

"Apart from this, the vice-chancellor incurs suspicion by strongly insisting on the deportation of the Brunswick family from Riga. Although this was promised in the manifesto, it was enacted hastily, without sufficient consideration. At present nobody who wishes the sovereign well would advise this course of action, and as long as I live and enjoy some influence, the former regent will not leave Russia. Russia is Russia after all and, since this will not be the last promise broken, why should the empress care what others say."

Lestocq's aspersions on the two Bestuzhev brothers showed the extent of his latent hostility. Chétardie expressed himself just as bluntly. "Ostermann was a rogue, but an intelligent rogue who knew well how to sugar his pills. But the current vice-chancellor is simply a half-wit. As far as the lord high marshal is concerned, perhaps he is not stupid, but he trusts Botta too blindly." But Chétardie, at least temporarily, had to yield place to the half-wit. He left Russia, considering it impossible to remain any longer after his role as mediator at the peace negotiations with Nolcken was rejected. Elizabeth parted with him as with an old friend, and made it clear that she had lost none of her liking for him, but she no longer relied upon the friendship of the French court.

To illustrate France's hostile intentions Bestuzhev referred to Prince Cantemir's dispatches. On January 7, 1742 Cantemir wrote to the empress "The ministry here expects the happy change in

Russia will have useful consequences for France, and if your majesty's own inclinations coincide with French intentions, I have no doubt that there will be displayed the most sincere interest in entering into closest relations with Russia. The primary concerns of French foreign policy are the queen of Hungary and the English. The most powerful efforts in France aim at the complete overthrow of the house of Austria; any country standing in the way is considered an enemy, and therefore liable to similar treatment.

"Because here Russia was regarded with hostility, enemies were incited against us to prevent us from acting on behalf of the house of Austria. French hatred for the English is based on much the same thing, although they do not actually say that it is reinforced by English prowess at sea and by flourishing trade.

"From this it will be clear to your majesty that if you intend to uphold our long-standing obligations to the Viennese and English courts, you must not allow yourself to be tempted by French friendship, for obviously they are in no hurry to reconcile Russia and Sweden without first thoroughly examining your majesty's intentions."

Regarding reconciliation with Sweden, Cantemir wrote in March "The French proposals are in no way compatible with the oft-repeated assurances about sincere and royal benevolence towards your majesty. Apart from these proposals, France has drawn up a plan for a triple alliance with Sweden and Denmark. France is inciting the Porte against Russia. It is thus clear that the old French aim of diminishing Russia's power still holds good. I am obliged to emphasize that all precaution against French guile is not only thoroughly desirable, but absolutely vital, because French declarations cannot be trusted. It is true that the danger presented by Holland and England might stop the French sending a naval squadron to the Baltic, an action which the Swedish ambassador is urging energetically.

"On the other hand French fears of a general war will not permit the slightest decrease in available land forces by sending even a few troops to Sweden's aid, but we should not be deceived into thinking this ability will prevent France doing any damage to us, or that France harbors any good intentions towards us."

In April, when news came about the renewal of war between Russia and Sweden, Fleury[5] and Amelot reprimanded Cantemir, saying that the decision to renew the war was taken by the Russian government in spite of the promise given by the empress to the marquis de Chétardie. The cardinal voiced this complaint courteously, but Amelot did not mince his words, calling Russia's action "hardly honest" (peu honnête) and a "sudden attack" (surprise). Reporting this to his court, Cantemir repeated the customary refrain. "From this we can be yet more sure of France's ill intentions towards Viennese interests and, I think, it can be reckoned a permanent feature of French foreign policy, that French interests demand a diminution of Russian power."

ENGLAND

With the coolness of the new Russian government's relations with France over the Swedish question, there naturally followed a rapprochement between Russia and England. While Russia's prime consideration remained relations with Sweden, England's main concern was with Europe as a whole.

The coup of November 25 produced on nobody a more disagreeable impression than on Finch, who saw in Elizabeth's accession to the throne a triumph for Chétardie and France, dashing all hopes his government had in Russia's intervention on Maria Theresa's side in the struggle for the Austrian succession. Apart from this, Finch could no longer remain in Russia, for the new empress was unable to deal amicably with a man who gave warnings about her to the previous government. Sir Cyril Wych was sent to Petersburg in his stead.

Russia's representation in London was changed at the same time. High Chamberlain Semeon Naryshkin replaced Prince Ivan Shcherbatov.[6] The Walpole government fell in consequence of the extreme stand it took on the policy of non-intervention, which at this time did not suit England either. The new minister of foreign affairs, Lord Carteret,[7] greeted the incoming ambassador with the following words. "Although the king was well satisfied with Prince Shcherbatov, we are pleased to have you here." Naryshkin asked Carteret if there was anything he wanted passed back to the imperial court in Petersburg. "His majesty the king," he replied, " desires nothing more than friendship with her imperial majesty. We are well aware of Russia's strength in European affairs. Many seek the friendship of your court, but no alliance would so accord with

Russian interests as alliance with the maritime powers. This is what
Peter the Great sought in order to maintain the balance of power
in Europe. I hope her majesty will not depart from those high principles. From no other country do so many empty ships sail to your
ports to be laden with your goods as from England. From other
countries boats may come with wine and other trifles, but such trade
will not be anything like as profitable in terms of hard cash as ours."

In March Naryshkin received instructions from Petersburg to
testify in general terms to Russia's immutable desire to maintain
the king of England's friendship, and to declare that the empress
commanded the revision of the Anglo-Russian treaty of alliance but
this matter was not yet finalized because of various problems arising
from her accession and her departure for Moscow. Naryshkin was
instructed to avoid giving any further details of the political situation, or about assistance for the queen of Hungary.

At the end of April Carteret told Naryshkin that the king, while
forbidding him to enter into explicit explanations, had ordered him
only incidentally to have the empress advised that, in her own interests, she return as quickly as possible from Moscow to Petersburg. The mere fact of her presence in Petersburg would be tanta-
mount to having thirty thousand auxiliary troops by virtue of her
proximity to European events. The queen of Hungary and the whole
of Europe only could be saved by the advice which the empress
could give to the kings of Prussia and Poland. Her return to Petersburg would scotch rumors put about by the French to boost Turkish
and Swedish morale, that Russia was reverting to character by
dismissing all foreigners from government posts and returning the
capital from Petersburg to Moscow. If a rumor the king heard was
correct, that the empress intended to go to Kiev in fulfillment of
a promise she made, the whole summer would pass without anything done, to the resultant advantage of the enemies of European
peace.[8] If the empress wishes to heed us, then together with Holland, our three countries will avert the European storm."

The renewal of the Swedish war prompted the Russian court to
communicate rather more explicitly with the English, and to bring
up once again the question of sending an English squadron to the
Baltic to defend merchant ships. Carteret expressed his view about
this to Naryshkin. "Our merchants are not demanding this, because
they are satisfied with written declarations given to me by the

Swedish ambassador in the king's name that our merchant ships can proceed in safety to all Russian ports. Moreover I told the Swedish minister frankly that the cloth these ships are bringing to Petersburg is for Russian army uniforms. Since Sweden always held England in high esteem, the promise of the Swedish king can be relied upon. But if our trade route is threatened in any way, we will be able to strike back with our squadron, which is prepared for any eventuality. It is unbecoming for England to send just five or six ships. If we send any, it will be fifteen, twenty or more. It is entirely up to the empress whether the vessels are sent. If she accepts our proposals, the ships will be ready as soon as she wants. The common interests of England and Russia require full agreement in general, and on the matter of urgent assistance for the queen of Hungary in particular."

In order to secure rapid Russian acceptance of the English terms, Lord Carteret wrote to Wych on June 8. "The king is aware of the influence of Count Lestocq, who is a natural subject of his majesty as elector of Hanover.[9] The king therefore wishes you to ascertain his attitude to his native country, and whether he would agree to serve the king, who in the event authorizes you to promise him a pension from us. You are also requested to make a similar proposition to the two Bestuzhevs. Neither of these gentlemen has any reason to be ashamed of accepting this kind of favor from the king, for nothing more is required of them than their cooperation in concluding a close alliance between the maritime powers and Russia for the restoration of peace in the north and the guarantee of the freedom of Europe, all of which is in complete accord with the true Russian interest."

Wych replied on September 9. "I have spared neither energy nor expense in winning Lestocq's friendship. I have spent many evenings with him and played him into our hands. He assured me that he will strive for a close alliance between Russia and England. I offered him a pension, which he accepted." The pension was £600 sterling

At the end of November Wych made confidential representations to the Russian court to the effect that his court very much wanted a frank declaration of the empress's intentions regarding Sweden, the restoration of the old ministry and of English influence. He announced England was prepared to collaborate fully with Russia, and to undertake joint measures. Wych was told that such a benevolent intention on the king's part was very satisfactory to the empress, and that she was ready to act with England jointly in Sweden to put it into effect. Since money helped a lot at representative assemblies in that country, the empress was prepared to allocate forty thousand rubles. Naryshkin was informed in London that Russia wanted to obtain the Swedish succession for the bishop of Lübeck, the administrator of Holstein.

Naryshkin was to pass this on to Lord Carteret with a request for cooperation. To dispose the king more favorably to such cooperation, Naryshkin was instructed to propose a marriage alliance between the bishop of Lübeck and an English princess. The Holstein minister Buchwald came to London for final negotiations. Naryshkin was ordered to act in this matter in strictest secrecy, in order not to jeopardize the arrangement by making a premature disclosure. Carteret told Naryshkin in reply that the French were allocating forty thousand pounds to Sweden so that its parliament would choose the duke of Zweibrücken as heir to the throne, whereas if Russia were to give forty thousand rubles and England as much again, it would amount to only twenty thousand pounds. Would the empress give still more money as necessity demanded?

"I am confident," answered Naryshkin, "that money is no object for the empress to carry out her wishes." "Our intention," Carteret continued, "was to obtain the Swedish succession for the brother of the present king of Sweden." Naryshkin replied that this would be extraordinarily difficult, in the first place on religious grounds, since the Swedes did not want a Calvinist. The second difficulty was a national antipathy towards the prince of Hesse personally. Thirdly, the French party simply would not agree. Consequently, to avoid the permanent loss of any influence in Sweden, only one course was left to England, to help Russia obtain the succession for the bishop of Lübeck, who could marry an English princess.[10]

Carteret agreed. "We shall be doing a great service if we succeed only in ridding you of the French." He let it be understood that the king earnestly desired to be a mediator in Russia's reconciliation with Sweden, particularly as French mediation was rejected. On Naryshkin's communiqué Bestuzhev commented, "When the mediation of one has been refused, there is no way it can be offered to another."

Meanwhile the promised revision of the treaty of alliance was completed and signed in Moscow on December 11 on England's behalf by Wych, and for Russia by Bestuzhev and Brevern. In the event of an attack on the English king, the empress of Russia was to send immediately ten thousand infantry and two thousand cavalry to his assistance, while under similar circumstances the English king was to send Russia a squadron of twelve ships, with seven hundred cannon. By mutual agreement this help could be substituted on either side by five hundred thousand rubles a year. If either of the parties were attacked while the other was at war, assistance was not obligatory. Nor was England bound to aid Russia in wars with Turkey or other eastern countries. Similarly Russia was under no obligation to help England in the event of an attack on its overseas territories. In Europe Russian troops would not be sent to assist the king in Italy, Spain or Portugal. After the pact was concluded Wych wrote to Carteret, "Lestocq is in receipt of a pension from France, but to give him his due, he has helped me considerably in arranging the speedy conclusion of our treaty."

DENMARK

We have noted help given Russia by Denmark in the previous reign. There was a long-standing defensive alliance between these two countries. But with the coup in Russia, which was so advantageous to the house of Holstein and consequently so dangerous to Denmark, Russians no longer could count on Danish aid.

Early in January 1742 Korf and Chernyshev wrote from Copenhagen that negotiations with England about the renewal of their subsidy treaty were unsuccessful. The change of government in Russia, with which the interests of the duke of Holstein were bound up, clearly called for a cautious reassessment by the Danish court, which naturally sought closer links with Prussia and Sweden than with England. Also in January Chernyshev had to leave for Berlin, while Korf remained by himself in Copenhagen. He reported from there that Danish fulfillment of alliance obligations to Russia could not be expected, but neither was it to be supposed that France would incite Denmark to war against Russia, because weak military and financial conditions would prevent Denmark from taking any action.

AUSTRIA

Consequently there was nothing to be feared from Denmark, and with England there was a defensive alliance. Yet this ally constantly talked about the need to maintain Europe's freedom by helping Maria Theresa. Nor were the English envoy or the English minister for foreign affairs the only ones to talk about this. Russian ministers did so as well. Trubetskoy, Cherkassky and the Bestuzhevs were all agreed on the need to come to Maria Theresa's aid, in spite of their antipathy for one another. But the empress would not hear of it. She could not suppress her hostile feelings for Austria, which in her mind was closely associated with the house of Brunswick. Immediately on her accession she told Chétardie that the Austrian envoy, Botta, with the active support of Prince Cherkassky, requested the assistance of thirty thousand troops for his queen. "I sent word to him," Elizabeth said, "that I am compelled myself to wage war, and the guiding principle is to think first of my own interests. I should like to know how the house of Austria might be useful to us, and what we might stand to gain from it."

"At present," Chétardie replied, "it would not be very useful at all. You may recall what I had the honor of saying to you a year ago. Had you not then been present to express your fortitude, the Viennese court, always hoping to guide Russia according to its own lights, would have succeeded in crowning the son of the prince of Brunswick, thereby completing a long term strategy initiated as far back as 1711 with the marriage of the tsarevich to the princess of Brevern."[11]

In this way the notion of a definite link between the Austrian and Brunswick houses was maintained skilfully. Elizabeth knew that the Viennese court had suggested to the previous government that she be declared the illegitimate daughter of Peter the Great and confined to a convent. It is therefore not surprising that Elizabeth could not refrain from schemes against the Viennese court. Thus when a quarrel arose among the envoys over seniority at the coronation ceremonies, she observed, "Botta has not the slightest reason to think highly of himself; if he starts giving himself airs, then he can return whence he came, since the friendship of those who stood by me earlier is dearer to me than the goodwill of his beggarly queen." When Prince Cherkassky and Bestuzhev both informed the empress about French intrigues in Turkey she replied that she did not believe it, but she knew that Botta had three hundred thousand rubles for the express purpose of bribing her ministers.

But still, such imperial outbursts did not obstruct the usual course of formal courtesies. On coming to the throne Elizabeth sent a message to the queen of Hungary and Bohemia, assuring her of her "true and inviolable goodwill." Maria Theresa told Lanczynski[12] in reply that she always derived great pleasure from news of any fortunate event in Russia, and it was with similar pleasure that she received assurances of unswerving friendship and alliance. For her part she would not fail to act in the same way. In conclusion the queen asked, "Have you not assured me of unwavering alliance?" Lanczynski repeated the assurance. "I am very glad," she answered.

When it became common knowledge that a coup took place in Petersburg, various rumors circulated [in Vienna]. Some were alarmed and remarked sorrowfully that there had been so many changes in such a short time; this latest change, it was thought, would bring the royal house here a lot of trouble because behind it all was France, intriguing through its ambassador and promising to reconcile Russia and Sweden. Thus their queen could expect no help from the present Russian government, even after peace between Russia and Sweden. Others maintained that the former government, in spite of close ties of kinship, had not helped the queen, but had been more inclined to the king of Prussia, with whom there were also links by marriage. Help might now be more readily forthcoming because the mother of the present tsaritsa[13] concluded an alliance with the late Holy Roman emperor [Charles VI], and the empress would not go back on her mother's policy.[14] Russia owed France nothing for the peace with Sweden. Russia was a strong country in its own right, populous and autocratic, and could deal with Sweden unaided without having to resort to an alliance with France.

Maria Theresa, it has been noted, found herself in a desperate position when France declared outright against her, and the king of Prussia concluded an alliance with the elector of Bavaria aimed at annexing Silesia to Prussia, and joining Upper Austria, Tyrol and Bohemia to Bavaria. At that time, according to Frederick II, a most advantageous and decisive event took place in the North. Sweden declared war on Russia and, with the consequent diversion of Russian forces, undermined all the anti-Prussian plans of the king of

England, the king of Poland and Prince Anton Ulrich.[15] King Augustus was carried along by the stream and aligned himself with the Bavarian elector's intention of destroying the house of Austria. The French and Bavarians entered Austria and invaded Bohemia, which the Saxons entered from the other side. The elector of Bavaria was chosen emperor with the title of Charles VII.[16] Thereupon Maria Theresa decided to rid herself of her most dangerous enemy, the king of Prussia, and concluded with him the Treaty of Breslau, sacrificing Silesia.[17]

Lanczynski took advantage of the elector of Bavaria's choice as emperor to raise the matter of the imperial title of the Russian sovereign, hoping that the Viennese court, despairing of keeping the Roman-German empire, would now agree to it. The state secretary informed Lanczynski that the queen would send Elizabeth a declaration with the imperial title, adding that Maria Theresa counted on Russian aid; Russia would not find a stauncher ally than the Viennese court, while France, along with other countries, merely deceived Russia, and would do nothing. If Russia allowed the queen's realm to collapse, Russia itself would incur thereby considerable harm.

Other notables told Lanczynski that his sovereign could easily win for herself immortal glory on three vital counts: by bringing peace to Europe, by satisfying Sweden by concession of some other territory at no cost to Russia, and by supporting the house of Austria, which was struggling for survival from enemy attacks on all sides. Peace should be concluded with the Swedes on the basis of the Nystadt treaty, for Russia could not desire any territory in stony and marshy Finland.[18] Moreover Sweden should be diverted to Pomerania, where compensation could be obtained. The Russian sovereign should send her troops to Pomerania to reassure Sweden, at the same time helping the queen by diverting Prussian troops for the defense of Stettin and neighboring towns; if she sent troops against Prussia, England and Holland would be forced to take a stand against France and subsidize Sweden.

It was uncertain what advantage the Russian court hoped to gain from friendship with the king of Prussia. Apparently attention should be paid to the remarkable increase in the strength of this monarch who soon would be in a position to field a hundred and fifty thousand troops, and for some time he cast covetous eyes on

Courland. France was sharpening envious teeth against Russia; having had its own way in Germany with the help of the king of Prussia, France also might proceed to embark upon some adventure against Russia in alliance with the same monarch.

In June Lanczynski reported that Austria was compelled to conclude peace with Prussia on unfavorable terms. The queen's chancellor, Ulefeldt,[19] told Lanczynski that "the English held a knife to our throats to induce us to make peace with Prussia, and we have conceded to all of the king of Prussia's demands. The best diamond[20] is snatched from the queen's crown without any guarantee of a secure peace. Perhaps like last time, Prussia will break the treaty without warning and attack. But what can we do? Extreme need compels us! We have no other way of raising more money."

PRUSSIA

It was above all to the advantage of Frederick II that the war between Russia and Sweden continue, since it would prevent their participation in the struggle for the Austrian succession. He was therefore not at all happy with Chétardie's attempts to bring the Russo-Swedish war to a conclusion, and neither was the French government. But not realizing that Chétardie had taken it upon himself to interfere in the matter without the knowledge of his government, Frederick was angry with the French court, and was astonished at its seemingly strange behavior. "I do not understand," he wrote to Mardefeld,[21] "why France is so busily engaged in stopping the war, when there is not the least advantage in extinguishing the flame ignited with such difficulty. On the contrary, it is to French advantage to keep Russia occupied in Sweden, thereby preventing either of them from becoming involved in European affairs."

On the other hand, Frederick was afraid that France, having reconciled Russia with Sweden, would begin to deploy their armies and use these forces to compel him to become subject to French control. For he knew very well that France would not accept the replacement of a strong Austria by an even stronger Prussia, but sought the breakup of Germany into small states. In his reports Mardefeld played on Frederick's fear of France, and as a result Frederick hastened to quit the war.

As far as direct contact between the new Russian government and Prussia was concerned, Elizabeth wrote to the king of Prussia as soon as she came to the throne informing him that she would avail herself of every opportunity to assure his majesty of her genuine and inviolable goodwill. Brakel was recalled from his post and died soon afterwards.[22] Gentleman of the Chamber Count Peter Grigorievich Chernyshev was appointed ambassador extraordinary in his place. The new envoy received the following rescript dated December 26. "Since the king of Prussia recently ordered his ambassador Mardefeld to demand the recall of Brakel, with whom he was not very pleased, you are to represent us to the king in a fitting manner, so that he shows us reciprocal indulgence. He has recalled from our court his ambassador Mardefeld."

But Mardefeld was not recalled, and Frederick II made every effort to gain the goodwill of the new empress. He reckoned that Chancellor Prince Cherkassky did not have long to live; that Vice-Chancellor Bestuzhev had powerful enemies and that the empress was not particularly well disposed towards him; that an important appointment in the department of foreign affairs was being prepared for a man who was close to the empress, Count Vorontsov, the husband of Elizabeth's favorite relative on her mother's side, Anna Karlovna Skavronskaia.[23] Consequently Vorontsov received from Frederick the order of the Black Eagle in the fall of 1742. At the same time Mardefeld announced that the king, in view of the services of the gentleman of the chamber, and the fact that he had the honor of being married to a relative of the empress, was anxious to express his high esteem for her majesty in making this award.

POLAND-SAXONY

Relations with the court of Poland-Saxony were dominated as before by the question of Courland.[24] With the changes in Petersburg there came a corresponding change of candidate for the throne of Courland.[25] The empress now ordered Keyserling[26] to support the candidature of the prince of Hesse-Homburg, a field marshal in Russian service,[27] rather than that of the duke of Brunswick. King August answered as before that he was very glad to be of help in fulfilling the empress's wish, particularly since he was on friendly terms with the candidate.

The former duke of Courland, Biron, was sent to live in Yaroslavl. But there was still an old pretender to the dukedom, who now sought to renew his claims. This was Count Maurice of Saxony.[28]

The empress favored the prince of Hesse-Homburg, but Lestocq and Chétardie were against him, since the German prince, through his marriage to the daughter of Field Marshal Trubetskoy, belonged to what they considered to be the enemy camp. Through Keyserling, Lestocq urged Maurice to come to Russia. Maurice appeared in Moscow after the coronation and stayed with Chétardie, who gave lavish dinners and suppers in his honor. Elizabeth received her former suitor very graciously, danced with him and took him on walks, but there the matter ended. After negotiations with the ministers the chancellor informed Maurice that the empress had derived much pleasure from his visit, but as far as the Courland question was concerned, her majesty repeatedly recommended the prince of Hesse-Homburg, and could not go back on her word. Since she had no intention, however, of attacking either the king of Poland, or the republic, or the people of Courland, but merely required that Courland preserve its ancient rights and liberty, her majesty would never act in any way against Count Maurice. With this reply the count left Moscow.

On the basis of secret information received from the Polish hetman Prince Radziwill and other well-intentioned Poles, Keyserling reported that many men, notably the elder Sapieha,[29] who was in receipt of a French pension, were trying to exacerbate the Courland question and other minor matters to sow dissent among the Poles. They were also making suggestions about assistance from Sweden and the large sums of money they would receive from other countries. These circumstances, they were urging, should be exploited, to strengthen the republic and restore it to its former glory. It was also being said, Keyserling's report went on, that Count Brühl[30] and Father Guarini, the king's chaplain, were devoted to Russia, but that the king thought otherwise. Since Keyserling's information came from Brühl himself, the ambassador suggested to him that it would be a good thing to assure the Poles of the king's sincere feelings for Russia. It would be easy to do so through the embassy sent to the empress to congratulate her on her accession. Brühl promised to do this.

Keyserling then put it to Grand Hetman Potocki[31] that the present situation in Europe might upset the peace of the republic, which depended on certain allies for support. The republic bordered on four strong neighbors. It must be decided which neighbor was most useful. Clearly Russia, since the empress was particularly well disposed towards the republic and sought the preservation of its peace and security. The hetman replied that in his opinion nothing could be better for the peace and security of the republic than friendship with Russia. In fact instructions were drawn up along these lines for Oginski, who was about to leave as ambassador to Petersburg with messages of congratulation.

Because of the confused situation in Europe the king could not travel to Poland,[32] and so convened the Polish Senate at the border town of Fraustadt.[33] Many Polish notables made for the town, and Keyserling was able to observe that the strengthening of Prussia produced a most disagreeable impression upon the Poles. The ambassador noted that while it was generally easy to find friends and supporters in a republican state, not one of the Polish dignitaries emerged as a follower of Prussia, with the exception of the governor of Bielz. Fear of Prussia lent the Poles a renewed loyalty for and trust in their king. Hetman Potocki, who always headed the anti-court faction, now declared that he and his confederates were completely at the king's disposal, and even presented him with a few hundred troops from his own host. It was fear of the Prussians which also explained their disposition towards Russia. Yet despite this widespread and positive attitude Keyserling did not rule out the possibility of the albeit small number of Swedish supporters finding a way to create unrest. For this reason he advocated the formation of a strong Russian party under the leadership of Tarlo, palatine of Lublin,[34] who should be supported financially. Hetman Potocki hinted that he was not paid all his pension; it would be advisable to keep him on our side.

The Swedish emissary Colonel de Bona went around the Polish dignitaries offering money for the formation of a general confederation, promising troops and supplies.[35] He demanded that Livonia be the theater of war against Russia, arguing that it would be difficult later to find more opportune circumstances.[36] It was discovered that Peter Sapieha, grand hetman of Lithuania, was attempting to aid the Swedes by raising and training troops, and persuading members of the Polish gentry to accept commissions in return for Swedish pensions. Young Orlik wrote to his father[37] in Jassy that Russia lost more than half its troops in Finland through disease, and that in Russia there was a strong party in favor of the deposed emperor. "We shall see," wrote Orlik, "what will happen at the next Sejm. We should prevail upon the king of Poland to join forces with his men and seize this golden opportunity to liberate his kingdom from Russian oppression, obtaining the return of Polish territory gained by Russia. He would succeed thereby in his general ambition to ensure that the Polish crown is inherited by his house."

But the king had no one with whom to join forces. For the most part the Polish gentry were completely out of sympathy with Swedish suggestions, and De Bona was arrested in Danzig. At the end of July Keyserling wrote that there was nothing to fear from Poland, and that the hetman would be constantly a staunch ally as a result of the goodwill shown by her majesty.

TURKEY

Another neighboring power, Turkey, was apparently more receptive to the blandishments of Russia's enemies, France and Sweden. Early in 1742 Veshniakov[38] reported that the French ambassador suggested to the Porte that Sweden began the war with Russia for Turkey's advantage, and was trying by every means to persuade the Turks to support Sweden financially, and to sanction a Tatar attack on Russia's borders. But the Turks did not allow themselves to be duped. "I have given a thorough appraisal of French treachery and Turkish weakness," wrote Veshniakov, "the English ambassador, with whose friendship and confidence I am now more than satisfied, is of considerable help to me."

In mid-April Veshniakov reported that war between Turkey and Persia was a foregone conclusion. This meant that the Porte was so preoccupied with its own problems that it could not possibly become involved in anybody else's. Even if the French were urging the Porte to support Sweden against Russia, in order to be secure from Russia during its own war with Persia, the Turks could not consent. Sweden's ambassador Karlsson, nonetheless, sought an alliance between Turkey and Prussia, on the strength of which Prussia would be permitted to raise an army in the Danube principalities. The Moldavian ruler, Gikah, supported Karlsson's view.

In September Miralem[39] informed Veshniakov that on French insistence the vizier was obliged to persuade the sultan of the need to help Sweden in accordance with the obligations of the alliance, if not by open force, at least with money. The sultan reacted angrily to this report, and sharply rebuked the vizier. He told him that he regretted that he had not ordered the beheading of the former foreign minister, who was the main instigator of this absurd alliance between Turkey and Sweden, and who had deceived the sultan with assurances that Sweden was just as powerful as Russia.

"When I was at war with Russia," the sultan continued, "Sweden was at peace. But when France felt compelled to support Russia, Sweden went to war. I do not want to hear about this Swedish alliance. My relations with Sweden are just the same as my relations with any other Christian country. Do not dare to remind me of the matter. It is not in my interest, and moreover it is against the law, since my treasury should be used only to support Islam and my subjects, not infidels. It is nothing to me if they all perish."

As a result of this the Porte informed Cardinal Fleury that Turkey was under no obligation to help Sweden, which had declared war on Russia on its own account, without informing Turkey in advance of the reasons, or demanding its good offices for its prevention, as the terms of the treaty required. The sultan could certainly not break with Russia, because there were not the least grounds for doing so. Moreover, if Turkey decided to violate peace with Russia, France, as guarantor of the peace, was bound to exercise restraint. Presumably the French guarantee was worthless when it was France that incited violation of the peace it guaranteed. This was a matter concerning only France and its relations with other Christian states, with which the Porte had no desire to become involved.

Apart from that, as Turkey was on the verge of war with Persia, it would be imprudent to provoke so powerful a state as Russia, which not only repelled Sweden with a mere quarter of its forces, but also brought about that country's utter ruin. The remaining forces might very well be deployed against the Porte in alliance with the shah. The causes declared by Sweden were hardly sufficient for bad relations with Russia, let alone war. Consequently the Porte was bound to deem this war unjust on Sweden's part, and could not therefore take any part in it. There was not much to say in reply to the Swedish ambassador's intimations that Sweden started the war for the Porte's benefit. If Sweden had the Porte's interests so much at heart, it should have taken Turkey's side in its own war against Russia, not two years after its conclusion. The Porte was fully justified in its anger at such suggestions, in which a complete lack of respect was clearly discernible, counting as they did on Turkey's stupidity and gullibility. Finally, even if the Porte wanted to act in some way out of respect for France, it was now in any case too late.

PERSIA

From Persia there came customarily remarkable reports. When the resident Kalushkin informed Nadir Shah of Elizabeth's succession, he replied that he was very glad to hear of it, and hoped that her majesty's state would be forever united. The throne of Russia, he said, was hers alone by law and by heredity, as the daughter of Peter the Great. He wished for this event, because he long knew of the empress's virtues. As a token of his joy he presented the envoy with a thousand rubles and a caftan with a sash and turban, a resident Russian student Bratishchev with three hundred rubles, and the interpreter with two hundred.

But with these civilities Nadir presented demands. (1) The two hundred horses destined for Persia and being kept at Kizliar should be released. Permission should be granted for the purchase of a larger number of horses and camels. (2) He was to be sent nine seaworthy vessels, three of which should be armed and with a full complement of powder and shot, manned by sailors and gunners, so that with their help the shah might root out dissidents living on an island in the Caspian sea. (3) The remaining seven [sic] vessels were to be laden with grain. Special agents would be sent to Astrakhan to purchase it. The grain should be delivered to the port nearest his camp, which was in its usual location near Derbent, for many Persian troops died from severe cold and starvation, not to mention the losses sustained in clashes with the Lezghi tribesmen,[40] who in the last battle had all but taken the shah himself prisoner.

Kalushkin as before could see no success for Nadir. The only likely outcome was destruction of Persia as a result of the reckless Dagestan campaign which the shah obstinately insisted on continuing. The resident wrote that the only way of moderating Nadir's demands was to move troops towards the border, and then pay no attention to the conqueror of India.[41] To satisfy Nadir and fulfill his demands was in no way compatible with Russian interests. Were the vessels to fall into his hands it would prove almost impossible to get them back. As long as the shah persisted in his desire to unleash the Persian fleet on the Caspian sea, Russian vessels would be always at risk. The Persians would try anything to attempt to acquire men and materials from them.

Kalushkin, dangerously ill as a result of the unpleasantness, his labors and all the deprivations he was experiencing in Persia, railed against Ostermann, who compelled him to endure all this rather than risk offending Nadir, even though it was clearly impossible to do anything with these barbarians by treating them with kindness and consideration. All the ambassador's calls for a bold and decisive policy towards Persia which would earn respect for Russia were scorned by Ostermann. Kalushkin even advised a temporary halt in trade with Persia to tame the shah's pride. Persian merchants must be obliged to come to Astrakhan; in this way Russian merchants would be freed from the violence they had to endure in Persia.

Kalushkin died but his suggestions were taken up by the new Russian government, especially in view of the abuse of the Russian consul in Riasche Arapovu, which convinced them that it was time to replace pleasantness with threats. Kalushkin's successor, the interpreter Bratishchev,[42] reported in July that the news about the continual movement of Russian troops towards Kizliar alarmed Nadir and took him down a peg or two. Like Kalushkin, Bratishchev stressed that there was nothing to fear from the Persians. "I make so bold as to report that there is no foreseeable difficulty in keeping so restless a neighbor in check. In order to capture the whole Persian camp we should need ten thousand or, at the very most, fifteen thousand regular troops and the same number of irregulars. There are many leading Persians, even eunuchs close to the court, who sincerely desire to submit to Russia. The men of Derbent and the town and country folk, who fear extermination at the hands of the tyrant, pray to God day and night for deliverance, and would consider submission to Russia a great happiness. Quite simply, there is scarcely anybody to be found in Persia who would not welcome Russian suzerainty."

In October Bratishchev reported that the shah intended to attack Kizliar, adding that all the mountain tribes were awaiting with impatience a Russian attack on the shah. Bratishchev's report on this general disaffection was confirmed by the unmasking of a conspiracy led by Nadir's son against his father's life. At the ensuing trial the son accused his father of wanting to have him poisoned. "The shah," wrote Bratishchev, "is in an immoderately bad humor and rarely hears things out; he only talks repeatedly about his son's crimes, complaining about everything that comes into his head. The whole camp is terrified, and nobody dares to go to the fearsome tyrant with their reports." Nadir had his son blinded.

Throughout November and early December Bratishchev continued to write about the shah's hostile intentions towards Russia. But then came news that these intentions altered on the advice of the shah's favorite, the mirza of Zekah and chief mullah, who pointed out that the Russians could advance against Persia by land and sea, and that the Andreevtsy and Kabardians[43] would be armed as Russian subjects. Finally Russia would raise the Dagestanis and the Turks. A Russian general already was in Kizliar with a large army.

In the second half of December renewed warnings of Nadir's hostile intentions were received from Bratishchev. Nadir had been convinced by certain individuals that Russia would be easy to attack. One such was an Englishman, Elton, who had built himself a ship on the Caspian Sea. Elton declared his readiness to transport men and munitions on this ship in the event of the shah leading an expedition against Russia. But evidently the strongest motive for a campaign against Russia was Nadir's desire to avenge the humiliation resulting from his ignominious defeat at the hands of the mountain tribes.[44]

V

THE REIGN OF ELIZABETH PETROVNA IN 1743

MORE EXILES RETURN

At the very beginning of Elizabeth's reign many who recently were disgraced returned from exile and were restored to their former positions. Memory of them was still fresh, and so they could well have had lively sympathizers. Not until early in 1743 was Anton Divier remembered.[1] He was a loyal servant of Peter and Catherine, and "suffered unjustly." His former rank of lieutenant general was restored, he was made a count and awarded the order of Alexander Nevsky. Second Lieutenant Alexis Shubin of the Semenovsky Regiment was banished, it was established, by Empress Anna for his connections with Elizabeth.[2] He returned to his regiment with the rank of first major, then was promoted major general for "unjustly enduring many years' exile in cruel confinement."

THE SENATE'S ACTIVITY

It is not known why the Senate was forbidden right at the beginning of the year to initiate proposals, either written or verbal, without the empress's personal written authorization. Four times in the course of the year Elizabeth attended the Senate, whose activity increased because of the procurators' reports on the state of disarray in several government institutions. For example the procurator general put before the Senate the report of Vasily Suvorov, procurator of the College of Mines, stating that at the end of the foregoing year 1742 the president of this college, arriving on the spot without calling a general meeting of the other members, drew up and signed an order for the release on bail of the factory worker Belov. This order subsequently was endorsed by the vice-president, one councillor and two assessors, but two other councillors and an assessor protested at Belov's release. There the matter ended but a little over a month later a deposition appeared, signed by the president and the assessors, calling for the case of Belov's release to be put before the Senate, since the other members of the college had no notion as to when this sentence was pronounced and signed.

There was no secretarial signature, from which they concluded that it must have been signed outside the college.

The procurator protested verbally and in writing about this handling of the matter, but he was not heeded. His protest was returned and the report on Belov's release was put before the Senate, which instructed that the College of Mines henceforth act correctly, not as in this case. The procurator's report alleging that the protocol was composed outside the college was to be examined in the light of the college's own submissions on the matter.

The College of Commerce decided to send Assessor Krasovsky to inspect the potash factories, but a subsequent announcement in its gazette stated that an officer from the Nizhny Novgorod government was to undertake this work, and that the decision regarding Krasovsky was to be reversed. The procurator blocked this new decision and demanded the implementation of the old. The college disagreed, but the Senate found in the procurator's favor. The procurator of Archangel government reported that secretaries were turning up at the office when they felt like it, with the result that suspects were being detained too long, while petitioners were having to endure unwarranted obfuscation and abuse. Moreover because of the chronic absenteeism of one secretary debts were not being collected, and when the procurator initiated proceedings against him, he was told very impolitely that "there was no way the governor could sack him."

The procurator of the College of Church Landed Property reported that some of its members never came to meetings, while those who came failed to deal with even the smallest matters, so matters dragged on. The procurator of Archangel government reported that the work of the police in Archangel and Vologda was not only desultory in the extreme and poorly supervised, but was on the point of complete collapse. The police force itself existed only in name, and nothing was being done to put this right. In April the procurator general informed the Senate that presidents and members of the colleges, chancelleries and government offices in Moscow were coming into work very late, at any rate not before nine in the morning, and so little work was done. The Senate ordered that designated working hours be strictly adhered to, but these orders had no effect. On November 1 the procurator general ordered an inspection of the colleges, chancelleries and other government offices at seven in the morning to ascertain whether work started at the regulation time, but the inspectors found not only none of the justices, but not even any secretaries. The offices were deserted except for the War College and the Provincial Chancellery.

Once more edicts were issued requiring regulation working hours, threatening fines for non-compliance. The procurators reported on the gross inefficiency of several of the colleges. But the Head Commissariat itself informed the Senate of a curious instruction it had issued. Without making any prior enquiries or asking for an edict from the Senate, it sent an order to the Belgorod government for the dismissal of the governor of Sevsk. The head of the commissariat was obliged to beg the Senate's pardon.

The Senate's negotiations with contractors for the works at Kronstadt form a curious feature of its activity in the year under discussion.[3] On June 3 building contractors were admitted to a meeting of the Senate. For a long time the senators tried to persuade them to construct the stone walls of the canal and cut the flagstones with payment by the sazhen. But the contractors refused, saying that no stonemason would undertake such piecework, they could not hope to recruit any, but they could find men to work for a flat rate of six rubles a month and, once work was started, having examined thoroughly the task at hand, they hoped after a month to be able to take on pieceworkers as well. The Senate found itself in a difficult position since it was forbidden by imperial decree to hire stonemasons for this work on a monthly or daily basis unless it was absolutely essential, but it had no alternative. Seeing the stubbornness of the contractors, the Senate decided to hire them at a monthly rate, so that in a month's time, on examination of the work in hand, they could recruit pieceworkers. This was to be carried out with the active participation of officers seconded to this work.

The senators again undertook to persuade the contractors to claim a realistic monthly salary and stressed that, while engaged on this work, they would suffer no hardship or delay in payment of their wages. If any had the slightest cause for complaint, they were to bring it directly to the Senate. But the contractors stuck to their demand for six rubles per man per month, saying that they could not hope to hire stonemasons for less. Furthermore they feared a recurrence of the fate which befell two contractors for their failure to provide the quantity of stonemasons required by contract, for which they were detained for about nine years at the Kronstadt construction office. The senators then made a final offer of five rubles a month, promptly announcing that by an edict of her imperial majesty stonemasons were to seek no other work in Petersburg other than at Kronstadt.

With this the contractors were dismissed. An order was sent to the Kronstadt construction office demanding that the Senate be informed which two contractors were meant, why they were detained, and why they had been held so long. On June 6 the contractors once more came before the Senate and declared that they could not concede more than ten copecks of the six rubles demanded, then said that fifteen copecks was the most they could concede. The Senate reported back to the empress, but since by June 21 no imperial decision on the matter was forthcoming the Senate ordered the Admiralty to make every effort to find other stone-masons and carpenters.

FINANCIAL MATTERS

The state was purchasing flour for two rubles per sack of nine puds; eight puds of groats cost two rubles eighty copecks. The Senate urged nineteen merchants to reduce these prices, but they refused on the grounds that in any case payment was not due until the following year, 1744.

The government's works were becoming expensive, and as always the financial machine operated slowly. The president of the Office of State Accounts reported to the Senate that his office was supposed to allocate large sums of money to very pressing projects but could not, since it was still owed 141,024 rubles by the College of Church Landed Property and 105,562 rubles by the Chancellery for Siberia. Yet despite repeated orders from the Senate to settle the accounts no money was forthcoming, only excuses. Arrears remained unpaid, while threats to the governors were unavailing. The Senate issued the Treasury College orders to secure recovery of outstanding state revenue without reference to the governors, and warned that failure to do so would lead to exaction of fines from all its members and secretaries.

The Senate learned that provincial and town governors and government officials were helping themselves to state liquor from taverns and firewood and candles from custom houses. A prohibition ensued. One German suggested the introduction of stamped cards with duty payable at fifteen copecks a game and the subsequent resale of such stamped cards, but the Senate rejected the proposal on the grounds that edicts of Peter the Great and Anna Ivanovna prohibited gambling.

The colleges of Mines and Manufacture were re-established and now operated as in Peter's day. Naturally the re-establishment of the Chief Magistracy followed, having been set up by the Reformer for the "assemblage of the disintegrated mansion."[4] Its work was resumed in May 1733 and Vasily Khovansky was appointed its high president.[5]

TRADE AND INDUSTRY

The new year began with the establishment of a commission of investigation into forged customs stamps. The commission found that many foreign merchants involved in this matter were importing from overseas into Russia goods bearing counterfeit customs stamps. Furthermore with the connivance of customs officials many goods were removed illegally from bonded warehouses and replaced with inferior and cheaper goods. The merchants confessed and were released, on condition that the admitted sum of defrauded customs duty, amounting to twenty-one thousand rubles, be paid double within a week. They would be let off only if the money were paid promptly.

On another matter, when it was a matter of securing prompt payment, the principle of strict adherence to the rules laid down by Peter the Great was waived in favor of an edict of Anna Leopoldovna. Peter the Great considered that the state had a monopoly interest only in potash and resin deposits, while other minerals he "gave over to the people," but during Anna Leopoldovna's reign pitch became once more a state monopoly. Now, on the basis of the edict calling for return to the legislation of Peter the Great, there was a move to allow free trade in pitch, but the handsome revenue obtained by trade in pitch made it too attractive a monopoly to relinquish.

It was only where religious matters were concerned that Elizabeth could not be prevailed upon to veer from the course charted by Peter, even if it appeared advantageous to do so. The Senate submitted a report stating that since the previous year's edict on banning

Jews trade suffered a marked decline, both in Little Russia and in the Baltic region. The state treasury stood to suffer a consequent drop in receipts from duty payable on such trade. "I have no wish to derive any profit from the enemies of Christ," was the empress's written retort.

Also faithfully adhered to was Peter's ruling that trade be developed by the spread of education and of clear understanding of the principles of dealing among merchants. The president of the College of Commerce informed the Senate that the college entrusted to Volchkov, secretary of the Academy of Sciences, the translation of an extract from Savary's trade dictionary from French into Russian.[6] Some of this work already was done, and Volchkov promised to undertake the rest, but demanded a fee of five hundred rubles for such a difficult piece of work. The college submitted that it would be to the glory of Emperor Peter the Great and to the great advantage of Russia's merchants, now and in the future, to have this book translated for the fee demanded, since its translation was conducive to increased state revenue and the enhancement of Russia's glory. The Senate directed that Volchkov undertake an accurate translation of the extract, and was to be paid five hundred rubles if he would not take less.

In order to increase revenue, it was deemed essential to set up a special government department for fishing industries on the Lower Volga and Yaik. Vice-President Raevsky was appointed director-in-chief of the Astrakhan Fishing Office. Under his control were the directors of the Saratov and Gurev Fishing Offices. The Moscow merchant Mylnikov was appointed personal private secretary to the director-in-chief at Astrakhan for five years, until the next review.[7] Fifty-five thousand rubles were allocated for increase of the industry's output, and Mylnikov was pledged to secure an annual revenue for the treasury of not less than fifty thousand rubles.

In the Southeast the government embarked upon establishment of a viable fishing industry. In the Arctic Ocean private individuals were fishing at great risk to themselves as far afield as remote Spitzbergen. In the year under discussion twelve peasants from the Mezensky district were returned to St. Petersburg from Lübeck by the Russian ambassador. They went walrus hunting on the "ocean island of Grumant,"[8] where their boat was broken in two and sunk by enormous waves. They were saved by a dory,[9] and taken on board a Dutch ship which took them to Amsterdam. The Russian resident sent them by way of Hamburg to Lübeck. The Admiralty issued them passports for their return to Russia, and provided them with rusks for the journey to alleviate their wretched condition.

It was noted with regret that the transfer of certain branches of industry from private hands to the state resulted in a drop in production. In June the empress put before the Senate a memorandum pointing out that nowhere was the manufacture of bricks and tiles satisfactory. The bricks were of poor quality, while the tiles were made only for appearance's sake. They had no strength in them, and where they were used for roofing cracks appeared, thus providing scant shelter. Production of these commodities fell into this sorry state after the death of the empress's parents, when the state factories were run down and taken over by private industry. The new private factory owners failed to observe the old manufacturing procedures, so that clay was not prepared in advance, there was a lack of forward planning, sheds for storage were not provided, and so forth. To put these industries back on a secure footing, it was decided that the architect Osip Drezin recruit in Italy two experts in brick and tile manufacture. These two were to be appointed architects and commissioned to locate suitable clay on crown lands on both banks of the Neva on the Moscow side, where new brickworks were to be built. Soldiers' children from the garrison school were to be apprenticed to the two Italians to acquire their skills.

The cloth and linen industries were thriving in private hands. The Voronezh merchant Postovalov invested forty thousand rubles in the establishment of a textile mill in that town in 1739. Apparently it was running well, and Postovalov was granted permission to open another factory, a paper mill. To assist him, the government gave him a stone house belonging to the treasury in Voronezh. A textile mill which was to have been handed over to the foreigner Ariolti was given to him, together with machinery and skilled workers from the factories confiscated from Sakharov and Plotnikov for "mismanagement of their cloth factories." He was permitted to buy an entire village of fifty households so that the peasants who inhabited it would be employed only in the cloth mill. In return for this assistance Postovalov was obliged to provide cloth for uniforms, in the first year not less than thirty thousand bales of cloth, with an increase in production over the following years.

Peter the Great's order concerning the manufacture of linen was reinstated. This required that linen be made in accordance with foreign demand. From one state factory 6,500 pieces were sold to a merchant, Timmerman, at 4 rubles 31 copecks apiece. On December 16 the empress, who was present at the Senate, gave a verbal order that the College of Commerce, together with the town council, find out why the price of silk and other products had risen so steeply.

The war with Sweden was over but the situation in Europe held out no guarantee of a prolonged preservation of peace, and no hope therefore of any significant decrease in Russia's military budget. In any case, the declared policy of return to the precepts of Peter the Great meant that care must be taken of his favorite creation, the navy, which was reported to be a very bad way. At the end of the year a shipwright apprentice, Ostretsov, sent the empress a report on the Admiralty, indicating that both it and the navy were in an extremely sorry state. The stores were completely exhausted, the harbors at Kronstadt were clogged with ships' hulls and silted up, there was no machinery for dredging them, the timber for masts had rotted away, and morale in the navy and in the shipyards was at a very low ebb. When the fleet would be required to put to sea against the enemy, provisions would have to be taken on board, brewing of beer contracted, pitch purchased, commercial vessels hired to transport these commodities, all at considerable cost to the treasury.

DOMESTIC UNREST

The war against enemies abroad was over, but the army was still needed for war against enemies at home. These were gangs of marauding brigands who, as before, were active in the eastern reaches of European Russia. Right after the New Year the Senate was informed of a petition from the landowners of Kazan. They requested the immediate dispatch of a staff officer with troops to round up fugitive peasants and root out brigands along the Volga, Medveditsa and Karamysh rivers and in the Saratov steppe. The Don ataman reported that all cossack settlements providing fugitives with shelter were destroyed, while fugitives hiding in large cossack townships in the forest were sent off to the St. Anne fortress, to Tsaritsyn and other places.

But in the fall the Nizhny Novgorod provincial chancellery sent word that robbers and brigands were appearing there in large bands, both by land and river, but for want of troops there was nothing the chancellery could do to rid themselves of them. The Senate gave orders for an appropriate body of troops to be sent from regiments stationed nearby. Robbery and brigandage was rife along the Petersburg highway, and not far from Moscow a naval officer was attacked and beaten. Even in Moscow a peasant named Zatsepliaev, together with eight house serfs and Telesnikov, a grenadier of the Imperial Life Guards, went beyond the Kaluga gates and the Don monastery and robbed two houses.

RELIGIOUS PROBLEMS

Apart from the pursuit of brigands the army also was called upon, again in Nizhny Novgorod province, to take action against the Mordvinians,[10] whose revolt stemmed form the following circumstances. Bishop Demetrius (Sechenov) of Nizhny Novgorod, making a visitation of his diocese, ordered the destruction of a pagan Mordvinian cemetery situated alongside a village church at Sarley in the district of Teriushev. The Mordvinians responded with a concerted attack on the bishop, whom they besieged in the cellar of the priest's house until the timely arrival of Christians from neighboring villages. Demetrius wrote in his report of this incident that the rioters were not Mordvinians but Old Russian idolaters who could not speak Mordvinian.[11] They spoke a Yaroslav dialect which differed from that spoken by the Nizhny Novgorod Russians. In any case First Major Jünger and his men were sent to the Teriushev district with orders to pacify the Mordvinians, failing which he was to report back and await further instructions. On no account was he to use force against them.

Jünger had no chance to carry out his orders or report back, for he was met by about one thousand Mordvinians, armed with bows, spears and firearms, who started firing upon his men. Jünger was compelled to retaliate and rout the insurgents. Thirty-five of them were killed and 136 captured, including thirty-one wounded. Five of his own men received injuries. Thereafter the Mordvinians sought pardon. Jünger was ordered to send the ringleaders, and Nesmianko in particular, to the provincial chancellery. The rest were to be pardoned and informed that if any wished to become Christians they were to apply to Bishop Demetrius. One hundred and thirty ring-leaders were sent to the regional office. Chief among them was the convert, Nesmianko-Krivoy, who was sentenced to be burned at the stake for apostasy from Christianity, for having torn off his cross and destroyed an icon. The Synod had to send the bishop an order not to force anyone to be baptized or give any other cause for griev-ance.

Russified, if not Russian, heathens attack a bishop, take on gov-ernment troops, a convert tears off his cross, smashes an icon and becomes the leader of an idolatrous uprising! Mention had been made of the fact that during Anna's reign the best means of paci-fying the regions of the old Kazan tsardom was reckoned to be propagation and strengthening of Christianity among the heathen population.[12] In 1740 Demetrius Sechenov, then only an archi-mandrite, was appointed to undertake this task in Kazan. During Elizabeth's reign he proposed to the Synod that at least thirty wooden churches needed to be built in areas inhabited by converts. This was because the newly converted were living as far away as eighty, a hundred versts or even more from Russian villages, and therefore nine thousand rubles ought to be allocated to the build-ing program, at an estimated cost of three hundred rubles per church. The Senate felt that this was too large a sum and authorized the College of Church Landed Property to grant only half the amount requested. The overall cost was to be reduced by having the churches built by the local inhabitants, including those who had no desire to become Christians. It indicated the cheapest means of procuring books, bells and other furnishings.

Sechenov's report to the Synod also suggested that before the churches were built there should be for every two hundred and fifty households two priests, one deacon and three catechists, who would supervise construction of the churches, give the converts religious instruction, teach their children to read, and generally introduce them to the Christian way of life. Meanwhile they would perform the basic rites as best they could, if only in improvised chapels. Priests were to receive thirty rubles and thirty chetverts of grain, deacons twenty rubles and twenty chetverts, and catechists fifteen rubles and fif-teen chetverts.

An edict of 1740 required converts to leave their villages if they lived alongside pagans. Sechenov, on the other hand, pointed out that in most villages it was the converts who were in the majority, and so to compel them to leave would be a travesty and a disgrace, since it would appear that they were being penalized for having accepted Christianity by being driven from their lands, and this would deter many heathen from following their example. Consequently, he argued, it would be better to resettle the pagans, since they would then "voluntarily" accept Christianity to avoid being deprived of their homes and lands. The Senate accepted this argument.

The Senate also agreed to restoration of the old arrangement whereby the converted slaves and serfs of heathen landowners were emancipated, while if the landowners themselves became Christians such slaves and serfs would be returned to them. The Senate further stipulated that those who accepted Christianity were released from all financial obligations for three years, and that such obligations be apportioned among those who remained heathens; that any of the new converts who were enslaved by debt to their creditors likewise were granted immunity; that heathens in prison for petty misdemeanors who were prepared to accept Christianity be pardoned and freed. Sechenov's report showed that in 1741 and 1742 there were 17,362 converts to Christianity.

Heathens were released from prison and not punished as long as they agreed to be baptized, and provided their motives for doing so were not suspect. The attitude of the schismatic leadership to those of their number who became Orthodox converts was rather different.[13] In the Kuznets district of Siberia eighteen schismatics burned themselves to death. Several others were apprehended attempting to follow their example, and promptly became Orthodox converts. But their leaders made representations to the Senate, objecting that these accepted conversion "solely to escape torment." They pointed out that they really ought to be flogged and interrogated about the eighteen self-immolators and their accomplices, and then be put to death for having failed either to prevent the immolations or to inform the authorities. But since they had become Orthodox converts they merely should be knouted as a warning to others.

The Senate directed that the leaders' case be examined strictly according to existing laws, including those which had not been observed, and the findings reported to the Senate. The converted schismatics were not to be molested, but merely observed to see that they were in fact adhering faithfully to Orthodoxy.

The Senate also had to moderate the zeal of the Archangel provincial chancellery. The diocesan chancellery reported that in the Mezen district and elsewhere there were populous hermitages where schismatics of both sexes, monks and secular clergy lived in hiding. In the informant's view they were from the gentry or upper merchant classes, and some were perhaps contractors who embezzled large sums of money from the treasury. The provincial chancellery sent a first major with a detachment of troops to round up all schismatics and their belongings and take them to Archangel, and burn their buildings. If they offered any resistance, they were to be persuaded by force; if they tried to get away, the troops were to open fire and prevent their escape. The Senate, on the other hand, ordered that the situation be handled with caution; there was to be no destruction or looting, and any military engagement was forbidden, on pain of court martial. Action was to be taken in accordance with the existing laws concerning schismatics. The Senate demanded to be informed by return messenger on what grounds and on whose orders did the provincial chancellery direct that schismatics be fired upon and their belongings impounded.

Since the Synod demanded release of newly baptized heathen and lifting of sentences imposed for petty crimes, it was natural that the Senate should ask the Synod whether it also followed that schismatics convicted of capital crimes be spared the death sentence if they adopted Orthodoxy. The Senate raised the question in connection with a newly baptized peasant, Stepanov, who had committed murder. The Synod replied that there was nothing in the patristic writings whereby a convicted murderer might be reprieved on acceptance of the Holy Church, for a conversion to piety gave deliverance only from eternal death; temporal power over the life and death of a convicted criminal rested with the civil laws.

But a short time after this pronouncement there arose another case. A peasant, Petrov, was sentenced to death for robbery. At his confession he declared himself to be a schismatic, but then was converted to Orthodoxy. Bishop Demetrius of Nizhny Novgorod proposed that he be reprieved and sent to a monastery as a model to others of the best way to salvation. Since the proposal came from a bishop, the Senate considered it necessary to inform the Senate and request "that the Holy Synod kindly consider how Petrov's case be dealt with, and report its findings to the Senate." The Synod gave a curious reply. "If the said Petrov is reprieved, the Holy Synod will assign him to a monastery for repentance." The Senate ordered that the convict's case be postponed until further notice.

Apart from dealing with matters concerning heathen and schismatics, the Senate had several unpleasant exchanges with the Synod. The College of Church Landed Property distributed among the monasteries of the Rostov diocese some retired servicemen. But the metropolitan of Rostov, Arseny Matseevich, would not accept them, on the grounds that retired servicemen hitherto lived on such monks' stipends as remained in consequence of Peter the Great's imposition of limits on the number of monks, but now all these stipends were allocated to newly professed monks. In his report Arseny indulged in abusive reference to the provincial governors, and to the secular authorities in general. The Synod ordered Arseny to stop using such insulting language, warning him that if he did not, he would be fined. But this did not satisfy the Senate, which threatened to inform the empress unless the Synod put a stop to such behavior.

Another exchange was in connection with the re-established law concerning the supervision of the observance of silence during church services. The Synod notified the Senate that this law was not entirely in accordance with that laid down by Peter the Great, and was at variance with the Ecclesiastical Statute in its requirement that fines in churches be collected by retired officers and soldiers.[14] They argued that this was a matter for the church and its pastors, and should be administered by the bishops, priests and clergy. The Synod was informed that the Senate's ruling was based on the law of Peter the Great and the view of the Synod as expressed on January 11, 1723. Peter's law stated that offenders were to be fined one ruble; the money was not to leave the church, but be used to maintain the church fabric, for which use laymen were more appropriate. The law clearly required laymen to collect the money, which was the usual practice during Peter's lifetime. The Senate considered it inappropriate for clergy and their acolytes to be watching out for those who broke the silence rule during the service. They referred the matter back to the Synod for further consideration.

A few months later the Synod complained that Governor Davydov offended Archbishop Mitrofan of Tver by summoning two seminary teachers to the provincial court. Questioned by the Senate, the governor explained that he received this complaint from a Lieutenant Vogt. This officer's stepson, the five-year-old Semeon Volkov, was walking near the town walls when he was seized by two teachers from the seminary. They carried him off to their cell in the archbishop's house, where they shrieked abuse at the little boy, stripped him naked and set about him with canes, beating him almost to death. On examination it was discovered that the boy actually was beaten very badly, and was ill as a result. Vogt stated that he had complained twice to the archbishop about the teachers, but nothing had come of it since they were the archbishop's close relatives.

The Senate ordered the Synod be informed that the governor's conduct in this matter gave no grounds for criticism. But the Synod objected that it did not accept Governor Davydov's explanation, and that the truth could not be established without further investigation, since the Tver teachers went abroad to train at their own expense in various languages, becoming valuable pedagogues. If they were not given satisfaction, there was great danger that other learned men would be afraid to come to Great Russia to teach in schools. Moreover according to the Statute, seminary teachers were not subject to the secular courts.

The archbishop of Tver brought a complaint against his governor, while in Kolomna the governor brought a complaint against Savva, his bishop, who forbade the parish priest of Svitiagin to perform religious rites because the peasants there disputed the bishop's claim to the land they worked. As a result, recently confined mothers were denied churching, and the dead their burial.

In spite of these conflicts, the Senate could not but agree with the Synod over the demand for expansion of religious education. The Synod pointed out that Russian noblemen and men of other ranks were teaching their children to read only the prayer book and the psalter from Russian books, but were using others for secular study. There were hardly any who attempted to teach "the knowledge of God and our duty towards Him, or the dogma of the Orthodox Christian faith, in which lies the true road to our salvation." The Synod demanded that the primer and catechism be taught, and that promotion be denied to any who did not know them. The Senate not only agreed but ordered that fathers who failed to arrange such instruction for their children be fined two rubles, or ten if he were a member of the gentry.

The Synod's beloved book *The Rock of Faith* was reprinted[15] but the Synod was not satisfied, and wanted to ban certain books coming to Russia from abroad since the time of the *Rock of Faith*'s suppression. It applied to the Senate, which in turn ordered that a book *The True Christianity* by Arndt,[16] printed in Russian at Halle in 1735, and a book on the decay of Christian life by an unknown author, neither of which were licensed by the Synod, be confiscated by the Synod. Furthermore in future all books printed in Russian abroad, either by Russians or by foreigners, should in no circumstances be imported into Russia, and a careful watch be kept for them at frontiers and in ports. Russians abroad for training or other business must be informed that they were strictly forbidden to translate such books into Russian, while within the empire no religious books might be translated into Russian without the Synod's permission.

In accordance with the spirit of the coup of November 25 it seemed an affront that the churches of foreign confessions were situated in Petersburg's most prominent street, the Nevsky Prospect. The empress decreed that more remote sites be found for them. Sites were found, plans drawn up and construction costs estimated. It was decided that the empress be asked to let the Protestant churches stay where they were for the time being, since estimates for building new ones showed that considerable public money would be needed, which presently was required for more pressing expenditure.

FOREIGN AFFAIRS

Beginning in October the court got ready to move to Moscow. For her imperial majesty's passage to Moscow the Senate ordered every coaching station be provided with two hundred horses by local merchants. To avoid making excessive demands on coachmen and merchants along the route for the supply of carriages, assistance was to be requisitioned from other towns and villages up to two hundred versts from the route the empress was to follow. The merchants and coachmen were to ensure that the horses were fitted with collars, reins and harness, and that they were properly fed and watered. For the conveyance of ministers, senators, the Synod, palace and other officials and the foreign ambassadors, local stations were to have five hundred carriages standing by. There came orders that an additional hundred carriages to supplement the two hundred already requisitioned be available at every staging post, to be provided by the coachmen and servants.

From Moscow the empress intended to travel to Kiev. It therefore was ordered that the road be improved and lodges built at the staging posts. But then it was found that the Little Russians could not undertake construction of lodges because of shortage of timber. Instead storehouses were to be prepared from Glukhov to Kiev for food and provisions.

The empress was visiting Moscow to celebrate the peace with Sweden. But what were the conditions on which this peace was concluded? The position adopted on foreign affairs by the empress and her entourage at the end of 1742 has been noted. Thanks to the clear bias towards Sweden expressed by the French government, and to the fact that the French touched on a most sensitive issue, namely Elizabeth's relations with Sweden before her accession, Lestocq and Chétardie lost the fight against the Russian aristocracy, and Chétardie was obliged to leave Russia.

At the beginning of November 1742 the supporters of France were heartened by the death of Chancellor Prince Alexis Mikhailovich Cherkassky, who at the end of his life expiated his past sins by his vigorous promotion of Russian interests.[17] But in fact his death served to further rather than damage these interests, since they were taken up by the gifted and energetic Bestuzhev, who now achieved independence. On the other hand, no one was certain in the first days after Cherkassky's death that Bestuzhev would receive overall control of foreign affairs. It is known that the vice-chancellor had powerful enemies who spared no effort to prevent him from becoming chancellor; but to do this they had to show the empress someone more, or at least as worthy, as Bestuzhev for this post. Their choice fell on Rumiantsev, but Elizabeth considered him neither competent nor sufficiently experienced. She wrote that though perhaps a good soldier he was a poor minister. Characteristically, Elizabeth postponed the troublesome task of appointing a new chancellor. Nevertheless Bestuzhev, though still officially only vice-chancellor, began to run foreign affairs on his own, and Brevern continued to serve him faithfully, as Ostermann before him.

Chétardie was no longer on the scene, but Lestocq had found himself another ally just as dangerous to Bestuzhev and Russian interests. This was Brümmer, a Holsteiner, marshal of the court of the heir apparent, Grand Duke Peter Fedorovich. The proclamation of Peter Fedorovich as heir to the throne happened quite suddenly. No one had known about it until the last minute, apart from Lestocq, Brümmer and Archbishop Ambrose Yushkevich of Novgorod. Clearly opposition was feared, and dissatisfaction from one side or the other.

But there was another, purely Holstein, matter close to Brümmer's heart. This was the succession to the Swedish throne, already refused by the grand duke, of his uncle, the bishop of Lübeck and administrator of Holstein during Peter Fedorovich's minority. It was obviously easy for Brümmer and Lestocq to persuade Elizabeth of the need to support the election of the duke of Holstein on Russia's behalf. The close kinship of the heirs to the Russian and Swedish thrones would remove the Swedish threat and stabilize the peace in the north. Elizabeth was also swayed by a bitter-sweet recollection of the help given by the duke of Holstein and the bishop of Lübeck to their cousin, who had been her intended, but whom death had taken from her.[18]

Lestocq, of course, strongly aided Brümmer in this matter since, with the election of the bishop of Lübeck, Sweden stood to gain a more favorable treaty, whereby Lestocq would have done something to earn his French pension. The Russians might also be counted on to favor the duke of Holstein's election as heir to the Swedish throne, provided that not too high a price was paid, and that Russian interests in concluding a treaty were not jeopardized; after all, kinship ties between countries by no means invariably guaranteed alliance.

CONGRESS AND TREATY OF ÅBO

In view of these considerations the choice of Russia's representatives at the congress of Åbo was a crucial one. Rumiantsev's appointment as a leading negotiator was not welcomed by Bestuzhev. Rumiantsev was the choice of the opposition faction, their candidate for the chancellorship in order to shut out Bestuzhev, who wanted to see Senator Prince Golitsyn made the second negotiator, but Lestocq sought the appointment of General Lübras. At first Elizabeth rejected Lübras on the grounds that he was a German. Nothing daunted, Lestocq retorted "But your majesty's father conducted negotiations at Nystadt through a German."[19] Elizabeth duly signed Lübras's appointment.

Mention has been made of the reply regarding peace terms taken from St. Petersburg by the Swedish deputation which came to announce the election of the duke of Holstein as heir to the Swedish throne. The congress of Åbo started in January 1743. A letter from Rumiantsev of January 30 indicated that disagreement between the Swedish negotiators Söderkrys and Nolcken was apparent, so Rumiantsev had found a convenient moment after dinner to engage Söderkrys in a frank conversation about past events, in the course of which he discovered to his regret that there was a lot the Swedish senator did not know; and what he did know had come from Nolcken, in whose hands clearly the real power lay. This meant, Rumiantsev argued, that the congress would be dogged by numerous disputes and stumbling blocks since Nolcken, as one of the supporters of the war, naturally would be bound to defend his case.

"What a pity," Rumiantsev told Söderkrys, "that your colleague is not such an honest fellow as you are." Söderkrys replied by requesting a frank account of the empress's intentions concerning the peace treaty. Rumiantsev repeated what the Swedish delegation already heard in Petersburg. Söderkrys replied that if it was impossible to have the duke of Holstein on the Swedish throne, the only possible alternative candidate was the duke's uncle, the bishop of Lübeck. In his view the best tactic at the conference was to make it sound as though the bishop of Lübeck was the duke of Holstein's own choice, adding that this would be acceptable to the empress as well. "This would also ensure that the recommendation would be more acceptable to the ministers of state," Söderkrys concluded.

As far as Finland was concerned, Söderkrys made it clear that Sweden would not give it up. Rumiantsev wrote that the peace negotiations would not go Russia's way without armed backing, and that the forthcoming campaign be prepared so that the enemy faced devastation of the Swedish coastlands. Rumiantsev intimated to Söderkrys that in the event of a successful outcome he could count on the gratitude of the Russian court.

From their very first conversation Söderkrys appeared complaisant. "Only all power is in Nolcken's hands," Rumiantsev wrote, "and he conducts affairs as he wishes, so that although a bribe to the avaricious Söderkrys might not be without effect, at present it would be premature." On February 16 Rumiantsev reported that the Swedish negotiators firmly rejected a peace formula based on the current territorial position (uti possidetis). They affirmed that the king and his ministers would go to any lengths rather than agree to this. Meanwhile the Swedes were trying to elicit exactly what concessions the Russians would be prepared to make if the bishop of Lübeck were elected. Rumiantsev asked the empress to furnish him with further instructions on the matter, adding that the Swedes could be relied on to engage in some kind of intrigue in the issue of succession, would use Finland as a bargaining counter, and then go back on their agreements. There was only one sure way of achieving peace, and that was firmness on Russia's part.

On February 22 the empress ordered a memorandum on the peace terms to be distributed to Field Marshals Prince Dolgoruky and Prince Trubetskoy, Count Lacy and the prince of Hesse-Homburg; Senators Admiral Count Golovin, Grand Master of the Horse Prince Kurakin, Senior Privy Councillor Naryshkin, Lieutenant Generals Prince Golitsyn and Prince Urusov, Privy Councillor Novosiltsev, Senior State Councillor Prince Golitsyn; members of the College of Foreign Affairs, Vice-Chancellor Count Bestuzhev-Riumin, Privy Councillor Brevern, Senior State Councillors Ivan Yuriev and Isaac Veselovsky. In addition, copies were to be sent to General Levashev, Count Mikhail Bestuzhev-Riumin and Prince Nikita Trubetskoy; to Lieutenant Generals Prince Repnin, Ignatiev and Izmailov.

Field Marshal Prince Dolgoruky proposed that the only part of Finland they would be prepared to concede to Sweden was East Bothnia. But if Sweden were prepared to accept the bishop of Lübeck, duke of Holstein, as heir to the throne, then Russia for its part would concede the Åbo region as well. Field Marshal Prince Trubetskoy took the view that the whole of Finland be retained at all costs. "It is out of the question to return Finland to the Swedish crown, no matter how good the reasons advanced for doing so. Not only would such a course of action be detrimental and inglorious for her majesty's armed forces, but it is also extremely important for the security of the Russian empire that its borders be pushed forward as far as possible. The current war demonstrates the danger of having an exposed frontier. Finally, once the Finns see that their country is being returned to the Swedes, next time they will resist Russian troops with all their might."

Trubetskoy went on to urge that if the Swedes refused to give up all of Finland, peace should be concluded, keeping Finland as far as Helsingfors and Nyslott; perhaps then the Swedes could be bought off. Another possibility was that Finland be a separate state under the rule of a neutral sovereign; no significant concession of any conquered territory would be made unless and until the Swedes elected the bishop of Lübeck to the throne.

In Field Marshal Lacy's view, only East Bothnia could be conceded, since it was a remote part of Finland, and was stony, marshy and barren. Admiral Golovin expressed the opinion that, if it was impossible to keep all of Finland up to the Gulf of Bothnia "with a living frontier," then Russia must be left Helsingfors and all of Nyland province. Helsingfors harbor was ideally suited for a naval base, since ships could winter there without any problem and if need be put out to sea in winter. Moreover ships could be moored more securely and easily in salt water.

Prince Kurakin expressed the opinion that at least the Åbo region must be retained, while Naryshkin thought that it would be in order to concede the area north of Vaasa. Lieutenant General Prince Mikhail Golitsyn felt that Russia's most vital interest lay in holding on to the coastal areas. The following viewpoint was expressed by Vice-Chancellor Count Bestuzhev-Riumin. "Almost the whole of Europe and our neighbors, Turkey and Persia, are watching keenly to see what kind of reparations and satisfaction we obtain for the naked aggression and heavy military losses inflicted on Russia by Sweden. Therefore the glory of the empress, of the Russian people and the interest of the state demand that every effort be made to obtain a treaty *on the basis of the present territorial position* (uti possidetis), even if it costs us as much as two million rubles to do so. In order to show the world that in retaining Finland, Russia is not seeking territorial expansion or an increase in revenue, but solely peace in the North, Swedish subjects should be accorded special rights of tariff-free trade in Finland. Should the Swedes fail to agree to this, then a form of government for Finland should be drawn up at the Åbo congress to prevent any clashes between the two sides. A guarantee for such an arrangement must be obtained from the other powers involved. This proposal would be eagerly supported by the Finns through their deputies at the congress, since they have no desire to offer themselves up as a sacrifice to Swedish vindictiveness. At worst, peace should be settled by keeping either Åbo or Helsingfors and the surrounding territory, with the provision that the Finns be given the option to move from Swedish to Russian-occupied land. As evidence of the vital necessity of this condition, one need only recall the fate of the Wallachian people after the treaty recently made with Turkey,[20] or the return to the shah's Persian provinces of Georgians and Armenians who relied on assurances we gave them;[21] in any future war with our neighbors we could hardly influence them with any promises.

"Finally, the present Swedish government, which was behind the war, must be overthrown, and its peaceful predecessor restored, otherwise Russia will never feel at peace.[22] The present government will intrigue with France, inciting such countries as Turkey and other enemies against us and, reducing us to a feeble state by a foreign war, once more take us by surprise with a treacherous invasion."

Brevern's opinion was that Finland was so important that, even if compelled to relinquish its claims temporarily, Sweden would never be satisfied until it possessed Finland, so that Russia would be in a constant state of unease. Moreover the other powers could not be expected to look on indifferently at such an expansion of Russia's territory and such an enfeeblement of Sweden. Troops would have to be based in Finland for its defence. Because of the size of the country there would have to be a considerable number. Feeding them would be difficult, because the country was so ravaged, and Finnish troops were unreliable. Russia needed peace, but if war with Sweden continued while peace was restored in Germany, other countries might well intervene in Russia's war to fish in troubled waters. It was, therefore, most desirable that the treaty negotiations be brought to a successful conclusion before the impending campaign, especially since the fortunes of war are in any case varied and unpredictable.

Count Mikhail Bestuzhev held the view that Finland must be retained and, following the example of Peter the Great, paid for in cash. If Sweden rejected this, we should review Russia's relations with neighboring states, especially Prussia, which was the most dangerous. In the absence of any apparent danger from Prussia, the war should be continued, but if Prussia did appear dangerous, a treaty should be concluded whereby Russia kept Helsingfors and the area around it, and Sweden proclaimed the bishop of Lübeck heir to the throne. Should this formula also be rejected, the bishop of Lübeck should be appointed sovereign prince of Finland under Russian protectorate. The other speeches contained nothing very remarkable.

Meanwhile the Swedish negotiators informed Rumiantsev and Lübras that the bishop of Lübeck would be designated heir to the throne only on the conditions that Russia return to Sweden all conquests and sign a defensive and offensive alliance. If the bishop of Lübeck and administrator of Holstein was elected, war with Denmark was bound to follow unless Russia guaranteed Schleswig, in which case the three northern courts could form an alliance. Finally, Russia was to give Sweden a subsidy.

Rumiantsev said that there could be only one answer to such proposals, namely that there was no point in his remaining any longer, and that the congress might as well break up. What strength had the Swedes gained over the Russians, that they could advance such proposals and demand subsidies? In the matter of succession they were free to act as they wished, but the empress would never return the whole of Finland.

At the beginning of March the Russian plenipotentiaries received a letter from Buchwald, the Holstein emissary who was in Stockholm. Buchwald wrote that there was imminent danger of the Swedes bypassing the administrator of Holstein, and instead offering the throne to the crown prince of Denmark or the prince of Birkenfeld. Consequently he urged that the peace negotiations be pursued with the utmost vigor, offering favorable terms to the Swedes. Rumiantsev wrote to Bestuzhev on the matter. "Clearly we do not need Buchwald's help in this matter. As far as he is concerned, we could concede Novgorod, as long as his duke is made king. For God's sake, my noble peer, such unfounded proposals must be scrutinized most carefully. Her majesty must be informed and briefed about everything the man writes, so that in future empty-headed opinions can be deleted in advance. It is true he frightens us with the notion that the Danish prince might be elected, but even supposing there be any truth in this suggestion it would be better for us to be at war with Sweden and Denmark than to conclude a dishonorable and unreasonable peace on the basis of the Nystadt treaty."

In accordance with the decision reached in Petersburg, Rumiantsev and Lübras informed the Swedish plenipotentiaries that if the bishop of Lübeck were chosen the empress would concede a generous portion of Finnish territory; otherwise she would concede nothing. Were Denmark to attack Sweden for electing the prince of Holstein, naturally honor would oblige Russia to assist, though it was unrealistic to suppose that once Russia and Sweden concluded such a treaty Denmark would attack them.

On March 28 the Swedish plenipotentiaries announced that their government was prepared to elect the bishop of Lübeck as heir, but wanted to know what the empress would be so good as to do for Sweden in return. The government hoped that the empress, taking Swedish needs into consideration, would grant commensurate favors, and would authorize peace terms on the basis of the treaty of Nystadt. The king hoped that Russia would take appropriate measures regarding other powers, in particular Denmark, or guarantee Schleswig, or conclude a defensive alliance against any country attacking Sweden for electing the bishop of Lübeck.

The Russian plenipotentiaries answered that the Swedes should first say how much of Finland they were prepared to cede to Russia. The Swedes indicated that they would cede all territory as far as Meidelaks. Rumiantsev and Lübras objected that even the area as far as the Kymen would be too little. The Swedes said that if Russia wanted to divide Finland equally, Sweden would have no alternative but to play into Danish hands and elect the crown prince of Denmark. The Russians announced they would concede East Bothnia, Åland and the district of Björneborg. The Swedes reacted to this with surprise and horror, declaring that in the interests of peace it would be better not to convey this announcement to Sweden, since an alternate candidate would be elected immediately.[23]

Rumiantsev wrote to Petersburg that hopes for peace were dim, and that the Swedes were dissatisfied with the latest boundaries proposed to them, the fixing of the frontier at Nyland. "Please give

the matter your earnest consideration," wrote Rumiantsev to Bestuzhev, "and let me know how it is to be concluded, for here I have
no way of knowing her majesty's intentions, neither do I know
which you consider to be the more desirable, war or peace. If peace,
further conditions must be attached to the concession, otherwise
events will take their own course. But please be sure to make preparations in good time for both the naval and merchant fleets, otherwise the Swedes might play some very dirty tricks on us. We have
very few troops here; in the area around Åbo and up to Vaasa there
will be no more than four thousand. Provisions at Åbo and Vaasa
will last only until the end of June." Meanwhile Buchwald wrote
from Stockholm that the Russian conditions had been received with
despair, that intensive preparations were being made for war, and
that the negotiators had been ordered to leave the congress unless
more favorable proposals were put forward.

On April 10 Rumiantsev and Lübras announced as an ultimatum
the concession of Finland as far as Nyland. On April 30 they wrote
to the empress that surely the peace congress would collapse before long, since there was no answer from the Swedes to the ultimatum, and that the only option left open to them was to quell the
proud enemy by force of arms. At the beginning of May Buchwald
wrote that the Swedes would never agree to the concession offered,
because they considered the province of Nyland and Fredrikshamn
harbor to be so important that if they lost them what was left of
Finland was of no significance. "There is no let up in their preparations for war," Buchwald's letter continued, "their army will
number thirty to forty thousand. ('Threats!' Bestuzhev noted in the
margin. 'Not as many as that!'). The fleet will comprise some
twenty-four warships. ('Not true!' Bestuzhev commented). If Denmark achieves its aims here, immediately the ten thousand men
standing in readiness in Norway will be dispatched to join the
Swedish troops, and together they will move on West Bothnia. The
remaining Danish troops will be used to attack Finland from Åland."

Bestuzhev observed that "formerly Buchwald wrote about nothing, but now it is all threats!" Bestuzhev was generally dissatisfied
with the way the matter was being handled. He was dissatisfied with
Buchwald, who was concerned only with the interests of the prince
of Holstein, and was trying to frighten the Russian government into
conceding quickly the whole of Finland in return for the election

of the bishop of Lübeck. Nor was Bestuzhev pleased with Rumiantsev, whom he reproached for his undue hastiness, and whose letter he answered somewhat brusquely. Rumiantsev was offended and wrote to him, "I would never have thought that your excellency would answer my humble letter in so unfriendly a fashion. Perhaps my artless pen did cause you offence, but I would rather you informed me in a friendly manner, not with such reprimands." When Rumiantsev and Lübras wrote to Petersburg that there was no hope of the Swedes abandoning their demands for Nyland, Bestuzhev's comment was "What bad prophets!"

But Bestuzhev could not do much about it, for it was the empress's ardent desire to see the bishop of Lübeck on the Swedish throne, and the earnest wish of all to see peace. At the April 24 meeting it was decided that "in view of the present state of Europe and our empire, it is both highly desirable and necessary that the war be terminated by a satisfactory treaty, because if the current war in Germany ends,[24] and the Swedes choose the crown prince of Denmark or the prince of Birkenfeld as heir to their throne instead of the bishop of Lübeck, there is grave danger that Prussia, Poland, Denmark, France, Turkey and other powers will intervene in the Russian-Swedish war, and continually aid Sweden. Moreover to continue the war would be very hard on Russia since even without this we have been in a constant state of war for several years. Therefore if the bishop of Lübeck actually is recognized heir to the Swedish throne Russia would be prepared to forego the Kymmenegard region,[25] including Fredrikshamn and Villmanstrand, as well as Savolaks, Nyslott and their districts, for these areas cover the districts of Vyborg, Kexholm and Olonets."

"It would be better for us," the empress replied, "to keep a little and what we really need, and to concede to the Swedes more of what is useful to them but unimportant to us. In other words, we should keep the province of Nyland and the Kymmenegard region, which are vital to us for direct access to our Estland, Ingrian and Karelian coastline. We should keep as much of the province of Kexholm as occupies the border established by the Treaty of Nystadt, while the Swedes should concede in addition all of Tavastland and Savolaks. In this way the Swedes will be left with more of Finland, but we shall have those parts vital to restrain our neighbors from attacking us, which is more to be expected at the coastline than at Olonets and Kexholm. In reply to the danger of possible intervention against us in our current war, we propose to the council firstly, God's help which for many years has been our country's true defence. In any case, there is no evidence of any danger, but should it arise we do have troops on our borders. It is said that to continue the war would be burdensome to our state; our reply is that, just as everything always was, so everything always shall be according to God's preordained will. We have seen, and see now, that the Lord God has aided our realm, as He does even now, and we may expect the same blessing from Him in the future. We wish nothing more from the council than that it should act now with the same spirit of fortitude as was displayed to us in the individual views expressed." The council answered that the conditions put forward by the empress were recognized to be the best, and thanked her for expressing her intention.

In the middle of May an answer came from Sweden that the king could not concede Nyland, but only the Kymmenegard region. On instructions from Petersburg the Russian plenipotentiaries agreed to concede Nyland, but demanded, in addition to the Kymmenegard region, Savolaks and Karelia. If this was not agreed the plenipotentiaries announced they would leave. This was on June 14. Meanwhile in Petersburg on June 8 the council considered the concession of Savolaks and decided "that the crown prince of Denmark should be prevented from ascending the Swedish throne and the prince of Holstein helped to do so. *In view of the weak negotiating of our representatives at the congress, as seen from their own communiqués*, the Swedes are to be granted Savolaks as far as the Kymmenegard region, with Fredrikshamn, Villmanstrand and Nyslott and their districts."

Alexis Bestuzhev-Riumin wrote to Cherkasov[26] a curious letter about this meeting of the council. "At yesterday's meeting a heated argument on two points was provoked by the procurator general, followed by Ushakov and Prince M. M. Golitsyn.[27] The first controversy arose over the statement that if the district of the town of Nyslott was on our side of the border while the enemy got nothing, it should be stipulated that five, or at least three, miles should be added to the town of Nyslott from Savolaks. At this there were shouts that nothing more should be conceded, and so on. Such was the uproar that the matter was simply left hanging in the air.

"The second dispute broke out over the statement that in view of the weak negotiating of our ministers at the congress, as seen from their communiqués, Savolaks would have to be conceded. Even though everyone joined in examining and condemning the weakness of the negotiating, in the end there was renewed shouting that it was abandoned by consent. Even Field Marshal Prince Dolgoruky, General Count Chernyshev and the others, apart from those mentioned above and Bakhmetev, again sought to have it included. They agreed over dinner at the field marshal's to set off again whence they had come, and prepared two documents, one containing the disputed point, and the other excluding it. Each would sign one or the other of them, according to the dictates of his own conscience. The procurator general arrived one and a half hours late. Meanwhile ten of them, including General Ushakov, signed the document containing the disputed point, leaving space for him. He was furious with everyone, particularly with me and the whole college for having signed without waiting for him, even though he was told that another document was drawn up without the disputed point, that it was up to him and his conscience which he signed. All the same, he raged for an hour and eventually, together with Prince Golitsyn and Bakhmetev, who had argued heatedly on the same matter, signed along with those who had not disputed it. I can vouch in all honesty that the quarreling and shouting I have described made this council meeting more like a cossack campfire."

Let us now turn to what was happening in Åbo. It was here on June 15 that Nolcken came to Lübras and tearfully begged him to strike out the conditions, and that the plenipotentiaries accept the responsibility. Rumiantsev and Lübras replied that they were not at all agreeable to taking responsibility for any alteration of the conditions. All they could do was suggest new ones, in the hope that the empress would approve them. They then suggested the cession to Russia of the whole Kymmenegard region, half of Karelia, and Nyslott. "We raised the matter of a part of Karelia," Rumiantsev and Lübras wrote, "in order that the Swedes might agree more readily to ceding Nyslott. Moreover we did not want to concede anything which we did not think would get us more in return."

The Swedes were not prepared to concede any more and after heated exchanges drew up a draft treaty whereby the Swedes guaranteed the election of the prince of Holstein as heir to the throne, with cession of the Kymmenegard region and all the estuaries of the Kymen river. Concerning Nyslott, the Swedish negotiators could undertake only to hope for approval, just as the Russians did concerning Savolaks and Karelia, even though they had an imperial edict concerning the concession of these territories. Russia was to undertake measures for Sweden's defense "as was discussed previously," in the event of an attack arising from the conclusion of such a treaty with Russia.

"This point has been the hardest of all for us," wrote Rumiantsev and Lübras in reference to this undertaking, "for your majesty's edict directed us to refuse it, and only to act when it became quite clear that this issue would effect the outcome of the entire congress. In our humble submission, however, the proposal is so drawn up that your majesty is not committed to anything since taking proper measures does not necessarily mean fielding troops, but simply entering into negotiations. Moreover the conclusion 'as has been discussed previously' refutes everything simply because what we actually said was that your majesty was not disposed to undertake any obligations in matters of peace."

On this basis a memorandum of agreement "on which to act" was drawn up and signed on June 17. The plenipotentiaries wrote, "We have been so bold, impelled by our humble and ardent sense of duty to the interest of your majesty and to the fatherland, and in particular so that the congress might be prevented from breaking up, and the Danes from uniting with the Swedes, precisely as your majesty commanded." The memorandum of agreement reached Stockholm only just in time because on June 22 about eight thousand Karelian peasants converged on the capital, calling for the crown prince of Denmark to be made heir to the throne. The peasants were dispersed by grapeshot. The memorandum of agreement was received four days earlier, on June 19, and on June 23 the king, the Senate and all four governing estates unanimously elected as heir presumptive Adolf Friedrich, prince of Holstein. At the same time this election was announced, peace with Russia was proclaimed.

The peace treaty was signed by the empress on August 19. The text read as follows: "The king of the Swedes concedes to her imperial majesty and to her heirs and to the successors of the Imperial Russian throne in complete, irrevocable and perpetual

possession the territory won in this war from the grand duchy of
Finland: the province of Kymmenegard with the towns and fortresses located in it, Fredrikshamn and Villmanstrand and, in addition, a part of Kirchspilia Piuttis, on this side and to the east of
the last arm of the Kymen river or Keltis, which arm flows between
the Great and Little Aberfors, and from the province of Savolaks
the town and fortress of Nyslott and the area around it with all
properties and rights."

A POPULAR VIEW

A curious document by an unknown hand concerning the war concluded by the treaty of Åbo has come down to us. It is in the form
of a conversation between two soldiers. At the time the army was
stationed on the Åland islands, before the signing of the treaty.
Soldier Simon is speaking to his comrade Yakov.

Simon: Why must we remain so long in such a wilderness, where
we cannot get hold of anything to eat, and even fresh water is in
short supply and contaminated? We can see Finnish cattle roam-
ing untended around the islands, there are no inhabitants in the
villages, but we are forbidden to take these cattle. As a result there
is discontent in the regiments, the number of sick has increased,
and some even are dying. Yet our commanding officers make no
attempt to improve our lot, or to have us transferred to better quarters. God be their judge! We would much prefer to have perished
fighting the enemy than starve to death here. If indeed the Swedes
invaded Russian territory, then they, in their pride and out of envy
of us, would not only slaughter our cattle, but would torture and
abuse our wives and children, and desecrate our churches, as they
did during the war in Little Russia. Do their cattle really count for
more than we do?

Yakov. Although the field marshal is a good man, because of his
age[28] he doesn't think about it, and the senior officers are afraid of
annoying him by drawing our plight to his attention. We have no
firsthand way of knowing what is actually happening in Stockholm
or at the peace congress in Åbo.

Simon. How our war with the Swedes is supposed to be going, and
how it will all turn out, it does not bear thinking about.

Yakov. Do you remember when we went to Poland to see that the
present king, August III, was elected in his father's place?[29] Our

commander-in-chief was General Lacy, now a field marshal. Even
though he was a foreigner, he was a good man.[30] As we approached
Danzig, we were joined by Field Marshal Münnich, a German by
birth and not of our faith. He treated us Russians badly, both soldiers and officers. Giving no thought to the losses incurred by our
country, he sent us into many unimportant battles, particularly to
Wielbark.[31] While he was drunk he took command of the best grenadiers and musketeers in the army. Only a small number of them got
back to camp, and most of those who did were severely wounded.
So many good soldiers were wiped out for nothing. When war was
declared on Turkey this same Münnich was given overall command
of the army, while General Lacy was promoted to field marshal and
sent to take Azov. So there we had two foreign field marshals,
something which never happened since Russia's beginnings, not
even in the reign of our merciful father, Emperor Peter the Great.
Under Münnich's command we went to the Crimea and out on to
the deserted steppe. Münnich inspected the Russians under his
command, in order to punish the officers and demote them without court martial. The most senior and distinguished colonels were
separated from their troops at gunpoint, and all for the most trifling
matters. For example, he would see an officer wearing a necktie,
and decide it was not white enough, as if there were anyone to notice
that in the steppe.

Then they undid the laws of Peter the Great. Our provisions were
reduced to nothing. Men weakened and died of starvation. Münnich
took no notice. Even though he saw many dead veterans lying before
him, he never expressed any regret, for they were not his peasants,
recruited from his own estates. As he did not own a single Russian
nobleman, what was there for him to be sorry about? He did not
reckon to settle in Russia for life, only to send the court communiqués about his own heroic deeds and to acquire thereby great
fame and wealth. And those days who knew anything about it at
court? The most important men were Germans, their friends and
relatives, while the Russian generals and senators counted for nothing. All they were interested in was whose head they could cut off
next, or whom they could at least send off into exile. Münnich did
not want to know about the intolerable existence of the Russian
people and often said, "Come now, batushka, there is nothing intolerable about the Russian people's existence."

The poor noblemen serving in the regiments were so down-trodden that all they wanted was release from military service, because they could not hope for promotion. If any were promoted it was only because Germans were in short supply. Even then they were subject to the abuse of Münnich and the other German generals, were called fools and rabble. It got to the point where in some regiments there was not a single Russian officer. Any German who joined up was assured of the rank of general, colonel, staff officer or captain at the very least. And it was the same in the civil service too. Eventually they had Russian affairs completely under their control. In Courland there were a few remaining journeymen and butchers, who were all made officers. In Mitava[32] I happened to be talking to a merchant, and the conversation got around to army officers. He said to me: "In your army there are more than a dozen common journeymen and men of base origin I know who are now serving as staff officers. Can it be that you have no Russian noblemen capable of serving?"

Simon. Tell me, were our Russian generals with Münnich on those campaigns? If they were, why did they not tell him about all these humiliations?

Yakov. At that time he was accompanied by generals who were almost all Germans, united by birth and religion. There were the two Birons, Löwendahl and others, while the only Russian regimental general was Rumiantsev. He was a good man all right, courageous and clever. He was a respected minister and a favorite general-adjutant of Emperor Peter the Great, and is now negotiating peace with the Swedes at Åbo. But what could he do? It was Münnich who had all the authority. The Russian colonels were shot and the generals reduced to the ranks, so Rumiantsev lived in constant fear of arrest and death. On the Khotin campaign Münnich called a meeting of his generals, including Rumiantsev. Rumiantsev contradicted his plan and pointed out that it did not serve Russian aims and interests. Münnich was so angry at him that he ordered this honorable and loyal man ignominiously out of his tent, and repeatedly wrote to the court complaining about him, trying to get him into trouble. It was God alone who preserved this good man and son of the Russian fatherland for his integrity and good deeds from such a scoundrel and from death.

After the Turkish war came news of Empress Anna's death and Biron's regency. I tell you, I could not have felt worse had I been mauled by a bear. Now poor Russia fell out of the frying pan and into the fire. Farewell to our Orthodox faith and our church leaders! They remained silent for ten years, and probably now always will remain so. Farewell Russian nobility, trained in arms by Peter the Great! For ten years you were forgotten and destroyed, and now you and your glorious deeds will perish. Farewell, factories and industries initiated by Peter the Great, along with technical skills: you are now in foreigners' hands! Soon we will be ordered to forget Peter's laws and acts, and set new intrigues in motion. The rest of my brothers, true sons of the Russian fatherland, ardently and keenly regretted it, frequently recalled in tears the rightful heir, Tsarevna Elizabeth Petrovna: is not all that was her father's now in the possession of foreigners?

Soon afterwards we heard that Münnich arrested Biron and sent him into exile with all his associates, including the Prussian, Bismarck. And we Russian soldiers gathered and cautiously whispered among ourselves that the devil had chased away the demon, but there was no escape from one or the other; that Tatar had cut down Tatar, but Russia needed neither of them. Almighty God destroys the perfidious counsels of foreign tongues, and His holy spirit brings back the spirit of Peter the Great, living in his daughter. He caused her to wrest her father's scepter from foreign hands, and rid us of the outrages and injustices done to the Russian nobility and to the whole people, to Peter the Great's pupils, whom he molded with his own blood, sweat and toil, but whom our former German rulers dismissed as being unfit to hold even the lowliest rank. But from his native-born Russians, Peter the Great made field marshals, admirals, ministers, senators and presidents. His initiative is preserved in entirety, and serves the needs of many.

RUSSIA AFTER THE TREATY OF ÅBO
1743

SWEDEN AND DENMARK

Peace with Sweden was concluded, but as a result Denmark started to rearm. When the Swedish ambassador asked why, he was told that it was for Denmark's own protection since, according to letters from Hamburg, Kiel and Stockholm, the return of Schleswig was to be demanded of Denmark, and Buchwald was talking about it. On receiving the report from Åbo, Bestuzhev observed, "These reckless threats from Holstein could lead to a new war which would be more disastrous than the last, and have less to show for it." The Swedish government demanded that the Russian ships be positioned nearer to the Sound to block the Danish fleet, and to enable the duke-administrator's safe passage to Sweden. It also requested that the squadron from Archangel which earlier was at the Sound should return to the North Sea, cruise towards Norway and harass Danish transports. It could winter in the Swedish harbor of Marstrand. "It is too late in the day," Bestuzhev commented, "to risk men and ships. What would be the point of wintering in a foreign port at the cost of at least one hundred thousand rubles, not to mention all the other obvious dangers involved?"

Rumiantsev and Lübras wrote to the empress. "As far as we can gather from what the Swedes are saying, they have no objection to his imperial highness (Peter Fedorovich) conceding Holstein to Denmark, for they have already referred to the laws of the Holy Roman empire which prohibit a sovereign of the Greek faith from ruling in Germany, so the Swedes would be happy to use this as a means of satisfying and pacifying the Danish court." The Swedish plenipotentiaries at Åbo consistently referred to this potential danger and demanded Russian assistance. Apart from the fleet, they requested that seven to eight thousand Russian land forces be sent overland to Sweden, not only to deal with the Danes, but also to maintain peace within Sweden. They declared that some of their regiments were unreliable. The hopes of the Danish court rested firstly on a party of peasants which immediately would join up with the Danish army, and secondly on some major revolution in Russia, for the Danish ministers told the Swedish ambassador who threatened them with Russia's strength, "It is true, Russia is strong, but is prone to revolutions and who knows what changes might soon take place there."

As a result of these reports, those who previously assembled to discuss the treaty terms received an edict from the empress on August 22. "Whereas we have received communiqués from our ministers plenipotentiary at Åbo that the Swedes requested our assistance in the event of current Danish mobilization leading to an invasion, we command your advice in a single communiqué as to the kind of assistance we might render the Swedes. It must be compatible with the honor and interests of the state. Such advice must be forthcoming immediately, and be reported to us, for time is running out. Elizabeth."

It was decided that the following suggestions be submitted to her majesty. First, that thirty galleys under the command of General Keith put about to Helsingfors, to remain there in readiness until cold weather set in, whereupon they should sail for Reval[1] and winter there; second, that the fleet under the command of Admiral Golovin spend September at sea and then sail to Karlskrona,[2] or further if possible, to join with the Swedish fleet in defence of the convoy bringing the heir apparent to Sweden. In the event of a Danish naval attack on the Swedes they were to be defended, and no Danish transports allowed to reach the Swedish coast. Then on September 3 the meeting decided that General Keith should sail with his regiments on the galleys direct from Helsingfors to Stockholm, where he was to winter.

The duke-administrator, who received fifty thousand rubles from the Russian court to cover his journey, safely reached Stockholm. Senior Chamberlain Nicholas Korf was sent there from Copenhagen to greet him. On November 21 Korf had an audience with the prince, who declared that he was not worthy of the honor the empress showed him in sending Korf to welcome him, and that apart from God he was solely indebted to her for his present position. Words could not be found to express the gratitude he felt, and he entrusted himself to imperial favor and protection. On November 30 two Russian regiments, the Rostov and Kazan, staged a triumphant entry into Stockholm, accompanied by martial music and unfurled banners. The old king [Fredrik I][3] expressed great pleasure, and there was general surprise at the fresh and alert appearance of the soldiers who, in spite of their prolonged and arduous voyage on the galleys, marched smartly and in good order. "I am well pleased," said the king, "that before my death I have seen and commanded such a splendid body of troops, a credit to their empress. Should need arise, I shall concede to no one the honor of commanding them in the field." On receiving from Korf and Keith the empress's document, the king kissed it.

THE FRENCH VIEW

Having found themselves up to this point in an ignominious position, the opponents of Russia's war were now triumphant, and sought to consolidate their triumph by eliminating completely all traces of French influence both in Russia and in Sweden. The members of this group, together with the Saxon ambassador Walther, convinced Korf that Chétardie was boasting of having scored a complete success in Petersburg through the favor of the empress. But at the same time he was claiming *impudently* that were Elizabeth to reject his suggestions and projects, he knew a way of overthrowing her, just as earlier he knew how to help her to the throne, although of course fate helped her more than he, because he had to stir up domestic discord and confusion in Russia. Chétardie was saying that on the strength of his standing with the empress he secured the rise of the Bestuzhevs, Brevern and Vorontsov, to win them over to the French side. But instead of being grateful to him for having lifted them out of the gutter, they made no attempt to fall in with his plans. So now he was determined to discredit them and bring them into disfavor and, if possible, deprive them of their good name and lives. The members of the old Russian party asked Korf for a minister to be sent to them who would defend and strengthen the position of good patriots and keep the supporters of France in check. The term "good patriots" referred to Mikhail Bestuzhev, as a man well acquainted with the French party and their intrigues.

France betrayed Sweden as earlier Poland, although on the other hand it should be noted that it was by no means anticipated in France that Sweden would behave so shamefully in regard to Finland. But whatever happened, France was in no position to help, since the

French handled their own affairs so badly in the war with Maria Theresa. As far as the north was concerned, there was only one option left to the French, to persuade the Russian court not to form an alliance with the maritime powers to assist the queen of Hungary. Further, France must strive, or at least appear to strive, to secure for Sweden the least unfavorable peace terms on the basis of Russia's demand for the election of the duke of Holstein as heir to the Swedish throne. After Chétardie's departure, d'Allion became France's ambassador. He worked in Russia under Chétardie, and was familiar with events there and the men behind them. But Chétardie was missed in Petersburg. The empress was bored, missing her meetings with the man who entertained her so well with his anecdotes and stories, while Lestocq and Brümmer, it goes without saying, lost no opportunity to strengthen the general desire to see the return of this diverting conversationalist.

Even at the end of 1742 Cantemir received a note from his court instructing him to make every possible effort to secure Marquis de Chétardie's return to Russia.[4] If he could not manage it, he was not to request the appointment of another minister to replace d'Allion. These efforts apparently proved unnecessary. Chétardie himself readily agreed to come back, as did Amelot. Months passed yet Chétardie did not return. The reason for this, no doubt, was Bestuzhev's stipulation that the empress not receive Chétardie in any official capacity unless the credentials he brought with him from the king recognize and styled her as empress. Elizabeth felt slighted by Chétardie's delay, and she instructed Cantemir no longer to seek his return to Russia.

In January 1743 Cardinal Fleury died from old age[5] and grief at France's involvement in a war from which there was no way out without losing face and honor. The king announced that there no longer would be a prime minister. Meanwhile important discussions were going on between Cantemir and Amelot about the election of an heir to the Swedish throne. Amelot stated that France would exclude only the prince of Hesse-Cassel, because of his devotion to the English court.[6] Any other prince would be perfectly acceptable to France. The king was particularly anxious that his conduct in the matter please the Russian sovereign, and so he wanted to be informed of her intentions as soon as possible. Cantemir reported to Petersburg that France would like to see the prince of Zweibrücken made heir, but that if this was not possible she would recognize willingly the lord bishop of Lübeck.

Cantemir sought closer ties with Controller General Vignory,[7] a man of strong influence in such matters. Vignory informed him that he always favored Franco-Russian friendship, but that the treaties of alliance between Russia and England and with the queen of Hungary and Bohemia now provided an obstacle to this friendship, as did the sumptuary laws, doubtless suggested by the English, forbidding Russian subjects to wear clothes made of rich material, which was damaging to French trade. Cantemir countered by pointing out that Russia's alliances with foreign powers were essentially of a defensive nature, and not aimed at a third power. Vignory himself must agree, he continued, that in the present circumstances the northern alliance with England was advantageous to Russia, while the alliance with the queen of Hungary was necessary for the whole of Christendom to contain the Turkish threat. Regarding the sumptuary laws, these were devised solely to serve the interests of the Russian people, and were not the consequence of any foreign suggestion. Vignory found these explanations entirely satisfactory, and suggested that to begin with there should be a treaty of friendship between France and Russia, followed by a treaty of alliance or a trade agreement.

But above all the Swedish question must be resolved. Cantemir at last informed Amelot that the empress's choice was the bishop of Lübeck, but that Russia would use only good offices to advance his cause. "That I can understand," Amelot told him, "but what I do not understand is why the Russian court enjoys much closer ties with England than with France, even though the French court is ready to cooperate with the wish of the Russian sovereign, while the English ambassador in Stockholm spares neither money nor effort to hinder the election of the bishop of Lübeck. I should like to know what kind of agreement the Russian court has reached with the English on this matter."

Cantemir answered that all this should be no surprise. It was perfectly natural that every ruler would wish to see the choice fall to a suitable candidate, and disagreement in one area need not necessarily lead to disagreement in others, as long as the courts employed only good offices in pursuit of their interests. Amelot also asked whether the matter of the election was tied up with the matter of peacemaking, because if it was, the candidate favored by Russia, depending on the peace terms, was assured of success; and if the terms were advantageous to the Swedish court, then he would start to press the Swedish embassy not to postpone the election of the bishop of Lübeck.

Cantemir replied that he did not know whether the empress intended to link these two issues, but that as far as he could judge he did not think she was prepared to pay too high a price for the election of the bishop of Lübeck. Cantemir also wrote to Petersburg on the matter. "I conclude from Amelot's repeated suggestions, firstly, that from fear of strengthening the faction favoring the prince of Hesse-Cassel, they are trying to alarm the Russian court into abandoning its English project; secondly, that they are anxious to reassert their good standing in Sweden by linking the issue of peace with that of the election, thus hoping to procure for the Swedish court the most favorable terms. With regard to this last point, I consider it to be in Russia's interest not to hold out any such hope to Amelot. Although I discern now a better attitude towards Russia in the ministry here, I still stand by my earlier view that every step taken by the French ministry is dictated solely by self-interest, itself determined by the lofty self-esteem of the people. Consequently it would be easy to put off the matter of entering into an alliance with the court here, politely avoiding discussions on the matter with the ministers.

"The improved attitude here towards Russia stems from the poor state of affairs in the French government, or else from the desire to isolate Russia from the other powers. In view of the first consideration it seems to me that whatever step the Russian court chooses to take, France would simply have to go along with it. Indeed we could treat any French complaint with indifference."

After the Treaty of Åbo was concluded Cantemir wrote, "The greater the glory accruing to your imperial majesty, the surer the peace that prevails in your realm and the safety secured for the future, the more dissatisfied with your success the court here becomes. This is because, on the one hand, it is realized that French standing in the North must be diminished considerably, and on the other, there are fears that your majesty will have an opportunity to help the queen of Hungary, which would be viewed as a considerable setback here. To these fears I ascribe the increased attention paid me by the ministry. Matters here are so bad that no matter how hard they try, they are unable to make their borders secure. The country's supply of men and money is exhausted, their military strength is deficient, the ministry is weak and incapable of handling such important matters, the generals untalented, the people poor and dissatisfied, and the king neglectful of affairs."

In August Cantemir dined with Controller General Vignory. The conversation turned to the king of Denmark's move against Sweden. "Taking into consideration the weakness of the Danish king," suggested Vignory, "and the absence of any hope of a foreign power coming to his assistance, presumably he is placing his hopes in some kind of revolution in Russia. Rumors are emanating from all sides about the possibility of such a revolution, as we already have informed her majesty on more than one occasion, and I consider it necessary to repeat that her majesty should pay due attention to these rumors." Cantemir replied that he received evidence from his court which proved the falsehood of these rumors.

Reporting on this conversation, Cantemir wrote "Earlier actions of this court do not allow me to suppose that the news put about here concerning an imminent revolution in Russia arises from its benevolent disposition towards your majesty. The repeated intrigues carried on here against our interests at the Porte are well known. Their machinations against us in Sweden and elsewhere would have ceased on the death of Cardinal Fleury had your majesty played into their hands, as they hoped at the time that you would. As it is, we can expect no sign of any good intention towards us, since almost everyone here is convinced that by next spring Russia's army will join with those of the queen of Hungary's allies. Consequently announcements here about impending revolution are being made either to discourage your majesty from joining the allies of the queen of Hungary by arousing your anxieties about the domestic peace of our country, or else in an attempt to free themselves from any suspicion of complicity in the event of some kind of disturbance in Russia."

Cantemir's reports served as a firm support for Bestuzhev, who on the basis of these reports immediately proposed to the empress that a close watch be kept on French relations. He alone, Bestuzhev insisted, could provide reliable information, and certainly not the empress's advisers in Petersburg, who could have no clear understanding of matters at such a distance. Bestuzhev was alluding to Lestocq and Brümmer, with whom d'Allion naturally had very close connections, as men who enjoyed the confidence of the empress as long as anyone could remember.

At the beginning of July d'Allion sent his government the following report. "On June 29 there was a ball at which her majesty told me that as she was walking in her garden the day before she encountered a guardsman who approached her with tears in his eyes, telling her it was being said that she planned to desert her loyal subjects and abdicate in favor of her nephew. Elizabeth told the guardsman that never had she been more surprised, assured him that this was completely untrue, and she would have whoever was saying so shot, even if he were a field marshal. She also related the incident to Brümmer, who suggested to her that such rumors had but one aim: to stir up discord between herself and the grand duke; it clearly demonstrated the necessity of ensuring that the prince's entourage was composed of men on whom she could rely completely. For my part I told her this rumor has circulated for at least three weeks."

D'Allion boasted to his government that, together with Brümmer and Lestocq, he wielded considerable influence in the resolution of the Swedish question, in spite of the standing of the Bestuzhevs and the intrigues of the English ambassador Wych. "*We* are undermining all plans for the marriage of the bishop of Lübeck to an English princess. Messrs. Brümmer and Lestocq told me that they recently persuaded the tsaritsa to write to the prince, telling him to think no longer about that marriage. At my instigation, and in pursuit of their own self-interest, both have redoubled their efforts to bring down the Bestuzhevs. They are awaiting with impatience the return of the plenipotentiaries from Åbo, upon whom they are counting to reveal sufficient secrets and mistakes. The intention of Brümmer and Lestocq, once Bestuzhev is overthrown, is to entrust the running of foreign affairs to General Rumiantsev and Mr. Naryshkin, who already is on his way here, and to Prince Cantemir, who will be recalled from France."

In point of fact, Chamberlain Semeon Naryshkin, ambassador in London, was recalled, but they did not manage to obtain the recall of Cantemir, who was suffering from a fatal illness. Informing his court of the lowering in prestige of Lord High Marshal of the Court Mikhail Bestuzhev, d'Allion wrote, "The marshal's stock, it is true, has fallen considerably, but it is recovering. This is a man whom his enemies will simply have to destroy, otherwise he will play a very considerable role in this state." In mid-August d'Allion reported that "the tsaritsa is firmly resolved to support the prince of Holstein in Sweden, and while there are no covert means the vice-chancellor will not use to keep her from decisive involvement in the matter, the influence he and his gang now exert is minimal. In the event of ministerial changes, General Rumiantsev will have a large part to play in the new arrangements, and although he himself is no supporter of the French, his wife can be relied on as an intriguer and a very skillful lady. Wych already has started to pay court to her." How come "the influence exerted by Bestuzhev and his gang" was "minimal" now?

THE LOPUKHIN AFFAIR

On July 21 a rumor spread around Petersburg that a very dangerous conspiracy was unmasked. Lestocq hurried from Peterhof to Petersburg. The empress, who on that day was in Petersburg incognito, remained there and did not go to Peterhof, although horses were at the ready. That night there were patrols on every street. Three days passed in anxious expectation. Finally, in the morning on July 25 General Ushakov, Procurator General Trubetskoy and Captain of the Guards Protasov arrested Lieutenant General Ivan Lopukhin, son of the former chief of the commissary, who was the man closest to Löwenwolde, and with whom he fell into disgrace.[8] Ivan Lopukhin's mother Natalia was placed under guard and their correspondence was impounded. On the same day the informers were interrogated. They were Lieutenant Berger of the Life Cuirassier Regiment, a Courland German by birth, and Major Falkenberg. They made the following statements. Ensign Berger said that on July 17 he was in the officers' mess, as was Lieutenant Colonel Ivan Stepanov Lopukhin. Together they left the mess for Lopukhin's home, where the latter told him of his grievance. "I was a gentleman of the chamber at the court of Princess Anna, with the rank of colonel.[9] But now I have the rank of lieutenant colonel, and where I go from here I do not know. Those scoundrels Lialin and Sievers have been promoted; one is a sailor and the other no more than a palace scullion. The empress rides out to Tsarskoe Selo for drinking bouts. She loves English beer and takes vulgar people there with her. She has no right to the throne, because she is illegitimate.

"The Riga guard which Emperor Ivan[10] and his mother have is very well disposed to the emperor, and what can the present ruler do with the three hundred scoundrels in her Imperial Life Guards Company? The former guard was stronger and did its job, but now it is easy for a change to be made. If Peter Semeonovich Saltykov could get in, he would beat the drum himself to signal it, even at the risk of subsequent dismissal from court.[11] In a few months' time there will be a change. My father has written to tell my mother that I should not seek any favor from the sovereign. For this reason my mother does not attend court, nor have I been since the last masquerade." On July 21, as he was passing Field Marshal Prince Trubetskoy's house with Berger, Lopukhin cursed the field marshal, and the prince of Hesse-Homburg as well. "The present ruler prefers common people, because she lives like a commoner herself," he said, "but most do not like her."

According to Falkenberg's report, Lopukhin said "The present members of the government are all worthless, not like the Ostermann and Löwenwolde[12] we used to have. Only Lestocq is a cunning rogue. Emperor Ivan will receive help from the king of Prussia, and our people, I hope, will not have to resort to arms." When Falkenberg asked whether this would happen soon, Lopukhin replied that it would. Falkenberg said to him that when everything turned out right, he should remember him, and Lopukhin promised that he would. Falkenberg asked whether there was not some important individual to whom he could escape in advance. At first Lopukhin said nothing in reply, but merely shrugged his shoulders. But then he said that the Austrian ambassador, Marquis Botta, was a stalwart supporter and well-wisher of Emperor Ivan.

On the same day Lopukhin was cross-examined before Ushakov, Trubetskoy and Lestocq, and admitted having spoken disparagingly of the empress. "I said that she went to Tsarskoe Selo because she liked drinking English beer. I also said that her majesty was born three years before her parents were married.[13] I did use those words about being ruled by a government of old women. Apart from that, I said nothing disrespectful, but I had the audacity to think that there might be welcome changes, since our former happiness would be restored." Lopukhin was not forthcoming about Botta. "Falkenberg told me," he said, "that Marquis Botta evidently did not want to waste his money, otherwise he would have come to the aid of

Princess Anna and the prince. To this I replied that he may yet do so."

Being confronted with his accusers, Lopukhin admitted everything. He was ordered to make a full statement of his criminal intentions. He requested time to think it over, and on the following day, July 26, stated that "Marquis Botta visited my mother in Moscow, and after he left she told me he said he would not rest until he helped Princess Anna. Botta also told her that the king of Prussia would help; he would see to it that he did. My mother repeated this to Countess Anna Gavrilovna Bestuzheva when she visited with her daughter Nastasia. I heard from my mother and father how upset they felt by what they suffered: their estates confiscated without reason, the father retired without his bounty, the son demoted from colonel to lieutenant-colonel."

Natalia Fedorovna Lopukhina was cross-examined. She stated that Marquis Botta visited her and told her that he was leaving for Berlin. "I asked him why, and what he had up his sleeve. He answered that whatever it was, he would not tell me. I did hear him say that he would not rest until he helped Princess Anna. My reply was that he should not plot to stir up trouble in Russia, but confine his activities to securing the release of the princess and her son, and permission for them to return to their estates. I said this because I was sorry for the princess, for she was very kind to me. Botta also said that he would do what he could to see Princess Anna on the Russian throne. But I made no reply apart from what I already stated. My husband knew nothing about this. I talked about what Botta said to Countess Anna Bestuzheva, who told me that he said the same when he visited her." Lopukhina was questioned at her home.

They next questioned Anna Gavrilovna Bestuzheva, the wife of Mikhail Petrovich.[14] It was, incidentally, her second marriage. Her first husband, since deceased, was Yaguzhinsky.[15] All she said was "What I said was no secret. For God's sake, let them (the Brunswick family) return to their own country!" But her daughter Natalia Yaguzhinskaia corroborated Lopukhina's testimony.

After these interrogations Ivan Lopukhin, his mother and Bestuzheva were imprisoned in a fortress, while Bestuzheva's daughter was placed under house arrest. In the fortress Natalia Lopukhina admitted that "my husband was present during the conversations with Botta, and when we questioned him further, he exclaimed 'You really want me to tell you Russians about this too!' And then he scolded me." Ivan Lopukhin was taken to the torture chamber, where he added that Bestuzheva said to his mother, "Nataliushka, that man Botta is terrible, but he can sometimes give us heart." On July 27 Ensign Moshkov stated that Lopukhin told him "Alexander Zybin informed my mother that the princess soon will be allowed to return home to Brunswick, together with her former staff, including the young Münnich. For that reason I shall leave the service, however that can be done, so that I can be one of her gentlemen of the chamber again. Do not fear, Moshkov! Perhaps the princess will be restored to her former position here, and we will all be happy once more. But if the princess is not freed, I hope there will be a war. When I am sent to fight, I will desert and go over to the Prussian army. Why should I fight against myself? I think a lot of men will not fight."

Next day, Zybin was summoned for interrogation. "I heard about the princess and prince," said he, "from Natalia Lopukhina. She said she was sorry for them and wanted them restored to their former positions. I tried to persuade her not to talk like that, since it could bring us trouble. 'Would it really be the first time you were in trouble?' was her answer."

That same day Bestuzheva and Lopukhina were confronted, and Bestuzheva admitted everything Lopukhin testified. On July 29 Sub-Captain Lilienfeld and Adjutant Stepan Kolychov of the Cavalry Guards, together with Chamberlain Lilienfeld's wife, Sophia Vasilievna, were cross-examined. The first two testified nothing new. "I used to meet Marquis Botta at the homes of Lopukhina and Bestuzheva," stated Sophia Lilienfeld, "and heard him express regret that the princess lived recklessly, which is why she lost her rule, and always obeyed Fräulein Julie.[16] We answered that this was quite true. The princess fell and dragged us down with her, and she brought the suspicion of the present sovereign on us. Countess Bestuzheva and Lopukhina said in my presence that her majesty lived in a common and undignified manner, constantly dashing around hither and yon. About the princess they said that it would be better for us if she were on the throne, and that maybe she would be. But if not, they should at least let her go." Sophia Lilienfeld implicated Chamberlain Prince Sergei Vasilievich Gagarin, but he admitted nothing, nor did Chamberlain Lilienfeld. Ivan Lopukhin was put to the rack and given eleven strokes, but he added nothing to his testimony. On August 11 he again was tortured and given nine strokes, but still made no new admissions.

His father Stepan Lopukhin told his interrogators "Marquis Botta often came to my house and said of the princess that it would be better all round if she were still ruler, whereas now there was considerable unrest, and the previous ministers were all dismissed; the empress will miss them later, for there will be none found to replace them. I said that this was true, but added that it would not be entirely satisfactory, since Germans would have taken over, because the princess would have looked no further. I told my wife that I felt aggrieved and dissatisfied with her majesty because I was wrongly arrested and discharged without my due bounty. I wanted the restoration of the princess because I felt it would improve my own situation. For having disdained my oath, I hold myself guilty before her majesty. About the senators, I said that there were only a few with any sense, and that the rest were fools, that nothing was getting done, and that this was bringing the animosity of the people on her majesty. When Emperor Peter II died I was sent for by Field Marshal Prince Golitsyn, Prince Dmitry Golitsyn and Field Marshal Prince Dolgoruky. They asked me whether his majesty signed a will. I told them that I had not seen any. Then they had a discussion about whom to elect to the throne. First they mentioned Tsaritsa Evdokia Fedorovna, but said she was too old, then Tsarevna Catherine and Tsarevna Praskovia,[17] but dismissed them with several rude comments. Field Marshal Prince Dolgoruky, I remember, then said of her majesty that she was born before her parents' marriage and that for this reason and others, which he expressed rather crudely, she could not be elected. So they resolved to elect Empress Anna."

On August 17 Stepan Lopukhin was put to the rack, and was suspended there for ten minutes, but said nothing new. Then his wife Natalia and Countess Bestuzheva were subjected to the same treatment, but they also added nothing to their earlier statements.

The interrogators informed the empress that Sophia Lilienfeld was pregnant, and asked whether they should confront her with those she implicated. Elizabeth wrote back personally. "I well remember Lilienfeld's wife testifying against Gagarin and his wife. They must certainly be taken to the fortress and the confrontation must take place, regardless of her infirmity. She cared little enough about our health, so there is no reason to take pity on bitches like her. Better her like were never heard of again, than they continue to breed."

Apart from those mentioned, others implicated were Prince Ivan Putiatin, Second Lieutenant Nil Akinfov and a noble, Nikolay Rzhevsky. A general assembly was convened at the Senate, attended also by the church leaders Archimandrite Cyril of the Trinity monastery, Bishop Simon of Suzdal and Bishop Stepan of Pskov. On August 19 the sentences were pronounced. All three Lopukhins and Anna Bestuzheva received the death penalty. They were to have their tongues ripped out and then were to be broken on the wheel. Also sentenced to death were Ivan Moshkov, Alexander Zybin, Prince Ivan Putiatin and Sophia Lilienfeld. Moshkov and Putiatin were to be quartered and Zybin and Lilienfeld beheaded for their failure to report the dangerous conversations they heard. For ignoring what he heard from his wife, Chamberlain Lilienfeld was to be stripped of his ranks and sent to his estates. Sub-Captain Lilienfeld, Second Lieutenant Akinfov and Adjutant Kolychov were to be reduced to the ranks. The nobleman Rzhevsky was to be flogged and conscripted into the navy.

The empress commuted these sentences. The three Lopukhins and Anna Bestuzheva were to be whipped, their tongues cut out, and exiled. Moshkov and Putiatin were to be knouted, Zybin whipped and exiled. Sophia Lilienfeld was not to be punished during her pregnancy, but was told that later she would be whipped and sent into exile. The estates of all concerned were to be confiscated. The rest were to be punished as sentenced, apart from Rzhevsky, who was to be conscripted into the navy without being flogged. The sentences were carried out publicly in front of the colleges' building.[18] In Siberia those exiled were kept under guard; they each received one ruble a day subsistence, apart from Ivan Lopukhin, Moshkov and Putiatin, who had to make do with fifty copecks. Stepan Lopukhin and his wife were allowed to take four servants with them, two men and two women, one of them a cook. Anna Bestuzheva and Sophia Lilienfeld were similarly allowed four servants each, while Zybin was allowed two, and Ivan Lopukhin, Moshkov and Putiatin one each. The servants were paid ten copecks a day.[19]

MARQUIS BOTTA

Those who made disparaging remarks about the empress's behavior and expressed regret for the fallen government, who desired its restoration and nurtured hopes that this might come about, were punished. But who aroused this hope, who "gave them heart" other than Marquis Botta, emissary of the queen of Hungary?

In September Lanczynski stated to Chancellor Ulefeldt the reasons for his court's displeasure with Marquis Botta. Ulefeldt listened in silence and with a grave expression. "I simply did not expect this," he said. "As state chancellor, and having at hand all Marquis Botta's dispatches, I can certify that always he has fulfilled the queen's instructions to regard your sovereign as a friend and ally. In his dispatches there is not the slightest trace of displeasure or evil intent. He relates events simply as they occurred."

Lanczynski replied that the complaint was not about dispatches, but the totally unacceptable and frequent private conversations which took place, about the audacious things said, the disgraceful language used, and the evil intentions stated, all of which must have been noted in Berlin. Ulefeldt protested that the other side should be heard, coming from one of such exalted rank. Shortly afterwards Ulefeldt explained to Lanczynski that the queen was most grieved to hear of the empress's displeasure, since she particularly valued her friendship, and strove always to fulfill the obligations of their alliance. But no accusation or justification of Marquis Botta could be made until he gave his own account. She expressed every confidence in the empress's sense of justice in the matter. Lanczynski replied that in the light of reliable and attested evidence, Botta had no defence.

In October Lanczynski had an audience with the queen herself. Maria Theresa spoke in a plaintive tone. "In order to upset our friendship with the Russian empress, my enemies have trumped up intricate but serious charges against Marquis Botta. But he is an intelligent man. How could he possibly interfere so brazenly in domestic affairs in Petersburg?"

Lanczynski replied that neither could his sovereign ever have believed Botta capable of such actions, had she not been presented with irrefutable proof. "As far as your proof is concerned," replied the queen, "those you arrested might well have accused Botta out of fear, and the whole matter have been arranged by my enemies.

But how can I turn him over to them, without first hearing what he has to say? Both in Constantinople and in Sweden I have made strenuous efforts on behalf of your empress. But it is clear that my enemies, with their treachery and their insinuations, have the upper hand." Count Ulefeldt told Lanczynski that in Paris there was more jubilation over the Botta affair than over the victory of their army, and that the French were crowing that now they could rupture the friendship and alliance between Russia and Austria.

When Botta arrived from Berlin a request was sent from Vienna to Petersburg for detailed evidence of the charges against him. Meanwhile a circular was sent to all the queen's embassies abroad setting out Botta's defense and reproaching the Russian court for so unjustly and unjustifiably proclaiming him guilty in the manifesto concerning the crimes of Lopukhina. The circular provoked considerable annoyance in Petersburg, as is evident from the empress's rescript to Lanczynski. "We should never have thought that the attempt to vindicate Botta would go so far in Vienna that all respect to us be set aside and a retaliation made on our own person for the alleged injustice done to Botta. We, it seems, are not equal, we and Marquis Botta. No matter what, they seek to justify Botta and base his innocence and the unfairness of our complaint on one thing, the established and unblemished reputation the marquis enjoys at the court of Vienna. The blotting of this reputation they consider a violation of all natural and national laws, whereas an insult to our imperial person they count as a matter of no significance. In Vienna Botta's innocence is established firstly on (1) his own reputation, (2) the orders given to him by the queen, (3) the testimony of the Berlin court and the circumstances there of Botta's ministry, (4) the absence of any written evidence against him. All they have against the marquis is the testimony of a few criminals apparently, very easily compelled by intrigue or by fear, or in the hope of escaping dire punishment, to give false testimony.

"With regard to the first point, we have no wish to dispute Marquis Botta's previous good service. We would only wish to point out that while here he did little to maintain his great reputation, for not only did he involve himself in numerous intrigues against us during the previous reign in a most ostentatious and brazen manner, but he continued to engage in just the same activities after our lawful accession to the throne. We never doubted that the orders and instructions issued him by the queen charged him to go about his business here in a very different manner, but this in no way serves to justify him. On the contrary, it clearly renders him liable to punishment.

"With regard to his conduct at the Prussian court, it is accepted that although Marquis Botta did not make any of his culpable proposals to the king himself, in conversations with others he often talked of an inevitable and imminent revolution in Russia. Finally, regarding the alleged lack of incriminating documentation compiled from the cross-examinations which took place, and allegedly extracted under duress. We ourselves were present at the cross-examinations, as we already informed the Viennese court, and ourselves can testify that the hearings were conducted properly, without the slightest compulsion or any other incorrect procedure. We consider that our own testimony and positive assurance constitutes sufficient proof.

"There remains the alleged lack of written evidence against him. It should be noted that in many instances criminals are unmasked without written evidence. Moreover written evidence itself is not always free from objection and dispute. Consequently there is no absolute necessity for written evidence, particularly in this case, when what Botta and his accomplices actually said was so dangerous that hardly would he commit his views to paper; even if he did, his accomplices most certainly would have destroyed anything they received. It is therefore unlikely that Botta corresponded with his accomplices, when he had fairly frequent meetings. In any case the whole affair consisted only of infamous directions, desires, conversations and counsels, all meriting severe punishment. All such intrigues in our empire always were and always will be completely unavailing in their attempts to provoke revolution against us.

"We consider that Botta deserves punishment for his audacious and inflammatory conversations and counsels against our person and majesty, especially in view of the fact that he was not simply a participant, but the main ringleader. It would be most gratifying to us if the Viennese court ceased its ambiguous and dubious assurances and give a short and precise account of its intentions and the satisfaction which we are entitled to expect."

But Vienna was not at all anxious to formulate so important a reply in haste, and Lanczynski was told that the queen was bound by laws from which she was not in a position to veer. A court of inquiry into the Botta affair was being set up, and very likely Botta would be convicted. The queen would be very pleased by his conviction and punishment to free herself from such an unpleasant predicament and, by thus satisfying the Russian empress, win her continued friendship. For the queen the fate of one or other of her subjects was of no significance!

But what if the court vindicated Botta? In German criminal law the extent to which the testimony of those interrogated could incriminate the defendant was laid down, and Botta would have to be tried according to German law. He swore that he had only permissible contact with the two ladies, with the elder Lopukhin he had conversations at his home, not more than five or six times, and with the younger he had no conversations at all. He was never at Lilienfeld's house more than once a year, and he did not know the other people mixed up in the affair. The empress's personal testimony was accepted with due respect, but it was hoped that her majesty would appreciate that even in the presence of their rulers criminals were bold enough to tell untruths in order to save their own skins, and that those whom Marquis Botta did not know at all clearly were lying.

In Vienna it was said that there was more elation in Paris over the Botta affair than over a military victory. Cantemir wrote to the empress that "the ministry here considers that after the exposure of the damaging and infamous schemes of Marquis Botta the French court should avail itself of any and every means to exploit the situation. At the very least they anticipate a cooling in relations between your imperial majesty and the queen of Hungary. In the circumstances they deem the presence of Chétardie at your imperial majesty's court absolutely imperative." Chétardie headed for Russia secretly. "The whole town," Cantemir wrote, "is as astonished as I am at his secret departure, and it is generally considered to be quite extraordinary behavior."

THE ENGLISH ATTITUDE

It is not difficult to see that the Botta affair produced quite a different impression in London. A treaty of alliance with Russia was concluded there at the beginning of the year.[20] Lord Carteret told Naryshkin that every effort must be made to restore the previous administration in Sweden. "In this way," he said, "our position will be strengthened by the presence of our natural allies, and conditions thus created for the successful fulfillment of our desires. The king of Prussia is much disquieted to hear of our friendship with you."

Wych, the English ambassador in Petersburg, informed the empress's ministers that his king was prepared to act in Sweden in concert with Russia, but first great caution must be observed in so delicate a matter as the proposal to the free Swedish estates of an heir to their throne, lest this played into the hands of the French party, and secondly to act without haste and from a position of strength. He did not say a word about the marriage of the bishop of Lübeck to an English princess. What primarily concerned England was whether the suitor would be a man of means. Carteret told Naryshkin that once the bishop of Lübeck was elected to the throne, Grand Duke Peter Fedorovich ought to cede him at least part of Holstein, because as Swedish heir the bishop would not receive more than five or six thousand reichsthalers a year for his upkeep. Naryshkin replied that the new Holstein ambassador would have some information about this. He was due in London soon to replace Buchwald, who left for Stockholm.

On the matter of expenditure in Sweden required to set up a strong party in favor of the bishop of Lübeck, Naryshkin declared that Russia would spend whatever was needed. But it was not simply a question of money. England was not happy with the treaty terms initially proposed by the Russian negotiators at Åbo. Russia rather should achieve peace with the lightest possible terms and the election of its candidate as heir to the Swedish throne. Russia, unencumbered by the war, could become involved in European affairs in accordance with England's aim.

"You can get what you want," Carteret told Naryshkin, "by making concessions, but if you push the Swedes too far you will force them into alliance with Denmark." Naryshkin answered that there was no chance of a close alliance between two peoples who hated each other as much as the Swedes and the Danes. The fact was that the Gulf of Bothnia was vital to Russia. "We desire with all our heart," Carteret continued, "that your affairs in the North be concluded with all possible speed. Your borders with Turkey and Persia are secure, and Russia could play an important role in Europe by joining us in assisting the queen of Hungary. But France will spare no effort to make it difficult for you to wind up your affairs."

Finally Carteret asked Naryshkin to inform the empress that the grand duke's marshal of the court, Brümmer, was corresponding with Nolcken, and that this correspondence was arousing the indignation of the friends of Russia and England. Moreover Buchwald snubbed the English ambassador in Stockholm, and was playing up to the French party there, providing it with money. The money was accepted, but brought Buchwald no advantage.

At his ensuing meetings with Naryshkin, Carteret repeatedly asserted that "it would be better if you did not press any large demands on the Swedes, but concluded a stable treaty. You could still have a good border even without the whole of Finland." Naryshkin referred to the Danish mobilization aimed at securing the election of the crown prince of Denmark as heir to the Swedish throne. He asked that an English squadron be sent to the Baltic to keep Denmark in check. "If France sends a squadron to the Baltic," Carteret replied, "we shall immediately send one after it. But Denmark presents no threat and its intentions are whimsical. Does Denmark want to renew the Kalmar union without Finland?[21] Without this duchy it will cost much to feed Sweden. It would be like taking a wife without a dowry. In any case, we have sent word that if Denmark attacks Russia, we shall send our navy in accordance with our treaty. Peace with Sweden and the election of the bishop of Lübeck depend on the empress. If the whole of Finland is given up, the bishop will be elected immediately, but if you concede only the area as far as the Kymen river, the Swedes will choose whom they like to succeed to the throne."

Naryshkin insisted that the English ambassador in Copenhagen be instructed to exhort the Danish government to remain peaceable, but Carteret replied with some annoyance, "We know perfectly well how to act in such cases. Our interests require constant cooperation with Russia, but it certainly would be improper for us to intimidate Denmark."

King George received very favorably Naryshkin's announcement that peace was concluded with Sweden, saying "I hope I did not make matters worse in this important matter by advising her majesty to give up most of the conquered Finnish territory in Russia's own best interests. As it is, her majesty has enough land. Had there been any further delay in making peace, the crown prince of Denmark would have been appointed heir to the throne."

"Although the French would have you think that we wanted to prolong the war,' said Lord Carteret, "your ministers are well aware that if there was anything over which we decided to contradict your court, it was only over our advice that the war be ended as soon as possible by suitable concessions. Before your plan to have the prince of Holstein on the Swedish throne, we intended it for the prince of Hesse-Cassel, but once we learned of your intention I was not so naive as to attempt the impossible. For you nothing is more profitable than to develop your trade through friendship with us, because you have many resources but little money. On the other hand, to stave off any Turkish threat you should cement your alliance with the queen of Hungary."

The question arose about the possibility of the bishop of Lübeck, now crown prince of Sweden, marrying Princess Louise of England, but at the time of his election and the peace negotiations in Åbo, Louise was promised in marriage to the Danish crown prince. This of course was quite unacceptable to the Russian court, particularly in view of the Danish mobilization threatening Sweden and Holstein. Naryshkin had an exchange on this matter with Carteret, who with his customary tactlessness declared, "What could be better than to marry Princess Louise to the prince of Denmark? He is self-sufficient, while the bishop of Lübeck has no land. Russia does not want to make him self-sufficient or any more powerful than the present king. He has little money of his own, and Sweden will not settle very much on him. Should he wish to marry any other princess of ours, we shall have to know in advance what kind of settlement he expects."

To Naryshkin's observation that the settlement would be sufficient, Carteret retorted "Perhaps you mean to give half; but the Swedes are not very rich. All we seek in the Danish match is a suitable husband for our princess. It is a purely family affair, on account of which we will not be any more favorably or unfavorably disposed to the Danish court. He is now asking for £80,000, but we intend to give him no more than half; that is, no more than our usual dowry. I cannot understand what it is you are afraid of, what can Denmark possibly do to you? Were the empress to conclude a treaty with the queen of Hungary, and then a defensive alliance with us, this would strengthen the accord with us to the true glory of her imperial majesty.... I am certain that Denmark will

undertake nothing against Russia. Only Grand Duke Peter Fedorovich's claims on Schleswig cause it some anxiety. Hence all the
noisy preparations, which are to protect Schleswig by rousing
Sweden into persuading the grand duke to drop his claims. Perhaps
France will give some prompting too."

INTRIGUES AGAINST THE BESTUZHEVS
While the English minister maintained that Russia should help the
queen of Hungary, it was learned in England that as a result of the
Lopukhin affair this help could not be counted on. Not only did it
give the Bestuzhevs' enemies a golden opportunity to overthrow
them, but it was also Chétardie's cue to hurry back to Russia in
order to hasten their disgrace, break the English alliance and play
Russia into French hands. On the subject of the Lopukhin affair,
Wych wrote to Carteret, "I can see the enemies of Lord High
Marshal of the Court Bestuzhev are doing their best to implicate
him in his wife's misfortune. If their scheming is successful, I shall
be very sorry to see the empress deprived of the advice of an
extraordinarily skillful and upright minister. He and his brother the
vice-chancellor advised the empress at the beginning of her reign
against accepting French mediation in Swedish affairs. The lord high
marshal of the court has been told to stay at his country house until
his wife's trial is over, but the empress continues as before to show
favor to the vice-chancellor, for the entire court is well aware that
he strongly opposed the marshal's marriage to Countess Yaguzhinskaia, and that relations between the brothers cooled as a result."

The efforts to destroy the Bestuzhevs are evident from d'Allion's
letter to Amelot, dated August 20. "I am not losing sight of the
Bestuzhevs' downfall for one minute. Brümmer, Lestocq and Procurator General Trubetskoy are no less preoccupied with this than I
am. Brümmer told me yesterday that he is prepared to stake his head
on the success of this matter. Prince Trubetskoy hopes to find a trap
in which to ensnare the Bestuzhevs. He swears that if he succeeds
in doing so he will see to it that they lose their heads on the scaf
fold."

Such efforts were being made in Stockholm as well as in Petersburg. "The French in Stockholm," Carteret wrote to Wych, "are now
trying to obtain falsified extracts from the interrogation of Gyllenstierna[22] at the last parliament in order to add to them material

damaging to Bestuzhev. Since they aim to send these forged documents to the empress, you should inform the Petersburg ministry about it, and do everything in your power to lay bare this base and frightful deceit. The Swedish deputies sent to Petersburg received instructions to try first of all to win the Bestuzhevs over to the French side with various flattering proposals, but if they see there is no prospect of success, they intend to use every means of intrigue, backed by a hundred thousand rubles put up by the French, to discredit the Bestuzhevs."

It was not easy to break the Bestuzhevs. Their enemies found themselves unable to exploit anything in the Lopukhin affair which might have thrown the slightest shadow of suspicion on the vice-chancellor, or even on the marshal. The empress was convinced of the innocence and loyalty of both brothers. They were supported by Razumovsky and Vorontsov, as well as by the most important ecclesiastic, Archbishop Ambrose Yushkevich of Novgorod, who managed to gain considerable influence at the court of the pious Elizabeth.

When it was evident that the Bestuzhevs emerged cleanly from the Lopukhin affair, Lestocq insinuated to the empress that since the marshal's wife was to be punished, her husband and his brother would have to be removed to positions from which they could not take revenge. Elizabeth retorted that she had absolute confidence in the loyalty and devotion of them both, and that there were many others who shared her confidence. These last words so exasperated Lestocq that he was bold enough to reply that he knew only one man who would defend the Bestuzhevs, and that was Vorontsov; but he was too young to be able to make any judgement, and his testimony therefore was unreliable. Elizabeth passed on this remark to Vorontsov, and he in turn told Bestuzhev about it. Lestocq did not give up, and several times went to the empress with his insinuations against the Bestuzhevs, but each time Elizabeth sent him packing.

The vice-chancellor, defended from Lestocq by Razumovsky and Vorontsov, found his own means of defending himself and counter-attacking his enemies by unsealing and deciphering the dispatches of the foreign ambassadors in Petersburg, and the instructions received by them from their courts. It was a means not, of course, devised by Bestuzhev himself, but which he borrowed from his

Western neighbors. Director of Posts Ash and Academician Taubert labored long and hard over the deciphering of dispatches. The vice-chancellor extracted the passages he needed, added his own comments, and passed them on to the empress.

Apart from the dispatches of d'Allion, his main attention obviously was focussed on those of Mardefeld, because he strongly suspected Prussia of making plans hostile to Russia. He was also interested in the dispatches of Neuhaus to Emperor Charles VII, who was emperor by the grace of France and Prussia, and who therefore had close ties with these two countries.[23] A dispatch from Neuhaus, in which he wrote to the emperor about the Lopukhin affair, was opened and read. He said that it was likely that Marshal Bestuzhev would be dismissed from court, but that in his clever way he would control every action of his brother the vice-chancellor. The latter commented, "The vice-chancellor, who did not see his brother for twenty-two years, from 1720 to 1742, directs his ministry with a mind of his own."[24] Neuhaus reported to his court that the vice-chancellor was completely devoted to Austria and England. Bestuzhev remarked, "This malicious suggestion Neuhaus makes very confidently for a man who had the effrontery to slander even her imperial majesty in an utterly unscrupulous manner, in spite of what he knows to be true, and to suggest that the vice-chancellor is suborned by the queen of Hungary. God the almighty and omniscient is aware of the slanders he already has committed, and those he is fabricating. May God soon be the judge and avenger of all his actions."

In October Neuhaus informed his court that Mardefeld received from his king repeated orders to inform the Russian ministers how offended Frederick II would be if Russia continued to reject all means of establishing accord with Emperor Charles. "The Prussian court," Bestuzhev commented, "is trying by whatever means it can devise to create a link between the courts of the Russian and Holy Roman empires, so that thereby Russia might be suspected by its old allies, leading to eventual disagreement among them, which the Prussian court will exploit by intrigue."

The kind of secret undertakings Bestuzhev suspected Prussia of engaging in are evident from a letter he wrote to Baron Cherkasov on April 30, 1743. "We have nothing to fear from the Turks, but if France intends to create some future diversion in Russia it might well be with the help of the king of Prussia, on whom a vigilant watch should be kept.... He might bribe the Courland nobility to have his brother elected duke. Provided the king of Prussia does not interfere in the Swedish war, a combination of Denmark and France will present no danger."

It was discovered from Neuhaus's dispatches that he was supported by Brümmer and Lestocq, the latter repeating to him the empress's references to his activities. In this connection, Bestuzhev wrote, "Lestocq and Brümmer, instead of reporting faithfully to her imperial majesty, as was proper, all that Neuhaus revealed to them, unscrupulously passed on to Neuhaus and other foreign ambassadors whatever they heard from her majesty."[25]

But it was very difficult for Bestuzhev to fight against Frederick II, who could use the situation to curry the empress's favor. As soon as news of the Lopukhin affair reached Berlin, Frederick wrote to his minister Podewils, "We must make good use of this propitious occasion. No expense must be spared to win Russia over to our cause and to have it at our disposal. The time is ripe, and if we do not succeed now, we never shall. That is why it is imperative that we clear the way by laying low the Bestuzhevs and any others who stand in our path, because once we have forged strong links with Petersburg we shall be in a position of strong influence in Europe as a whole." Frederick sent to Petersburg well meaning advice from which the empress could discern the king of Prussia's increasing sincerity towards her. He urged her to banish Ivan Antonovich and his whole family, and expressed surprise at the casual lack of haste with which the matter was being handled. He further suggested that if Elizabeth wanted to have the heir to the throne under her thumb, she should not marry him off to a princess from a powerful house but rather from a minor German house, which would ever after be indebted to the empress for its good fortune.

Botta was transferred by his court from Petersburg to Berlin after the Treaty of Breslau,[26] but Frederick demanded that Maria Theresa withdraw him from the Prussian court in consequence of the Lopukhin affair. This action was presented by Mardefeld as evidence of his king's great sympathy towards Elizabeth, who was very gratified by it. If Mardefeld's account can be believed, she solemnly declared at table that the king of Prussia was the most perfect monarch in the world. Mardefeld guessed that his dispatches were being read, and in his anger forgot that Bestuzhev prided himself on being the agent of "the most perfect monarch in the world." He wrote to his court that "all letters sent abroad from the Russian empire still are being opened. I hope that those who stick their noses in my letters in time will find them being rubbed in the dirt. I would just laugh it off, were the scoundrels not ascribing to me what they read in the letters of members of their gang. I am not violent, nor am I quick tempered, but in due course I shall find out the rascal who has thought this up, and run him through with my sword."

The Bestuzhevs' enemies were given new heart by the long-awaited arrival of their most powerful ally, Chétardie. On November 28 Mardefeld wrote to his court, "Chétardie unfailingly will overwhelm all his political rivals and leave them with bloody noses. He has dined with me, and is coming round for supper this evening." The empress received her old acquaintance and his amusing company very well, albeit as a simple nobleman, for since he bore with him no letter of credence from his king with the imperial title for Elizabeth, he was obliged to remain *without portfolio*, as the expression was; that is to say, that he could not be recognized as ambassador.

Shortly after his arrival the empress sent him a birch rod and a note saying that he deserved to be punished like a little boy for having played so carelessly with gunpowder. Chétardie actually bandaged his hand, telling everybody that it was a powder burn; but everyone knew that it was not with gunpowder that he hurt his hand. No one was as infuriated at Chétardie's return as d'Allion, who saw in him the man who would push him aside, undo the work he began and, in the event of success, make himself out to be its sole architect. D'Allion could not restrain his anger and on meeting Chétardie upbraided him for coming back to Russia, where everyone detested him. Vorontsov, he said, passed on to the Bestuzhevs all the unfavorable comments Chétardie made about them, and only he, d'Allion, could be of any use to France in Russia. Chétardie flew into a rage, and in turn reproached d'Allion for his less than honest dealings. D'Allion screamed in reply that Chétardie was a scoundrel. Chétardie struck him in the face, whereupon d'Allion attacked him with his drawn sword. Chétardie seized hold of him to restrain the blow, and sustained a wound in his hand. At this point servants rushed in and separated the opponents; but the marquis's hand did not heal for a long time.

All the same, this episode by no means deprived Chétardie of the opportunity to act with Brümmer, Lestocq and Mardefeld against the Bestuzhevs. But the vice-chancellor took his own measures. On December 23, when making his report, the vice-chancellor submitted a request to the empress. "From the time your imperial majesty first graciously entrusted the affairs of state to me, and even before, I have been obliged to endure from my enemies base accusations and all manner of godless slander. I have been variously accused of being in Austria's pay, and in England's and, depending on circumstances against your interests, in Denmark's. These same enemies of mine are compelled by their own consciences to admit that by the grace of God I have never been the slightest bit neglect-ful in the performance of the duties entrusted to me, either in European or in Asian affairs.... I make so bold as to throw myself humbly at your majesty's feet and to beg your protection against the slander that I was somehow involved in the recent hideous conspiracy. I request you order an inquiry into each and every accusation brought against me.... And if any of these evil suggestions cause your imperial majesty to have any doubt or mistrust in me, then whatever success in my affairs might be expected, I shall not only be very greatly humiliated, but all my pure-hearted and manifold labors and endeavors will be confounded utterly and reduced to nothing."

The petition was submitted to evince assurances that no such doubt or mistrust was entertained by Elizabeth. The assurances were of course given, because Bestuzhev remained in his former post. Bestuzhev was now left alone, because his brother the marshal had to leave the court and Russia for the time being, as a result of the case against his wife. But he left the country on a diplomatic mission to Berlin, a very important posting, where he could all the more successfully and vigilantly preserve both Russia's interests and his own.

Meanwhile the Russian ministers and foreign ambassadors travelled in hope and fear to Moscow, where the empress intended to spend the year 1744. In the ancient capital the issue of the final preeminence of either Chétardie or Bestuzhev would be resolved, an event preoccupying all Europe.

THE REIGN OF EMPRESS ELIZABETH PETROVNA
1744

ADMINISTRATIVE INEFFICIENCY

On January 16, 1744 Elizabeth was present at the Senate and on the twenty-first left for Moscow, where she attended the Senate another three times in the course of the year.

During this year the Senate had occasion to deal with a matter of direct concern to itself. It was reported that a servant of Count Golovkin called Tatarinov, in a fit of temper at one of his friends who stated his intention to submit a petition to the Senate, cursed the institution with unbefitting language. The Senate ordered Tatarinov to be knouted without mercy as a warning to others, citing the article of the legal code concerning dishonor brought on boyars, lords-in-waiting and members of the council by ordinary people.

Immediately on arrival in Moscow the procurator general complained to the Senate that officials and civil servants were turning up late for work. The procurator of the College of Manufactures reported that it was even a rare event for his staff to turn up at all, so that in addition to other matters awaiting decision, there were thirty-two convicts being detained there. The Senate directed that all members of the colleges were to be summoned and *reprimanded*. Those failing to answer the summons under the pretext of illness were to receive a visit from an official and a doctor from the Senate for verification of the claimed illness.

On August 3 the procurator general informed the Senate that after an inspection of the colleges and chancelleries on that date it was found that very many staff failed to arrive at work on time. It was ruled that such defaulters were to be sent to the Senate for a reprimand and a warning that if they continued to arrive late, they would be fined. Reprimands and threats were unavailing. On September 20 the procurator general again produced a long list of defaulters. Those on the list were ordered to account for their absence. But on October 9 Trubetskoy reported that not one answer was received. Meanwhile the day before again it was found that many were absent; moreover on this same day, October 9, a soldier sent to the College of Justice on Senate business came back and reported that there was not a soul at the college.

Other disorders were reported by the procurators. In the College of Commerce there were frequent arguments, quarrels and slanging matches between the president Prince Yusupov and the vice-president Melissino, who reported he was seriously attacked and verbally abused by Prince Yusupov. The procurator of Novgorod reported that no accounts either were drawn up or submitted for the collection of the soul tax for the years 1737 through 1743; nor were any accounts kept for supplies for many years, no records of serfs maintained for twelve years, and the outstanding tariff payments and alcohol duty for the years 1730 through 1743 amounted to 476,884 rubles, while the chancelleries still owed 13,270 rubles. Although he frequently had drawn the attention of the provincial chancellery to this, the only answer he received was that because of the sustained negligence of earlier governors and civil servants and the current pressure of work it was impossible for them to correct the previous years' accounts. The procurator asked that a certain number of civil servants be specially assigned to draw up and audit the neglected accounts under the direction of someone particularly reliable. The Senate granted this request.

SALT SHORTAGE
Right at the beginning of the year the Senate and the procurator general had to devote all their attention to a serious hardship for the people, namely shortage of salt. It was produced at the Stroganov saltworks in Perm, but supplies ran out because the water level in the salt pans fell critically low. On February 13 Privy Councillor Baron Stroganov and his brothers applied to the Senate for government aid in view of the losses they sustained. In particular they requested immediate recruitment of 9,500 workers, stressing that without such assistance there was nothing they could do to maintain the required production of salt. They found it impossible to obtain sufficient freed laborers with stamped passports.[1] After bargaining Stroganov compromised and agreed that the government supply him with five thousand workers drawn from the local inhabitants, and then pressed for an additional 4,500 workers. The Senate

agreed, and sent Major General Yushkov to supervise the immediate production of salt.

Meanwhile the population at large suffered a shortage of salt, aggravated by hoarders among the soldiers who used to get to the shops first, pushing others aside. The procurator general informed the Senate that in the Moscow shops, state salt was sold mainly to men of various ranks,[2] soldiers and hoarders, while peasants and other ordinary people were scarcely able to buy any. Such was the crush that many could not buy any at all. He himself went to the shops at eleven in the morning of February 8 and found that there was no salt on sale, and a large crowd of peasants and other common people who told him that they could not obtain any salt for several days. On the recommendation of the procurator general the Senate ordered that state salt in the shops be sold only to peasants and other common people. Soldiers were not to be served in the shops, but were to be allowed to buy salt only by arrangement with the War College and other army headquarters once a month. This was designed to stop the growth of a black market in salt among soldiers and hoarders. Nor were members of the upper classes to be sold salt in the shops, thus avoiding delays in sales to peasants and other common people. They were to make their purchases of salt at a separate outlet. If officials sold salt to hoarders who in turn resold it at a higher price, both the officials and the hoarders were to be knouted without mercy. Inspectors were sent to the towns to root out and prosecute hoarders. Finally hasty arrangements were made to have reserves of salt sent to Moscow from Petersburg.

But the salt crisis was not curtailed by these measures. In May Baron Alexander Stroganov announced that because of the enormous losses they sustained, running into many thousands of rubles which they had no hope of recouping, it proved impossible for him and his brothers to purchase the timber necessary for the salt manufacturing process, or to make other vital arrangements for salt manufacture in 1745. In February they were charged transport costs of five copecks per pud for the shipment of frozen salt from Balakhna to Yaroslavl, whereas they could not pay more than three and a half copecks to cover all expenses. Similarly this year contractors were asking five and a half copecks a pud to transport salt from Nizhny Novgorod to Moscow; but now that the price fixed by decree was five copecks per pud, including all expenses, there were no

contractors to be found. Not only were they unable to make arrangements for production for 1745, they did not know how they were
going to be able to continue production for the rest of the current
year. Nor were they in a position to distribute the salt already
arrived from Nizhny Novgorod to towns upriver. Accordingly they
asked for their business to be taken over by the state. For the salt
supply this year they were relying on generous financial assistance,
without which they could not hope to continue production.

Stroganov presented a problem too difficult to resolve. The
Senate made no immediate response, and further approaches were
unavailing. In September Privy Councillor Alexander Stroganov and
Senior Chamberlain Baron Sergei Stroganov were called to the
Senate and told that salt sent from Nizhny Novgorod to Moscow
in May and June was not supplied by them, and that the salt coming
to centers near Moscow stayed there a whole month without being
brought to Moscow, so that there was none for sale to the public.
They were instructed to make every effort to supply Moscow with
salt, and threatened with fines if they failed to do so. The Stroganovs
replied that the salt trade was causing them heavy losses, and asked
the senators to act on the application they submitted, asking to be
relieved from responsibility for salt manufacture.

In November the Senate told Baron Alexander Stroganov that he
was to have salt ready for distribution in 1745 to Nizhny Novgorod
and towns upstream. Stroganov replied that they petitioned the
empress to be relieved of the salt works, but that meanwhile they
would try as far as possible to implement the Senate's direction,
with an undertaking to report back should they be unable to do so.

It will be recalled that the empress reached a decision the previous year regarding the Senate's report on the works contracts at
Kronstadt.[3] The contracts were drawn up again, for hitherto they
resorted to the compulsory requisitioning of workers from the provinces for state building projects. At this point, since the matter was
still pending, they decided to renew the old custom. General Lübras,
who was in charge of the Kronstadt works, requested the Senate in
April to have 1,033 highly skilled stonemasons sent to him, not like
those sent in 1742, less than a half of whom were found to be
skilled. But the Senate rejected the request on the grounds that it
would be impossible to make such arrangements without creating
too long a delay before work at Kronstadt actually got underway;

if more than half of the men previously sent proved unsuitable, it only went to show that many were put to a lot of trouble to no purpose whatsoever. Labor was to be hired on a monthly basis by voluntary agreement.

CLOTH MANUFACTURE

There was considerable concern in the Senate over cloth manufacture for the army by Russian factories. The Head Quartermaster reported that the Moscow cloth manufacturers undertook to supply cloth in accordance with patterns made at Bolotin's factory. They guaranteed a supply of 178,500 arshins, but when the deliveries were made quality controllers rejected 1,509 of Bolotin's 1,800 arshins, thirty-eight of Serikov's two hundred and twenty-seven of Tretiakov's eighty. Those not rejected barely made the grade, with the exception of Bolotin's. The president of the College of Manufactures said he found the quartermaster's high rejection rate very suspicious. The War College suggested that, in view of the wrangling between the Head Quartermaster and the College of Manufactures, quality control should be entrusted to the College of Manufactures alone, or the cloth mills given over to the complete control of the Head Quartermaster.

The Senate ordered that the cloth be checked by the Head Quartermaster, in conjunction with the College of Manufactures; the manufacturers were to be required to improve their quality in accordance with the specifications indicated; if there was no immediate improvement in quality they would be penalized not only by a cut in prices, but they also would have to shoulder the cost borne by the treasury for imported cloth. A few months later the quartermaster again complained of the poor quality of cloth, apart from Bolotin's. Even though his product was much the best he was paid the same as the rest, to his considerable annoyance. Justice demanded that the rest be paid less, and Bolotin more. The Senate ordered a survey of cloth prices in the marketplace, and of the discrepancy in value between the cloth the merchants undertook to produce and what they actually produced. By way of a fine they were to be paid according to lower estimate rather than the price they initially were guaranteed. Bolotin could not be paid more than the fifty-eight copecks per arshin fixed by imperial decree.

At the end of the year the question of cloth manufacture arose once more. The Senate ordered that Bolotin and his partners produce cloth in 1745 for fifty-eight copecks per arshin, according to the 1743 specifications, which Bolotin himself devised in his own factory. The other manufacturers who proved unable to furnish cloth of the standard set by Bolotin were required to follow the patterns devised by Serikov's mill. As these were less demanding, they were to be paid only fifty-six copecks per arshin. Bolotin and his partners were to receive an interest-free loan of thirty thousand rubles for the reconstruction and repair of their mill, to be repaid over ten years in cloth production. The manufacturers concerned were based mainly in Moscow, which grew into a great commercial center, since generally the cost of living was much lower than in Petersburg. For example, a Moscow merchant called Zalessky took over two silk factories from the manufacturer Solodovnikov. One was in Petersburg, the other in Moscow. Zalessky asked permission to transfer the Petersburg factory to Moscow, since it was prohibitively expensive to maintain. The College of Manufactures passed Zalessky's request to the Senate, which retorted that the college could have granted permission on its own initiative, and that the Senate should not be bothered with such applications in future.

LABOR SHORTAGE

We have pointed out repeatedly that the main obstacle to flourishing industry and development of other aspects of national life in the new Russia was labor shortage. Despite awareness of the value and profitability of free labor, it was frequently impossible to find. The Moscow cloth manufacturers Bolotin, Yeremeev, Tretiakov and Serikov informed the College of Manufactures that they could not man their mills; there was no free labor to be found; landless peasants for sale, particularly youngsters, were difficult to come by, while landowners would not sell their own peasants, apart from those they considered to be no good; the mills were in dire need of youngsters aged between ten and fifteen to work as spinners. Similarly silk manufacturers and others asserted that their greatest problem was labor shortage.

On the basis of these complaints the College of Manufactures sought the Senate's agreement to the employment in Russian factories of men of various ranks[4] who would emerge from the current census, that is to say, clerics' children, men of illegitimate birth, and emancipated serfs. The college proposed that all in these categories without exception be transferred from the soul tax lists and ascribed to the factories. The Senate disagreed, because instructions relating to the census directed that men of various ranks be registered as they wished in trading quarters and with guilds; the more able bodied among them were to be conscripted; otherwise they were to be sent to landowners and to factories.

ROBBERIES AND VIOLENCE

There were no workers to engage in honest labor. But at the same time countless were involved in dishonest and corrupt practises which the government was powerless to combat, again through shortage of manpower. Every time the Senate delivered a reprimand to the police the reply was that it was in no condition to preserve order, because of the lack of troops at its disposal. But more and more it appeared that disorder was instigated and perpetrated from the ranks of the army; its rougher elements took advantage of the fact that they were armed, whereas the rest of the citizenry was not. In Petersburg a Little Russian nobleman called Leshchinsky was killed. He was living in Count Chernyshev's house, in which soldiers of the watch also were billeted. On the other side of the Moscow River soldiers one night broke into the house of the merchant Petrov, set upon his wife and niece, ran them through with their swords and made off with his belongings. The Senate recognized that the Gendarme General Chancellery was insufficiently firm and thorough in its investigations; as soon as they heard of the incident, they should have sent someone to investigate, the Guards regiments and War College be requested to have every soldier and dragoon searched for trace of the stolen property and be required to provide evidence of their whereabouts on the night of the break-in.

On July 27 the empress announced in the Senate that the police headquarters were failing to exercise proper control. In Moscow there were all too frequent incidents of disorderly conduct and, what was worse, ordinary people were having their homes broken into and plundered. Furthermore the amount of sturdy beggars was on the increase, feigning various illnesses and begging alms. In many places there were no turnpikes, and people were failing to carry lanterns at night; nor was the peace with Sweden correctly observed by illuminating the houses, at least to the extent of placing candles at the windows. By way of justification, the police referred to incidents such as that occurring on September 8. At five that afternoon a fist fight broke out near the Earthen wall on the other side of the Yauza. It was twice broken up by the police. But the guardsmen organized a fight between factory lads and others. When a mounted patrol arrived to stop the fight its commander was attacked by the mob armed with stakes and rocks and was beaten almost to death. The instigator was a soldier of the Izmailovsky Regiment. If this was the situation in the capital, how must it have been in the provinces?

In Dmitrov district, in the hamlet Semenovskoe belonging to Major Doktorov, robbers and murderers were identified among his peasants. A detachment of troops with an officer was sent to arrest them, but they returned empty handed with fourteen of their number seriously wounded by the beating they had suffered at the hands of the Semenovskoe peasants. Another good officer was dispatched with his men with orders to meet any resistance by firing only wadding, in order to intimidate them. Every effort was to be made to secure their arrest without bloodshed, but if resistance continued after this show of strength, no quarter was to be given.

News came from Astrakhan that two boatloads of robbers, in all more than fifty men, had fallen upon three teams of commercial fishermen and robbed them of large seagoing boats, cannon and gunpowder, declaring their intention to put to sea. On the Vetluga patrimony of Count Golovkin the bailiff was killed in Nikolskoe village, also known as Baki, and the accounts office pillaged. All this happened in broad daylight and on an estate of 1,668 peasants. At midsummer the Senate was informed that robbery was on the increase along the highways near Moscow, especially along the road to Vladimir. Not only were travellers held up, but entire villages came under attack. Major General Sheremetev reported that robbers came by night to Sokol, the district he administered, to the village of Voskresenskoe, where they looted and set fire to his house, took money and assaulted the bailiff. In the same district they set fire to two villages. The leader[5] of the gang was called Knut. Prince Khovansky, high president of the Chief Magistracy, reported that a large mob of robbers descended on his Suzdal estate, Pestiakovo.

They burned down the church, his house and the homes of the peasants, killed five peasants and fatally injured another four.

On the basis of these reports the War College made arrangements for troops to be stationed at regular intervals along the Volga, from Tver to Astrakhan, to keep the brigands in check. Similarly troops were posted along the Oka, from Kaluga to Nizhny Novgorod, and in the governments of Belgorod, Voronezh and Archangel. The Senate ordered an inquiry into the activities of those hitherto responsible for policing the areas in question, and demanded to know why they were so feeble as to have allowed the number of such criminals to increase, and why the provincial and town governors were making no attempt to eradicate them.

After a month the Senate was informed that according to a report of Ivan Kain, an agent known to them, three robbers and a "hetman" were apprehended in Moscow. The robbers declared that "Hetman" Knut, formerly Posulikhin, and his gang of thieves, whose activities were centered mainly around Nizhny Novgorod, were now aboard merchant ships sailing towards Kolomna. Fifty dragoons were sent there immediately.

Troops also had to be used against rebellious peasants. In a village called Rogachevo, near the Trinity monastery of St. Sergius, as well as in other villages belonging to the St. Nicholas monastery on the Pesnosha, the peasants refused to obey the monastic authorities. They stabbed the captain sent to pacify them, and gave the soldiers a severe beating. The Senate gave orders specifying that a Russian officer be sent to deal with the matter. The peasant disturbance was put down successfully. Its participants explained that the reason for their truculence was a rumor that peasants ascribed to monasteries were granted freedom.

In another incident, on Countess Anna Bestuzheva's estate in the district of Pskov, the peasants arbitrarily elected their own bailiff Trofimov and drove out his predecessor Zalevsky. Lieutenant Colonel Golovin and his men were sent from Pskov to restore order. Initially he sent a small detachment on ahead to arrest the self-appointed bailiff and his accomplices, but was met by a mob of about a hundred and fifty peasants armed with guns, spears and pole-axes who opened fire on the soldiers, who returned their fire, killing one peasant. Six others were arrested, and the rest scattered. The next day another detachment was sent to try and persuade the peasants to surrender, but they responded by opening fire and wounding a soldier. The soldiers fired back, wounding a girl and arresting five people, among them Trofimov's mother. The rest took to their heels once more. The arrested peasants declared that among the rebels was a soldier from the Izmailovsky Regiment who was committing numerous crimes. The next day three hundred peasants attacked a detachment of one hundred and twenty-six men, killing a soldier and wounding three others. The soldiers opened fire, the peasants ran away, and twenty-two arrests were made. Thereafter resistance ceased, and the peasants began to register in acceptance of their subjugation; in all 731 peasants did so. At first the bailiff went into hiding, along with the elder and the tax collector. Then Trofimov was captured, only to escape from his guards by slipping his shackles. He subsequently turned up in Moscow and personally petitioned the empress against Golovin. The empress sent him to the Chancellery for Investigations.

SYNOD ACTIVITY

The Synod was grappling with its own problems. On April 13 there was a general meeting of both governing bodies, the Senate and the Synod, to discuss the request of the Kazan Tatars for permission to rebuild their mosques. Records showed that 418 of the 536 mosques in the Kazan government were destroyed. In addition the archbishop of Kazan stated that by the Synod's ruling of 1743 he was forbidden to sanction the construction of new mosques, and was ordered to demolish those built after this ruling. It was reported from the Astrakhan government that the destruction of mosques was risky; Muslims long subject to Russia might take flight, and those from elsewhere be discouraged from settling in Russia. It was decreed that mosques be demolished and not rebuilt in places where Russians and converts were living, so that they would not be exposed to pagan influences. Pagans were to be transferred from those villages to others inhabited solely by Muslims. If all mosques were demolished there was risk of unrest spreading among the areas where members of the Greek Orthodox church lived among Muslims, and where Christian churches were built, and that such churches might be subjected to persecution. It therefore was decided that two mosques be built in the Tatar quarter of Kazan, and that mosques be erected in villages populated exclusively by Tatars, with no

Russians, and with a population of two to three hundred. If on the basis of this reckoning there remained an excess of mosques, they were to be demolished immediately.

Councillor Yartsev was sent to Kazan government to look after the interests of the converts and to encourage pagans to adopt the Christian faith. He reported that the converts had to endure wrongs from everyone. They were subjected to forced labor and were enslaved by indentures. If anyone desired to free himself, the landlords sent reports against these inarticulate converts, who not only could not understand these legal technicalities, but also could not understand the Russian language very well. At the instigation of the landlords the governors dealt with these converts unmercifully. The petitioners were imprisoned for half a year and forced into "reconciliation" with their landlords, meaning that they were compelled to accept enserfment. Those freed at Yartsev's insistence received no compensation. Hauliers robbed them of their carts and they were given no provisions or travelling allowances, while their own provisions and fodder for their horses were taken from them.

They were terribly ill-treated by the pagans, who forced them to pay the taxes from which they were exempted for three years; they were subjected to military service under the command of pagans; they were falsely reported to local chancelleries and as a result were rounded up, kept under prolonged arrest and almost beaten to death. Yartsev registered protests on all these counts, but the provincial governors completely ignored him.

Yartsev extolled Archbishop Dimitry of Nizhny Novgorod to the same extent as he deplored the provincial governors. Dimitry, he claimed, showed indefatigable zeal in his diocese for converting the heathen and protecting converts from ill-treatment by pagans. Yartsev demanded an armed escort because only then would he enter a pagan village so that those seeking baptism would come forward without fear. Without such an escort it was dangerous to call on those wanting to adopt Christianity, for in many places the unbaptized opposed the edict, roundly cursing Yartsev and threatening to assault him. A company of his soldiers actually were attacked. Without the presence of an armed detachment pagans were intransigent, refusing to move to their designated places of resettlement.

Of the pagans, the Muslims were the most opposed to conversion. In many districts where pagans were elected to positions such as hundredmen, elders and chosen men, they subjected converts to intolerable abuses, beating them mercilessly and exacting all kinds of taxes from them. The Senate consequently directed that to promote this godly task an officer under Yartsev's supervision be assigned to the governments of Kazan, Nizhny Novgorod and Voronezh. They were to ensure that converts suffered no ill-treatment or malice.

THE SCHISM

Another problem was the schism.[6] At Volokolamsk twenty peasants were apprehended making their way towards the Polish border at Vetka at the instigation of the son of a cannon founder called Yamshchikov from Rzhev Volodimirov. Yamshchikov undertook to escort them to Vetka for five rubles a family, and taught them how to pray in the manner of the Old Believers.[7]

This sect, noted during Anna's reign, was not extinct, despite harsh measures. At the Bogoslovsk hermitage, sixty versts from Moscow, a large crowd assembled at the bare garden cell of the superior. Among them, it should be observed in passing, was Princess Daria Fedorovna Khovanskaia.[8] They all sat on benches, the men on one side and the women on the other. They sang the words "O Lord, have mercy upon us! Jesus Christ, have mercy upon us! O most Holy Mother of God, beseech Thy Son and our God that Thou mightest save our sinful souls on earth!"

During the singing the merchant Ivan Dmitriev jumped up from the bench and began to quake and spin around for more than an hour. "Believe me," he said to those present, "when I tell you that the Holy Spirit is upon me, and that it is not my own mind that causes me to speak, but the Holy Spirit." He went up to those he knew, called them by name saying "May God help you, my brother (or my sister), how are you? Pray to God at night and do not fornicate, do not go to weddings or baptisms, drink neither wine nor beer, where songs are sung, do not listen, do not watch prize fights." To those whose names he did not know he said "Pray for me, my brother!" As he went away from them, he said "Pardon me, my friend, if I have angered you in any way!" He then took a slice of bread, broke it into pieces, put it on a plate together with some salt and, pouring some water into a glass, handed it round, instructing them to eat it from their hands with a sip of water from the glass which they were to kiss, making the sign of the cross as they did so.

After this, all present took each other by the hand and ran round in a circle, jumping up and down. This practice they called "the ship." They rotated clockwise, chanting the same prayer as before, flailing themselves with axe handles and cannonballs which lacerated their flesh. Frightened by this beating, Princess Khovanskaia left with her retainers, and did not return. The remainder continued to dance and mutilate themselves in the manner described throughout the night and dispersed at dawn. The superior Dimitry was arrested, and testified that he was taught by Alexander Golubtsov, an apprentice at a textile mill, while he himself was still a novice at the St. Andrew monastery in Moscow in 1732. Golubtsov took him up the Yauza river to a meeting of ten men, who prayed using two fingers to make the sign of the cross. Golubtsov told him that his first baptism was effected by water, and his second by the Spirit, and that those who did not receive this second baptism would not go to heaven. The superior also stated that during worship some beat themselves with staves, while others cut themselves with knives inserted in sticks. It was discovered that even after the suppression of the heretics in Anna's reign there were some who continued to meet at St. John's monastery. Although the heretics repudiated legal marriage and forbade those already married to have intercourse (according to them intercourse was a sin instituted by Adam and Eve), the teacher and organizer, Grigory Sapozhnikov, nevertheless had a relationship with one Feodosia Yakovleva.

At the meetings held in Grigory Sapozhnikov's house, the host spun round saying "Pray to God, the wrath of God will come upon you, you will be arrested, tortured and beaten, the bishops and judges will attack you, but do not submit or swear loyalty to them, but endure steadfastly, for God and the All-Merciful Lady will liberate you."

Feodosia Yakovleva stated that she heard from her followers that Our Lord was to be found in Yaroslavl in the person of a peasant called Stepan Vasilievich, who held sway over heaven and earth, and whom they referred to as Christ. His wife, Afrosina, was deemed to be the Virgin Mary. Stepan and his wife were taught to believe this by another peasant, Astafy Anufriev.

In order to assist them in their struggle against the schismatics, the Senate petitioned the empress to publish two books by Feofilakt Lopatinsky, *An Inquiry into the Schismatic Beliefs of Dmitry Rostovsky* and *Objections to the Answers of Feofilakt Lopatinsky's Immolated Schismatics.*[9]

THE SYNOD

In the year under consideration the Synod had the good fortune to receive the edict removing it from the College of Church Landed Property, and all revenue from the lands belonging to the Synod, the church and the monasteries now was to become subject to the authority of the Synod, as was previously the case. It was to have control over expenditure as it had during the time of Peter the Great, with the sole exception of the Zaikonospassk monastery school,[10] which was to be maintained by a separate fund.

This meant the end of the Synod's wrangles with the College of Church Landed Properties, but not with the provincial governors. There was the case of a friend of the governor of Pereiaslavl-Zalessk,[11] Prince Shchepin-Rostovsky, who arrested and tortured a priest so harshly that subsequently he fell sick and died of his injuries. The Senate ordered a thorough investigation and summoned Shchepin to Moscow. Not long after this incident, the Synod submitted to the Senate a long list it received from Bishop Luke of Kazan. This list gave details of assaults by the civil authorities on church personnel. At the same time the Synod complained that provincial and town governors were continuing to try ecclesiastics in their civil courts.

But then there was the case of Archbishop Varlaam of Viatka, who boxed the ears of a governor, Pisarev, who reported that he was attacked by the archbishop's servants and by schoolboys wielding staves. He succeeded in beating them off and managed to arrest two of them. The governor was questioning them when the arch-bishop appeared in the chancellery and abused him in the most forthright terms, finally slapping him in the face. In his statement the archbishop recounted how the governor was his guest at dinner on December 6, together with his son, a second lieutenant home on leave from the Izmailovsky Regiment. The son ordered the singers to sing the dirge "Eternal Memory"[12] and, taking up a mug of beer, said to the merchants who were there "Hey, what scum you merchants of Khlynov are!"[13] Then he went to the cell of the archbishop's treasurer and tried to give him a whipping. Three days later, December 9, the governor's son beat the archbishop's secretary almost to death; next, the monastery's steward and baker were picked up off the street and taken to the governor's chancellery for interrogation. There the drunken governor and his son ordered a fire prepared in the torture chamber. Then the archbishop arrived at the governor's chancellery, but the governor answered his admonition in the most obscene language, so the archbishop struck him on the cheek.

REVISION OF THE BIBLE

On its arrival in Moscow in February the Synod received from the empress an edict which put it in some difficulty. "Whereas we deem the matter of corrections to the Bible, already long in preparation, but as yet not completed, of pressing need both to our church and to our people; in consideration whereof we charge and require, by this our edict, all members of the Holy Synod to resume the task of preparing the Bible for publication from the time our edict is received, working every morning and afternoon, apart from holidays, so that if possible its correction will be complete by Easter. We further charge that on completion of such emendations we be informed, and that the emended version not be printed without our express command. We also desire herewith that all necessary prerequisites be taken in hand, and most particularly that the paper for printing be procured from the mills of Councillor Zatrapeznov and Assessor Goncharov and from other suitable purveyors. Furthermore we command the participation in this enterprise not only of members of the Synod, but also of learned men of the ecclesiastical estate. For carrying on current affairs pending within the Synod's competence, which presently are fewer than at other times, certain of the Synod's members are to be assigned, and are to report to the Synod on those weighty matters occasionally arising, and seek a decision."

But Easter drew near, and still the work of revising the Bible was not complete. In July Ambrose of Novgorod petitioned the empress to be excused by reason of illness from further work on the project "because I have a sickness in my head which ill befits me to undertake the task at hand." In the event the matter was to drag on for several years.[14]

A BRIDE FOR GRAND DUKE PETER

Elizabeth was unable to pay too much attention to the fact that her edict remained unfulfilled because at this time she was preoccupied with an important family matter which, in view of the current tension in Europe, inevitably was bound up with political intrigue. The empress, plagued by the sympathy still felt for the Brunswick family, as witnessed first in the Turchaninov affair and later in that of Lopukhin, wanted to arrange the marriage of the heir to the throne, Grand Duke Peter Fedorovich, with all possible speed, but the importance of making the right match, both from her own point of view, and in the interests of others, will be understood readily.

As far as Brümmer, Lestocq, Mardefeld and Chétardie were concerned, it was vital that the young grand duchess chosen, together with her relatives and retinue accompanying her to Russia, did not act counter to their aims and influence by acting in accordance with those of Bestuzhev, whose choice fell on Princess Marianne of Saxony, daughter of King August III of Poland, since such a match would accord fully with his policy of pursuing an alliance between the maritime powers and Russia, Austria and Saxony, to keep France and Prussia in check.

As soon as Bestuzhev's designs for the princess of Saxony became known in the enemy camp, they hastened to find another candidate for the marriage. They put forward Sophia Augusta Frederika, daughter of the prince of Anhalt-Zerbst,[15] who was in Prussian service, and Elizabeth of Holstein, sister of the bishop of Lübeck, heir-elect to the Swedish throne. "Thanks to Lestocq and Brümmer," wrote Chétardie to Amelot on December 10, 1743, "the Saxon ambassador Hersdorf could not obtain twenty-five thousand Russian auxiliaries in exchange for the English subsidy."[16]

Hersdorf also proposed that the grand duke marry the daughter of the king of Poland. Hearing of this, Brümmer and Lestocq put it to the tsaritsa that a princess from a strong house could hardly be counted on to be pliable, and it was essential to select one for whom this marriage would represent genuine good fortune. They also encouraged church leaders to impress upon the empress that Orthodoxy would be more endangered by a Catholic than a Protestant match, and therefore nominated the princess of Zerbst.[17] Lestocq came to see me yesterday evening and informed me that the matter was settled, and the tsaritsa secretly sent ten thousand rubles to the princess of Zerbst, to get her to come here immediately."

In a letter to the princess of Zerbst's mother dated December 17, New Style, Brümmer wrote the following. "I trust your excellency

Princess Sophia of Anhalt-Zerbst (1740)

Rosina Lischevska

is fully confident that I have not ceased, from the moment I arrived in Russia, to strive for the good fortune and high standing of the illustrious ducal house of Holstein. Let others judge whether I have been successful or not. Having long nurtured a deep respect for the person of your excellency, and having always wished to assure you of my esteem not merely with words, I have been seeking day and night some signal way of advancing your cause and that of your illustrious house.

"Knowing the generosity of your heart and the nobility of your sentiments, I do not hesitate for a moment to reveal to your excellency a matter which I would ask you to keep strictly secret, at least for now. During the two years I spent at this court, I have had many occasions to talk to her imperial highness about your excellency and your virtues. I have long been exploring various means and using various channels to bring matters to the desired conclusion. After prolonged and persistent efforts, I believe that I have succeeded at last in finding a way of fulfilling and securing the complete happiness of the house of Holstein. It now remains for your excellency to conclude the matter which fortunately I have been able to set in motion. At the behest of her imperial highness, it is my duty to inform you that your excellency, accompanied by your eldest daughter, should leave for Russia without delay. Your excellency will understand of course why her highness so urgently desires to see you here as soon as possible together with your daughter the princess, about whom much good is spoken. There are occasions when the voice of the people is truly the voice of God.

"At the same time, our incomparable monarch expressly directs me to inform your excellency that the prince, your husband, should not on any account come with you. Lest your excellency be embarrassed and in order that you might have several dresses made for you and your daughter the princess, and so that you might commence the journey without delay, I have the honor of enclosing with this missive a letter of credit. To be sure the amount is modest, but I should explain to your excellency that it is deliberately so, since it is feared that a more ostentatious remittance might excite the attention of those observing our actions. Lest your excellency lack anything essential on your arrival in Petersburg, I have arranged for a merchant called Lüdolfd to advance you two thousand rubles in case of need. I guarantee that once you arrive here safely, your excellency will not want for anything."

Brümmer indicated in his letter the number of people the princess was to bring with her: one lady in waiting, two maids, a chef (in this country an indispensable item, as Brümmer put it), a communications officer, and three or four lackeys. Brümmer provided the princess the explanation she was to give for her departure to Russia. "All your excellency needs to say is that duty and respect demand that you go to Russia, both to thank the empress for her graciousness towards the house of Holstein, to visit the most perfect of sovereigns, and to receive her kind favors personally. So that your excellency is acquainted with all circumstances relating to this matter, I have the honor of informing you that the king of Prussia is privy to the secret. Your excellency is at liberty to speak with him about it or not. But as for me I respectfully urge your excellency to speak to the king, since in due course you will reap the benefits which naturally flow from this course of action. Monsieur Lestocq who of course has been working with me and is very devoted to the interests of the house of Holstein, asked me to convey to your excellency the profound respect in which he holds you. To give him due credit, I should tell you that in the matter of your excellency's interests he has conducted himself as a man of honor and your zealous servant."

On December 21 Brümmer sent another letter, urging the princess to come as quickly as possible and "strike while the iron is hot." Chamberlain Naryshkin was sent to meet them and to deliver a letter from Brümmer to the princess's mother in Riga. "I receive daily inquiries from the empress," he wrote, "wanting to know whether I have any news of you, whether you have passed through Danzig, and when you may be expected in Moscow. My usual reply is that if your excellency had wings, you would use them, so as not to waste a minute." Brümmer pressed the princess to take his advice, and to show the empress on her first meeting with her "an extraordinary and more than complete respect" (une déférence extraordinaire et plus que parfaite), particularly by kissing her hand. Brümmer also informed her that the grand duke knew nothing of the imminent arrival of his aunt and her daughter

The intended did not know that a bride was underway but the king of Prussia was fully aware of the matter, and at the end of

December wrote to the princess's mother, stressing that she should head immediately for Russia, where a wonderful destiny lay in store for her daughter. He boasted that the idea of a match between her daughter and the heir to the Russian throne originated with him, and demanded that the matter be kept strictly secret, especially from her husband the prince and Chernyshev, the Russian ambassador in Berlin. The princess replied that she was fully prepared to accept the king's advice, but that on one point she was unable to comply fully—she could not conceal the purpose of her journey from her husband.

Frederick himself described his view of the affair. "Of all Prussia's neighbors, the Russian empire deserved the most attention as the most dangerous, being strong and close. Prussia's future rulers also will have to seek the friendship of these barbarians. The king employed every means to obtain Russia's friendship. Empress Elizabeth intended marrying off her nephew the grand duke, and although she had not made her final choice, she was more and more inclined towards Princess Ulrike, the king of Prussia's sister. But the Saxon court wanted the grand duke to accept Princess Marianna, second daughter of King August. Nothing could be more opposed to Prussian interests than to allow the formation of an alliance between Russia and Saxony, and nothing worse than to sacrifice a princess of royal blood to edge the Saxon competition out.

"Another way was devised. Of the eligible German princesses, the princess of Zerbst most suited the interests of Russia and Prussia. Her father was a field marshal in royal service, her mother a princess of Holstein, sister of the heir to the Swedish throne and aunt of the Russian grand duke. There is no need to go into detail concerning the negotiations. Suffice it to say that the efforts required to bring it off were as if it were a matter of greatest significance for the world. The bride's father himself opposed the marriage; being an ardent Lutheran of the early Reformation type, he did not want to see his daughter become a schismatic, and only gave his assent when a priest of the utmost patience demonstrated to him that the Greek faith was almost the same thing as the Lutheran. In Russia, Mardefeld was so skilful in concealing from Chancellor Bestuzhev the action he initiated, that the princess of Zerbst arrived in Petersburg to the great surprise of Europe, and was received by the empress in Moscow with clear signs of pleasure and friendship."

This account contains obvious exaggerations and attempts to inflate the actually rather modest significance of his own part in the matter. It is a curious claim that the original idea for the marriage came from the king of Prussia rather than from Brümmer, considering the latter's devotion to the "ducal house." Brümmer might well have made Mardefeld a party to his secret, but there was nothing for Mardefeld to do in the matter. Any action involved was initiated by Brümmer and Lestocq; besides such action was scarcely necessary, for Elizabeth had vivid and tender memories of her late intended, and it was clearly a source of considerable pleasure to have the niece of him she was to have married as a bride for her nephew.[18]

Practical as well as emotional considerations were satisfied because, given the current European situation, it was certainly most advantageous to select a bride for the grand duke from an insignificant house, whose interests could have no influence on political events; the marriage was concluded within the family. It was simple enough to keep it a secret, since it directly concerned only three or four people, all equally anxious to let it go no further than themselves. That the match was made without any difficulty is seen most clearly from the fact that Frederick could not point to one obstacle, apart from the initial opposition of the bride's father.

ARRIVAL IN MOSCOW

Be that as it may, the princess and her daughter reached Petersburg on February 3, 1744, and Moscow on the ninth. Acting on Brümmer's advice, the princess kissed the empress's hand saying, "I lay at your highness's feet my profoundest gratitude for the honor done to my house." "What I have done," replied Elizabeth, "is a trifle compared to what I would have wished to do for my family; my own blood is no dearer than yours." A lively conversation ensued which the empress abruptly curtailed, withdrawing into another room. The princess later was told that Elizabeth, being very much reminded of her cousin, could not restrain her tears and left the room in order to hide them.

FREDERICK II AGAINST BESTUZHEV AND THE BRUNSWICK FAMILY

Quite clearly the arrival of the Zerbst princesses was a source of shock and dismay to Bestuzhev, who recently suffered the loss of his valued friend Brevern, who died suddenly the previous January.

The princess's mother naturally turned to the men she considered to be her friends and protectors, namely Brümmer, Lestocq, Mardefeld and Chétardie, who in turn warned her against Bestuzhev as her bitter enemy, to be feared above all. In this way the number of the vice-chancellor's enemies multiplied, and this increase took place precisely at a very dangerous time, when his enemies were doing all they could to bring about his downfall, or at least to ensure that his powers were curbed.

Early in January Chétardie wrote to Amelot. "A group of us, consisting of Mardefeld, Brümmer, Lestocq, General Rumiantsev, Procurator General Prince Trubetskoy, their associates and myself, have agreed to get General Rumiantsev made chancellor. He would then, as head of the colleges, be empowered to keep Bestuzhev in check. If not, we shall have to set up a council or a cabinet drawn from the College of Foreign Affairs with the number required to prevent the vice-chancellor controlling them all."

All these moves against Bestuzhev were mainly to the advantage of Frederick II, to whom it was vital at this time to draw Russia into an alliance, or at least force it into neutrality. Austria's military success in the war with Emperor Charles VII[19] and the bankruptcy of France, which proved incapable of defending its ally, aroused considerable anxiety in Berlin, for if permitted to gain strength Austria would not leave Prussia in peace without recovering Silesia. Saxony was anti-Prussian and anti-French because of the deception practiced by these two countries and because Prussia, having gained Silesia under the terms of the Treaty of Breslau, did not allow King August to win any share of the spoils.[20] Saxony, therefore, was drawing closer to Austria.

To check Austria's successes and to keep Silesia, Frederick considered it imperative to launch another attack on Maria Theresa under the pretext that he was obliged to assist the emperor. But how would this pretext be viewed in Russia? In order to assure a favorable Russian attitude it was essential for Frederick to destroy the Bestuzhev group, which was constantly talking about his dangerous intentions. "Caution and prudence," Frederick wrote to Mardefeld, "most certainly demand that I forestall the enemy (Austria), which seeks to preempt me. I see no security either for myself or for the empire as long as matters remain where they are now. If I have to go to war against the queen of Hungary alone, I always shall emerge the victor, but the essential condition (conditio sine qua non) is Bestuzhev's overthrow. I can do nothing without your skill and your good fortune. On your efforts depend the fate of Prussia and of my house."

At the same time Frederick needed to free Sweden from Russian and to replace it with Prussian influence, so that if need be Prussia could use Sweden against Russia precisely as recently France did. Two marriages in Russia and Sweden served to fulfill these aims: the marriage of the heir to the Russian throne to the princess of Zerbst, and the marriage of the heir to the Swedish throne to Frederick's sister Ulrike. "Once the empress decided on the princess of Zerbst as the grand duke's bride," Frederick himself wrote in his memoirs, "it was no great problem to press her to agree to the marriage between the Prussian princess Ulrika and the heir to the throne of Sweden. Prussian security depended on these two matches."

But Frederick had yet another concern about Russia. Knowing Elizabeth's personal antipathy towards Austria and Saxony, he did not think that she would decide to offer active help towards Maria Theresa and King August against Prussia. Consequently it was important for Prussia that the Russian throne continue to be occupied by Elizabeth, and after her by her nephew, married to the princess of Zerbst, a devoted supporter of Prussia. Hence Frederick II's efforts to deprive the Brunswick family of the possibility of regaining the Russian throne, for the Austrian sympathies of this family were well known. At the end of 1743, talking to Chernyshev about the Botta affair, Frederick instructed his ambassador to convey to the empress the sincere advice that she "remove the Brunswick family, now in Livland, to some place where no one would be able to trace them, and so that they would be forgotten about in Europe. This would be easy to effect, since no power in Europe will come to their aid."

In January 1744 Chétardie wrote to Amelot. "Mardefeld is instructed by the king to seek a secret audience with the empress in order to point out the imminent danger threatening her, and to impress upon her the urgent necessity of averting it. He is to press for the removal of the Bestuzhevs, and to emphasize the absolute necessity of returning Prince Anton of Brunswick to Germany, and of sending his wife and children to various places in Russia, so that no living soul might know of their departure or of their whereabouts.

Otherwise if Prince Ivan and his family continue to live near Riga,[21] England, Denmark, Hungary and Saxony would lose no time in fulfilling the intention on which their fondest hopes are based.[22]

"Such counsel the empress might only have received from her father, for if she acts unjustly and abuses her power by detaining a free prince (Anton of Brunswick), then good politics demand that his wife and children be similarly treated. His family in any case has increased with the birth of another prince, as the empress has told me in confidence. In my opinion, the advice of the king of Prussia is sincere, taking into consideration his fear of Russia. He knows the empress's weaknesses, and is sure that in her reign Russians will receive preference."

The fatherly advice was taken, the Brunswick family being transferred to Ranenburg. At the same time Chétardie urged his government that no expense be spared in the matter of bribery, and that apart from Lestocq, who already received a gift of two thousand rubles from the king, and the two ladies, the empress's chaplain and members of the Synod needed to be bribed to bring influence to bear upon the superstitious Elizabeth.

YOUNG CATHERINE

Just as Brümmer, Chétardie and their associates were busy undermining Bestuzhev in anticipation of the help which the princess of Zerbst was to afford them, a totally unexpected event caused them considerable anxiety. In the middle of March the young princess fell dangerously ill. It is best to hear the princess's own account of the causes of her illness and its course because this account provides the reader with a first opportunity to meet the future Catherine the Great (Catherine le Grand). In the fourteen-year-old girl we may discern the first glimpses of the strong will and clear understanding of her position which later characterized the outstanding empress.

"On the tenth day after my arrival in Moscow, the empress went to the Trinity monastery. I was given three teachers: Simon Teodorsky, who was to instruct me in the Orthodox religion, Vasily Adadurov for Russian, and Lodé for dancing.[23] In order to get on faster with my Russian, I got up at night when everyone else was fast asleep, and sat over the books Adadurov left me. As it was warm in the room, and I had no experience of the climate, I studied in bed barefoot. So it was that on the fifteenth day I was gripped with an illness which all but dispatched me to the next world.

"While I was getting dressed to go to dinner with my mother at the grand duke's, I began to feel feverish. With difficulty I asked my mother to allow me to go to bed. When she returned from dinner, she found me almost unconscious, with a very high fever and an unbearable pain in my side. She thought I had smallpox and sent for the doctors, who decided that I should be bled. But she did not want to hear of it, saying that her brother died of bloodletting in Russia when he had smallpox, and that she did not want the same thing to happen to me. As my mother and the doctors argued, I lay unconscious, groaning from the terrible pain in my side, while my mother scolded me for being so impatient. Finally on the fifth day of my illness the empress returned from the Trinity monastery. She came straight from her carriage to my room, and found me unconscious. She was accompanied by Lestocq and another doctor. Hearing their opinions, she ordered them to bleed me. As soon as this was started, I came around and, on opening my eyes, I saw that the empress was holding me in her arms. For twenty-seven days I hung between life and death. Finally the abscess on my right side burst, and I began to get better. I immediately noted that my mother's behavior during my illness produced a very bad impression on everyone. When she saw that I was in a bad way, she wanted to send for a Lutheran pastor. When I was told of this later, I said 'What for? I should prefer Simon Teodorsky to be sent for. I would very much like to talk to him.' He was brought to me and our conversation, which took place in everyone's presence, greatly pleased those who heard it. As a result the empress and the whole court were completely won over to me. The empress often wept on my account."[24]

According to Chétardie, those who viewed the marriage of the grand duke to the princess of Zerbst with disfavor, and wanted to see the Saxon princess the heir's bride, were incautious enough to display their delight during the illness of the young princess of Zerbst. This greatly annoyed Elizabeth, and she told Brümmer and Lestocq that the supporters of a Saxon match stood to gain nothing, even if she had the misfortune to lose such a good child, since she would never accept a Saxon princess. In case of just such a misfortune Brümmer had in mind another bride for the grand duke, the princess of Darmstadt, whom Frederick II also suggested in the event the princess of Zerbst proved unacceptable.

CONTINUED MOVES AGAINST BESTUZHEV

The young Zerbst princess recovered, and the intrigues against Bestuzhev gathered momentum. Emperor Charles VII made Razumovsky, Brümmer and Lestocq knights of the Holy Roman empire. The king of Prussia bestowed favors and gifts on Razumovsky's younger brother, Kirill Grigorievich, who was being educated in Berlin. But it was much more important for him to win over to his side a more influential person than Razumovsky, namely Vorontsov. Chétardie put it to Brümmer, Lestocq and Mardefeld that Vorontsov enjoyed the complete confidence of the empress at this time, and that there was accordingly not a minute to be lost in bringing him over to their side, otherwise Bestuzhev would gain the upper hand. Lestocq, he suggested, should put aside personal feelings and tell Vorontsov that he held him long in the utmost regard, but that he was unable to place confidence in him, seeing that he enjoyed close links with Bestuzhev, a malicious enemy of the empress and of the house of Holstein. By making such a declaration it would be easy to open Vorontsov's eyes to the vice-chancellor, and then excite his ambition by indicating to him the possibility of his becoming chancellor, thereby using him as a means to overthrow Bestuzhev.

Lestocq and Brümmer declared themselves ready to act according to this scheme, while Mardefeld went to Vorontsov without delay to bait the trap. "I have come to you," he told Vorontsov, "to lay bare the secret of my heart. I cannot endure without heartfelt pain the present state of affairs in Russia. The only way of alleviating this situation is for you to enter the ministry. The sincerity of your intentions and the nobility of your heart will be a more reliable and a better guide than any knowledge and experience, and because of your qualities the empress will find in you the help to avert the dangers threatening her. She would also find a powerful help in friendly relations with my master the king, but at present efforts are being made to sow dissent between them. The vice-chancellor quite clearly has come out against us, and I tell you now that I no longer shall have any pity for him. I will also state that as long as he alone controls foreign affairs, my court will not have any confidence in anything that the empress does or says."

"From this it follows," Vorontsov observed, "that we shall either have to send him off to some distant foreign court, or else assign more members to the Council for Foreign affairs; but were I to take him on single-handed he would surely be the ruin of me if he is the man you say he is."

"The first course of action would be better," answered Mardefeld, "but even in the second case, no matter whom you appointed, they would be dependent always on you, because you enjoy the empress's trust. Initially they would help you with their experience, but after a while you would be able to get along without them. Out of friendship towards you, I am bound to observe that you should consolidate your position. But would it be secure if Princess Anna ever succeeded to the throne, which might very well happen in the present circumstances? Or could you deem your own position secure when the grand duke succeeds the empress? Believe me, he would never forgive you your close friendship with the enemies of his house. If you do not believe me, ask the grand duke himself. Quite clearly you can only assure your own future and that of your children by openly supporting the empress's occupancy of the throne and the order of succession laid down by her in Russia and Sweden. My master the king has bestowed on you the Order of the Black Eagle, and sent you his portrait set in diamonds. You can be sure that this will not be all." So that Vorontsov could be certain of the truth of Mardefeld's words, the grand duke was asked to tell him Bestuzhev was the enemy of the house of Holstein, and that the empress herself told him so.[25]

But Bestuzhev, evidently standing alone before his enemies, had in his hands a powerful means of defense. All these dispatches of Chétardie were intercepted, and their code deciphered with the assistance of Academician Goldbach. The vice-chancellor took the opportunity to pass on to the empress in his report all these curious documents with his own comments and rebuttals. For example, where Chétardie wrote that he and his friends were counting on the help of the princess of Zerbst, Bestuzhev observed, "The king of Prussia, urged on by the French court, has instructed his minister, Mardefeld, to undertake this unprecedented persecution of the vice-chancellor and these attempts to effect his undeserved ruin, in collusion with Marquis de la Chétardie. They carry on in so shameless a fashion that they have intrigued to involve the princess of

Zerbst, apparently in all innocence. They have acted so scandalously, and it is clear beyond doubt that particularly they have turned his imperial highness the grand duke also against the vice-chancellor. Being in so wretched and miserable a state my only comfort lies in the fairness of her imperial majesty, who with her generous protection will not allow the vice-chancellor to become an innocent victim."

Chétardie wrote that Bestuzhev, infuriated at the arrival of the princess of Zerbst, so forgot himself as to say "We shall see whether such marital alliances can be concluded without consulting us, the overlords of this state." Chétardie also wrote that Bestuzhev brought over to his side the archbishop of Moscow, who pointed out to the empress the illegality of the grand duke's marriage to the princess of Zerbst, on grounds of consanguinity,[26] and to suggest another bride, the princess of Saxony. "It is impossible," Bestuzhev commented, "to think of anything as malicious as the allegations made by Marquis de la Chétardie and his associates Lestocq and Brümmer against the vice-chancellor. All that has to be done to show that these are nothing but shameless and fabricated lies is for her imperial majesty to ask the archbishop of Moscow or any other cleric to testify under oath whether any such comments were made by the vice-chancellor concerning the marriage to the princess of Zerbst, or whether he ever had with any of them any specific conversation at all on this subject."

In one of his dispatches Chétardie said that Bestuzhev and his party showed themselves just as angry with the Berlin court as with France. "It is true," Bestuzhev noted, "that the vice-chancellor no longer trusts either the Prussian or the French court. Prussia is more dangerous than France by virtue of its proximity and its greatly increased strength. The vice-chancellor, however, has shown not the slightest anger against either, despite the fact that both are working to bring about his ruin; he has only been discharging his sworn duty in all respects."

In connection with the interrogation of the Livonian Stakelberg, who had made derogatory comments about Russia in a Königsberg inn and predicted a new revolution, Chétardie wrote that apart from Ushakov they also were hoping to appoint as interrogator Procurator General Prince Trubetskoy. "Is it in accordance with customary practice at court that a foreign ambassador not only creates his own faction and meddles in matters of domestic policy, but even goes so far as to interfere in the business of the Secret Chancellery? Her imperial majesty might be pleased to consider the consequences of this state of affairs," was Bestuzhev's notation.

Chétardie boasted that he had drafted a reply to be sent to General Keith in Sweden concerning the local situation, and that before a meeting of the Council on Foreign Affairs he conferred with his associates as to how to carry out his plan, and that this plan actually was carried out with a few emendations. "That a foreign ambassador," commented Bestuzhev, "has himself worked out and written an answer (actually amounting to an order) to a general of the Russian empire and now, it transpires, to a minister, is so utterly incomprehensible that the imagination boggles at the possible consequences! It is surely absolutely without precedent to receive directives from a foreign ambassador indicating the manner in which his aims and advice are to be acted upon. Her majesty might consider the value of those who divulge secrets, and the future benefit of such an assembly to the Council of her imperial majesty and to the state. It is also quite without precedent that matters be concluded in Council according to the prescripts of a foreign ambassador, and that he should know exactly how these are discussed and amended. General Keith must be confused as to which instructions he is supposed to act upon, those issued by the College of Foreign Affairs, or Chétardie's representations which purportedly inform him of her imperial majesty's sentiments."

Chétardie wrote that Elizabeth would be acting against her own interests should she fail to remove a vice-chancellor who considered that Russia's salvation lay only in an alliance with the maritime powers, the queen of Hungary, King August and his supporters, and who without the slightest twinge of conscience declared himself against France, the king of Prussia and any supporter of the French and Prussian courts. Bestuzhev commented by way of justifying his policy, "But this is a traditional Russian course, pursued by Peter the Great himself."

Bestuzhev found his most powerful line of counterattack in those passages of the dispatches where Chétardie made derogatory remarks about the empress herself. Although he was on the best of terms with her, the French minister was vexed that Elizabeth would not fall in fully with his plans by sacrificing her vice-chancellor to satisfy the

Franco-Prussian party. Chétardie constantly complained about Elizabeth's weakness, her laziness and her aversion to affairs of state. In his words, Elizabeth was in the habit of accepting her ministers' views only to save herself the trouble of having to think for herself. Her goodness was never properly understood, and always based on blind trust in others. Elizabeth's only real concern was for her own pleasures, and her main reason for wanting peace was so that she could squander the money on these pleasures which otherwise might have to be used to finance war. The main pleasures, according to Chétardie's list, were being in love, having her slightest whim gratified, changing her dresses four or five times a day, and being waited on hand and foot surrounded by lackeys in her palace. Any man superior to those daily surrounding her was an immediate source of anxiety. The prospect of having to attend to the slightest bit of formal business alarmed and angered her. Laziness and the fear of finding in new ministers an efficiency which would not at all suit her own lack of discipline caused her to stand by the vice-chancellor, and so on. All these extracts from the dispatches were set before Elizabeth.

THE BRIDE'S MOTHER

In May the empress again went to the Trinity monastery, taking with her the grand duke, both Zerbst princesses, Lestocq and Vorontsov. The young princess noted that for some time now the empress had been behaving very coldly towards her mother. After dinner one evening at the Trinity monastery the empress followed the grand duke into the princesses' rooms and called the princess's mother into another room, where they were joined by Lestocq. The grand duke and the young princess sat down by the window to await the return of their elders. After a lengthy interval Lestocq at last appeared and approached the grand duke and the princess, who were laughing about something. "You will soon be laughing on other side of your faces," he said. Then he turned to the princess and added, "You'd better pack your bags, you're going straight home." "Why?" asked the grand duke. "You'll find out soon enough," Lestocq answered, then left. The empress entered looking flushed and angry. She was followed by the princess, whose eyes were red and tear-stained. When the grand duke and the young princess jumped down from the high window sill, the empress laughed, kissed them both and went out.

CHÉTARDIE EXPELLED

Soon afterwards another not entirely unconnected scene took place. Early on the morning of June 6, at half past five, there appeared at Chétardie's apartments General Ushakov, Prince Peter Golitsyn, two officials from the College of Foreign Affairs, and Kurbatov, secretary of the college. Chétardie came down to meet them, clad in his dressing gown and wig. Ushakov informed him that he came on the orders of the empress to make a certain announcement. This was read out by Kurbatov and directed Chétardie to leave Moscow within twenty-four hours. Chétardie demanded the evidence on which this order was based, whereupon Kurbatov read him all the extracts from his letters where he spoke of the need to bribe government and church leaders, and made insulting references to the empress. Having listened to them, Chétardie said that it remained to him only to fulfill her majesty's will, and that *"although he regretted her majesty's decision in this matter, once it was taken, he was grateful for the graciousness with which her majesty was pleased to make her intention known to him."*

"While this was taking place," Ushakov wrote in his report, "it was clear that as soon as he saw General Ushakov, his face fell. While the extracts were read to him he was so embarrassed that he was unable to utter a single word by way of apology or justification. He merely looked at the original documents and, recognizing on them his own hand, had no desire to look any further, being completely confused. Both the expression of his face, the words he stammered out and the tremble in his voice betrayed the guilt and trepidation he felt. Nothing worse was done to him, as Chétardie's words just quoted indicate. It was quite apparent that in view of his established guilt he expected more serious consequences."

The delighted Bestuzhev wrote to Vorontsov at the Trinity monastery, enclosing a copy of Ushakov's report. "From the enclosed your excellency will be able to see the happy outcome of Andrei Ivanovich Ushakov's commission, on which I have the honor of proffering my congratulations. In all honesty I must report that I never expected the degree of confusion shown by Chétardie. He really was extremely embarrassed. He was quite unable to collect himself, did not think to ask the company to be seated, let alone offer any explanation by way of self-justification. He stood with downcast eyes, sighing deeply and coughing. He evidently never thought so much compromising evidence was amassed against him. When it was read out to him he listened in silence, and on being shown the originals he covered them with his hands and turned away, not wishing to look at them."

After Bestuzhev the man who derived most pleasure from this turn of events was the English ambassador, Lord Tyrawley,[27] who replaced Wych. "I have not had a free moment during the Chétardie affair," he wrote to Lord Carteret, "because it poses the question whether England or France emerges the victor. When we revealed Chétardie's actions to the empress and portrayed him as a ridiculous as well as a dangerous figure, it acted very quickly upon her. The princess of Zerbst, whom I dubbed the queen mother (a sobriquet which so pleased the vice-chancellor that this is how he always refers to her), apparently foresaw Chétardie's disgrace. It is said that on this account she wept for several days before the blow fell. Chétardie's fall was decided before Elizabeth left for the Trinity monastery, and during the journey Vorontsov held her to her intention. Now we shall have to see how this development will affect those who were Chétardie's close friends: Brümmer, Lestocq, Trubetskoy, Rumiantsev and his wife."

Ten days later he wrote, "Our main aim now is to continue the undermining of French interests set in motion by Chétardie's expulsion, and to bring down the French party once and for all, particularly Lestocq and Brümmer. I am confident that we can manage this, but we need a little time. I was with the vice-chancellor on June 16 and he said to me that he just dispatched a courier to Berlin and Stockholm with orders for his brother, and the ambassador in Sweden, Lübras, to break off negotiations for a quadruple alliance between Russia, Prussia, Sweden and France, as well as that other alliance proposed by Mardefeld, a triple alliance between Russia, Prussia and Sweden, which France was to have joined. Apparently after Chétardie's departure the princess of Zerbst tried to persuade the empress to conclude this latter alliance. But Elizabeth told her to be silent, saying that it was none of her business, and that she had ministers who would advise her about relations with other powers.

"I wanted," continued Tyrawley, "to recover for the king the pension which Lestocq so little deserves, and spoke to the vice-chancellor about it, but he advised me to continue to award the pension to Lestocq to mask my real opinion of him."

Later Bestuzhev changed his mind, fearing that Lestocq would refuse the offer of a pension and then boast about it, all the more so as Frederick II spread a rumor that Tyrawley brought six hundred thousand chervontsy to Moscow.

CATHERINE'S WEDDING

The princess of Zerbst was told not to meddle in affairs which did not concern her, but Lestocq's attempts to frighten the young princess by telling her that she should pack up her belongings and return to her homeland was in vain, for the empress did not change her plans for her in the slightest. Towards the end of June Archimandrite Teodorsky was to finish his religious instruction. The mother of the princess of Zerbst wrote to her husband in April, "I can testify to the fact that their Orthodox teachings, apart from a few outward ceremonies, are very much like our own. They do not accept the veneration of saints, but good deeds are taken for a sign of faith." In May the princess wrote to her father that "since I find almost no difference between the Greek and Lutheran faiths, I have decided to become an Orthodox convert." She was anointed as such on June 28, and took the name Ekaterina (Catherine) Alekseevna. The event was reported from Moscow in the Petersburg News. "Her highness of Anhalt-Zerbst has received daily instruction from a certain archimandrite in the teachings of the Orthodox confession of the Greek faith. At noon today, in the presence of her imperial majesty and of his imperial highness the grand duke, and in the company of the assembled ecclesiastical, civil and court dignitaries, she publicly accepted the confession of the Orthodox Greek rite, after which she was anointed by his grace the archbishop of Novgorod and named Ekaterina Alekseevna. On completion of this ceremony her imperial majesty bestowed on the princess a clasp and diamond-encrusted icon worth several hundred thousand rubles. It is impossible to describe the zeal and decorum with which this most worthy princess conducted herself throughout the solemnities described, so much so that her imperial majesty and the majority of those present were scarcely able to restrain their tears of joy."

On the following day, June 29, on his name day, the grand duke was married to Catherine Alexeevna, who received the title of grand duchess. "Her imperial majesty," her mother wrote of this occasion, "intended to seat me at dinner beside her and the young couple

Grand Duke Peter and Grand Duchess Catherine
following their betrothal (1744)

Johann Christoph Grooth (1716-1749)

beneath the canopy. But our inveterate enemy in her Council, and for whom this whole day was unbearable (Bestuzhev), being either so stupid and fanciful as to imagine that I would make a fuss and thereby incur the empress's displeasure, or else wishing to hurt my pride, schemed so successfully that the ambassadors made it clear that were I to dine with the empress under the canopy along with them, they would keep their hats on. They claimed, you see, that according to protocol they should come immediately after the grand duke and his bride, but not after me." As a result, the princess dined alone in the gallery.

On July 26 the grand duke together with his wife and mother-in-law left for Kiev, followed the next day by the empress herself, who returned to Moscow on October 1. She was accompanied on this journey by the newly-appointed vice-chancellor Vorontsov, newly made a knight of the Holy Roman empire, while Bestuzhev, now chancellor, remained in Moscow. He found his income was not enough to support his new position honorably, and so he requested the empress for a grant of land in Livonia bringing him an annual income of 3,642 efimki. He wrote to Vorontsov that if the empress refused his request, he would be compelled "to crawl back to his old wooden hovel, and to have his customary conferences with foreign ambassadors and discuss them when possible at the empress's table."[28]

But much more important was his correspondence with Vorontsov on foreign affairs.

FOREIGN AFFAIRS
1744

FRENCH REACTION

It is not difficult to imagine the effect of Chétardie's expulsion on the French court. Cantemir was no longer was in Paris; he died March 31, leaving his secretary Gross as *chargé d'affaires.*[1]

On June 30 Gross informed the minister of foreign affairs, S. Florentin, that Chétardie not only attempted to suborn church and state leaders, but even dared to describe her imperial majesty in the most bold and brazen manner, and to claim that the empress dealt with him like an ordinary offending foreigner. The empress hoped therefore that the king would not only demonstrate his disapproval of Chétardie's behavior, but duly would acknowledge her majesty's moderation and condescension in not wishing to take advantage of Chétardie's position as a man entitled to no diplomatic immunity, so that friendship with Russia might continue. For her part the empress was prepared to reciprocate, in any event to offer his majesty her consideration and special respect.

S. Florentin, who interrupted Gross's speech several times, answered that Chétardie hitherto was considered a prudent man, so that his enemies must have managed at last to score a victory over him. Gross observed that the empress dealt with Chétardie on the basis, not of any slander, but of his original letters, and that he could not offer any justification. When informed of the empress's decision his face fell, registering embarrassment and confusion, and he plainly considered himself very lucky to have been treated so leniently. Florentin objected that a change of expression did not necessarily signify guilt; it could have been a result of Chétardie's surprise at the underhand manner of his treatment, since the key to his code was taken from him. Gross replied that no key was taken, but means of obtaining it were found.

RELATIONS WITH PRUSSIA

But France now no longer was the main object of Russia's attention. Bestuzhev declared openly that Prussia was more dangerous than France "by virtue of proximity and greatly increased strength."

In Berlin at this time Russia was represented by the chancellor's brother, Mikhail Petrovich Bestuzhev-Riumin, as emissary extraordinary. This is how on June 28 he reported the impression created in Berlin by Chétardie's expulsion. "When I gave Count Podewils reliable information about the matter, and he read the written declaration, it was clear from his mien and what he said that this news worried and pained him, for he asked me questions which in the circumstances appeared most unseemly. For example he wanted to know whether Marquis de la Chétardie actually departed and, if so, whether he left a secretary behind, and whether his way home lay through Berlin. I answered that Chétardie was instructed to leave on the express orders of her imperial majesty, and that I had no information whether he left behind a secretary. Nor could I say which route he would take home, since that was up to him.

"Later, while dining at the house of the Saxon ambassador Bülow, Podewils proved quite unable to master the regret he felt at the news of Chétardie's expulsion, so that it was plain for all to see. Von Borck, the *chef de cabinet,* took the news more calmly and said that the French were like that: if they were given an inch they would take a mile. He went on to say that her majesty's magnanimity and moderation in the way she dealt with a man accused of such flagrant and major crimes would not find enough praise here. Moreover it was acknowledged that the firmness of purpose she showed and the wisdom of the action she took would redound to her eternal credit and to the greatest respect and consideration in all the courts of Europe.

"That the Prussian court played no small part in Chétardie's intrigues can be demonstrated by the following evidence: (1) I am informed that the king was very troubled about the news about Chétardie, since he expected quite a different outcome. It was not so much a matter of disappointment at his expulsion, but that he did not succeed, and that such a strong faction was unable to bring down the ministry. If Baron Mardefeld was mixed up in the Chétardie affair and a complaint is brought against him by your majesty, his recall from Petersburg will cause the king no difficulties. It is clear from this information that Mardefeld and Chétardie were in collusion. (2) General Lübras, who enjoys the king's special favor, told me that the king asked him whether there was some new conspiracy in Russia, for he heard there was a considerable degree of unrest. He was hoping within the next three or four days to receive news of some important event by special courier, and suggested that the British ambassador had £200,000 available to ensure that something happened. Yesterday several of my old friends and acquaintances told me how extremely glad they were about Chétardie's expulsion, since they could now hope that the king would leave them in peace, which is what they all wanted here. From such conversations it is obvious how much the court here fears Russia, which alone is capable of restraining the king of Prussia from further scheming."

On July 14 Bestuzhev sent the following curious report. "Privy Councillor von Roth came to me and told me in the king's name how pleased his majesty was with me but not with my brother because (1) Russian ministers at foreign courts are not dealing frankly with their Prussian counterparts and (2) the vice-chancellor is frustrating the completion of a triple alliance between Russia, Prussia and Sweden. He also said that the English were boasting that their ambassador took six hundred thousand chervontsy to bribe the vice-chancellor and others, and that this money was given to the vice-chancellor for him to distribute as he saw fit. The king instructed me to be told all this so that I would reassure my brother privately that as long as he did not oppose his majesty's interests the king would show us both his gratitude. I was told further that the king would use the first opportunity to talk to me about this himself, which he did two days later. I was invited along with other foreign ministers to a ball and dinner given by the queen, at which the king also was present. His majesty came up to me and spoke very softly so that nobody else could hear. He repeated what von Roth told me except that, according to the king, the English ambassador Lord Carteret[2] claimed that a hundred thousand guineas were brought into Russia to set up a party, and that this money was given to my brother to distribute as he thought best.

"I answered that it might very well be that England was making such claims, and this I did not dispute, but I found it hard to believe that my brother was given this money, and if it were true, he deserved the most severe punishment. I asked whether his majesty would have any objection to my communicating all this to my sovereign. The king answered that this was not why he told me about it, for he had no wish to get involved or become compromised. All he wanted me to do was to write to my brother in a private capacity to warn him what the English court was about, and to suggest that he might treat the king with more consideration and respect."

Frederick II urgently needed a radical improvement in his relations with the vice-chancellor. Austrian success in Alsace forced him into war earlier than he wanted.[3] His plan was to invade Bohemia by various routes, but to do so he had to pass through Saxon possessions. Since the king of Prussia declared he went to war only to support Emperor Charles VII, the latter demanded from the elector of Saxony free passage of allied Prussian troops. But Frederick II did not wait for the Saxon government's permission, and took his troops through its territory to Prague. August III protested at such violation of his territory, but in vain.[4] It is easy to imagine the effect of the king of Prussia's action on the allies of Maria Theresa.

Informing the court of the latest Prussian moves against Austria, Bestuzhev wrote on July 21, "Even in its present state Prussia poses a considerable threat to its neighbors, and if the king further strengthens his position by typical efforts to expand his frontier at every convenient opportunity, the influence he stands to gain in Poland and Sweden will make Prussia a formidable danger to Russia. It is therefore in the interests, not only of your majesty, but also of our present and future security, to prevent the further strengthening of Prussia, the more so since only Russia is capable of doing so. In my opinion the danger is so real that measures must be taken before it is too late."

Bestuzhev followed this up by writing "May it please your majesty to note the haughty terms and arrogant self-assertion with which the Prussian court seeks to justify with baseless excuses its current 'belligerent *démarche*' before an impartial world. All this vividly demonstrates how little we should rely on Prussian pacts and promises."

Constantly pointing to the fearsome growth of Prussia's strength, Bestuzhev wrote, "I remember when I was a student at the academy here, that the king's grandfather had no more than twenty thousand troops; his successor brought this number up to eighty thousand,[5] and now it stands at a hundred and forty thousand. If he extends his frontiers any further, he will have two hundred thousand troops. The Prussian king is attempting by every possible means to cajole and lull your majesty into a false sense of security to ensure you take no part in European affairs, but as soon as he achieves his aims and acquires something else, then, quite apart from the fact that he may well annex the Polish part of Prussia, he will gain an enormous amount of influence in Poland and Sweden by reason of both family ties and proximity. His ambitions perhaps aspire to placing one of his brothers on the Polish throne. Together with France, he will attempt to reduce Russia to its former frontiers and incite the hostility of the Swedes and Poles. I have heard first-hand that when someone asked the king whether Russia would oppose this enterprise, the king replied: 'I have as much to fear from Russia as an unborn child in its mother's womb.'"

Bestuzhev wrote to his brother the chancellor in the same terms. "As it is getting very late in the day, I think it best that the court here be given a jolt and kept from attacking Austria. This can be achieved by strong representations from me to the effect that Russia fully intends rendering the queen of Hungary the assistance guaranteed by treaty, and that mobilization is underway, both of our troops and the cossacks, who are feared greatly here. Our obligations to Austria and our own interests require that measures commensurate with the honor and dignity of the empress be taken immediately, the more so since the Prussians play with pacts and in their unscrupulous fashion hold nothing sacrosanct or inviolable. They have, for example, with utter impudence and complete contempt, broken the Treaty of Breslau, guaranteed by Russia and England.[6] They are accustomed to attacking their allies while at the same time reassuring them of their friendship. It seems to me essential, *mon cher frère,* that if we have not yet decided on any definite policy, you and your colleague should settle on the surest and most useful course of action for Russia, and implement it forthwith. Count Podewils said recently that the king told him he understood from me that our court has no intention of getting involved in European affairs. My reply was that the king never had any such reassurance from me, and that in any case I could only have given it with the authorization of my own court. But I can see how this misapprehension might have arisen. When the king was talking to me once about the duplicity of the English and the deceit of the Austrians with their Treaty of Belgrade,[7] he added, 'Am I not right in thinking that your court will not get involved in the present European crisis?' I answered I had no idea of her majesty's intentions except for a general desire that peace in the north not be violated. I am writing to you about this because you know very well the sort of scheming and intriguing they are capable of here."

In London on August 9 Lord Carteret told Prince Shcherbatov, "The king of Prussia has torn off his mask. He has done violence to the elector of Saxony and attacked the queen of Hungary, in violation of the Treaty of Breslau. Please draw the empress's attention to the king of Prussia's moves, and urge her to take immediate measures, together with her allies, to stop him becoming stronger, for this accession may prove dangerous also to Russia."

In September the king himself told Shcherbatov "in the most forthright terms" how much Europe's present affairs depended on the decisions of the Russian empress, and that she easily could have a great impact by frustrating the king of Prussia's plans. But even before the receipt of these suggestions Bestuzhev wrote to Vorontsov in Kiev on August 11 about the "unexpected and dangerous actions" of the king of Prussia. "Just bear in mind," the chancellor wrote, "that this is something I referred to before. Look into it carefully, and you will find that I was telling the truth. When her imperial majesty takes the trouble to investigate the matter and graciously recalls what I have almost always pointed out when I had the honor to make my humble reports, I am certain that her majesty herself will acknowledge graciously that it was not in vain that I made constant reference to the lack of trust the king of Prussia deserved, and to the fact that his conduct and actions should be most definitely the object of our country's attention.

"Clearly this king, being the closest and strongest neighbor of our empire, is the most dangerous. We all wish he were not so erratic, aggressive and excitable, or his views and actions not as manifest to the world as they actually are. But what has been observed during the short time of his reign?[8] He was the initiator of the ill-fated war in Germany.[9] This was begun in bad faith with the most unctuous assurances of friendship and aid, and was ended in equally bad faith.[10] This prince drew up a peace treaty, the terms of which were unfavorable to France, the emperor and the king of Poland and elector of Saxony, while he secured Silesia for himself. When the terms of the Treaty of Breslau were being ratified your excellency will remember the extraordinary vigor and astonishing effrontery with which he sought her majesty's endorsement of this

treaty here. Hardly was this endorsement received than he unilat-
erally and without the slightest provocation took it upon himself
to violate the peace terms, wantonly breaking his word not to involve himself either directly or indirectly in the war. Can such a
prince be trusted, when he plainly has little regard for his own
solemn promises, undertakings and obligations? What might other
countries expect? What are we to expect when this prince, always
full of new projects, is happy so to deal with us? The honor and
glory of her imperial majesty demand that our obligations to our
allies now be fulfilled. Even if her majesty did not have such obligations, the interests and security of her empire clearly demand
that actions becoming daily more menacing not be treated with
indifference. For if my neighbor's house is on fire, I am naturally
obliged to help him put it out for my own safety, even if he were
my worst enemy; and of course I would be doubly obliged to do
so were he my friend. Her majesty thereby would be following the
celebrated policy of Peter I, which brought our country so much
benefit. It would bring her empire so much credit, that no one would
dare attempt to attack us in future. Moreover it would secure for
us the friendship of other countries, which is as essential to us now
as it was to our forbears.

"The stronger the king of Prussia becomes, the more dangerous
will it be for us. We cannot foresee the possible consequences of
such a powerful, frivolous and erratic ruler of so vast an realm. The
new ties the king acquired by the marriage in Sweden of the crown
prince to his sister need to be watched. Your excellency might take
note from the summaries you have of my reports that continually
I have pointed out to her majesty that this match might sooner or
later prove disastrous for the Russian empire....[11] The welfare and
security of the empire consists, not in deserting our allies, for they
are the maritime powers which Peter the Great always strove to
cultivate, while the king of Poland and elector of Saxony, and the
queen of Hungary (because of the respective positions of their
territories) naturally have interests in common with our empire."

Vorontsov replied with the pleasant news that Count Fleming,
sent by August III to the empress in Kiev, was well received, and
that on his departure Elizabeth herself said "Reassure his majesty
that I shall always remain his true and faithful ally, and that in the
event of any attack upon his lands I will not fail to come to his

immediate aid." Vorontsov also sent a copy of his remarks on foreign affairs he submitted to the empress, and these turned out to
accord completely with Bestuzhev's views. In his memorandum
Vorontsov suggested that Frederick II had secret plans to conquer
Bohemia and partition it with the emperor. "In view of the increased
strength of the king of Prussia, and given that he is cunning, se-
cretive and aggressive, what guarantee is there that he will not
undertake some enterprise against Russia? He might start by attacking Poland, and not only acquire towns and land but, forming con-
federations, overthrow the king of Poland and replace him by force
with his own candidate.[12] This would leave him free to pursue all
kinds of as yet unfinished disputes and claims in Ukraine, Smolensk
and Livonia. What would we do then? To stop him, we would need
the help of other powers. But is it not already too late to attempt
to do so, when none of the neighboring countries is in a fit state
to offer him any resistance? Might not one add that the Swedes and
the Danes would do nothing to stop us being attacked? So if no
attempt is made to prevent the king of Prussia from carrying out
his designs the misfortunes which are bound to follow, including
the final loss of Livonia and other calamities, do not bear thinking
about. We now must realize that it is not only the French and Prussian clamors for the relief of their troops (and if we are reliably
informed, the king of Prussia sent an express emissary to Turkey
to conclude an alliance and to incite war against the kingdom of
Hungary and Russia), but also the Turkish sultan himself and the
Persians, who will not pass up a suitable opportunity to go to war
against a Russia threatened on all sides. How are we then to defend
ourselves? When all our allies, as mentioned above, are rendered
incapable of affording us any help, it is beyond the wit of man to
see what hope of salvation there is for us.

   "Even though your majesty is personally greatly disappointed by
the evil intentions and actions of the loathsome Botta, it would be
very dangerous for the general interests of your state to allow the
fall of the house of the queen of Hungary, considering the very
frequent and erratic shifts in European politics. Moreover the Hungarian house is essential to Russia to create a diversion in the event
of any war with Turkey, and perhaps even more so in view of all
the military and territorial advantages which the kings of Prussia,
Spain and France, the emperor and several other minor German

princes stand to gain from the present war. Not one will give your majesty any thanks, but merely acknowledge an obvious blunder and ultimately set in motion all the misfortunes I have described in order to force Russia, whose mighty strength they so envy, back to its former frontiers. In this way they will seek to prevent any future participation of Russia in European affairs."

Vorontsov proposed the following measures. (1) Russia must assume a strong position by deploying large numbers of troops on the Livonian and Polish borders. The empress should then declare herself the intermediary between the warring factions. (2) Russia must come to an agreement with its allies, including Holland; lest the allies "leave Russia to shoulder the whole burden alone, a plan of action should be decided upon." (3) The Russian emissary in Poland must put it to the king and the magnates that the empress would be prepared to come to their aid in the event of an attack on their territory, or in case a confederation was formed.

Bestuzhev was delighted with this memorandum. "I am pleasantly surprised," he wrote to Vorontsov, "to find that your painstaking consideration of current European problems contains points of view which are in such complete accord, not only with my own views, but also with those of other members of the college, that together we could not have produced anything better to serve the interests, glory and honor of her imperial majesty. If this arrogant neighbor (I mean the king of Prussia) will not be mollified, then sooner or later, as your excellency rightly observes, we shall meet him in our Livonia with an even greater force than he has now (although he is extremely dangerous as it is)." Bestuzhev indicated Sweden, and Vorontsov Poland, as places where it was vital to combat the king of Prussia's intrigues.

SWEDEN AND DENMARK

Money was sent to Stockholm for the upkeep of Russian troops as early as the end of 1743 in order to deprive malcontents of an excuse to complain about excess burdens. General Keith, who on Korf's return to Copenhagen also had diplomatic responsibilities, sent word back to his court about the effect created in Stockholm by the empress's generosity. The crown prince told him that he considered the Russian sovereign the sole author of his well-being, and her latest act of generosity confirmed him in the position he attained through her majesty. The king himself with a happy expression told Keith that the empress deigned to bestow generous New Year gifts, and that he was hard put to it to find words to express his gratitude and to match the extent of her bounty. Nevertheless, he continued, since he was in military service from his boyhood, and in spite of his advanced years, he now felt enough strength to repay the empress's kindness by taking up his sword on her behalf, should a suitable opportunity arise. Along with him, he concluded, the whole of Sweden would be eternally obliged to the empress, and never forget her favors. The senators said that this would stop the mouths of those evil thinkers who maligned the sending of a Russian auxiliary corps.

Keith wrote that remitting money was just as important as dispatching troops, since money would persuade the majority of Denmark's supporters to melt away. It was these supporters upon whom Denmark would rely to plan an attack on Sweden.

At the same time some rather unpleasant news arrived in Petersburg from Stockholm. The king informed Keith of the crown prince's intention to marry the king of Prussia's sister, and of his request for the empress's consent. The heir himself wrote to the empress "as a son to his mother," asking her consent to this marriage which "accords with his friendly disposition towards the Berlin court." Elizabeth replied in January 1744, "This is a matter which depends mainly on the good intentions of your royal highness and the assent of his royal majesty and the Swedish lords. If this arrangement promises to further the growth of paternal and filial sentiment between his majesty and your highness, it is seemly and acceptable to us." A family connection between the crown prince and the Berlin court was potentially all the more dangerous, for the Swedish people's goodwill towards Russia could not be counted on. For this reason there was strong temptation for the crown prince to act ungratefully towards his benefactress in order to acquire popularity among the Swedish people, particularly since matters with Denmark were settled

On April 1 Keith wrote that Gyllenborg[13] and Nolcken already were asking when the repatriation of the Russian auxiliary corps might be expected. Rumors were spreading in Sweden that the empress wanted to leave two or three regiments for the crown prince in place of a guard. In Keith's opinion, these rumors were fostered by malevolents who wanted their countrymen to believe that the crown prince did not trust them, and intended for his own safety's sake to surround himself with alien troops. Keith reported that the two significant parties in Sweden, the French and the English, of which the former was the stronger, included the majority of the nobility and nearly all townsmen. The church was divided more or less equally between them, while the peasantry still did not entirely abandon the idea of union with Denmark.

"Of all these factions," Keith wrote, "I cannot say which best represents your majesty's interests. The king has only a small following, which is not in a position to take any significant steps. If your majesty will permit me to make an informed observation regarding the continued presence here of Russian troops, I am bound to state in all honesty that this is a matter demanding the utmost care and caution. I humbly beg leave to refrain for the time being from making any proposals; time can be gained through the arrangements they themselves have made. I can draw out the embarkation of troops onto the galleys until the end of May without giving the Swedes any grounds for concern, and if your majesty then permits the garrison to continue at its post here, the pretext of lack of provisions will provide me with a reason to stay longer, waiting for the arrival of supplies from Russia."

Peace between Sweden and Denmark finally was concluded. The Swedish government suggested to Keith that the Russian troops, now no longer needed, might leave Sweden. It would be best were they to leave before harvest or, even better, before haymaking. When Keith stated that supplies from Russia were expected any moment, the ministry immediately undertook to issue provisions from their own stores. On informing the crown prince that he received orders from the empress to remove the Russian troops from Sweden, Keith received the reply "I am very glad to hear it because some here have ascribed your long stay in this country to me, and are beginning to grumble about it and about me."

Keith had to leave Sweden with the Russian troops. In his place General Lübras was appointed ambassador extraordinary to Stockholm. He was a participant in the congress of Åbo and apparently was neither liked nor trusted by Bestuzhev. Consequently it must be concluded that his appointment was arranged by the chancellor's opponents. Lübras travelled by way of Berlin from where, on June

25, he wrote to the empress about a conversation he had with the king. Frederick II told him that he was very disturbed about the Russian court, because the empress was exposed to many disagreeable and dangerous opinions expressed by malevolent and disloyal men. In the same report Lübras wrote that he spent forty-eight hours with the king in Potsdam, and had long conversations with him. He would be forwarding reports of these later.

"In forty-eight hours," commented Bestuzhev, "he did not think to write what the king talked to him about, but perhaps the news about Chétardie will change Lübras's dispatch entirely."

Lübras's dispatch finally arrived, dated June 28. It reported that the king repeated his grave anxiety about the state of affairs at the Russian court. His main concern was that, whatever intrigues were being hatched around her, the empress hold the throne. "I know for certain," Frederick II said, "that such powerful disturbances are going on at court and among the people that something unexpected soon will come to light. I have evidence before me that Lord Tyrawley has at his disposal six hundred thousand chervontsy for purposes of bribery. I await my courier with impatience. What is happening in your ministry? Who will be chancellor?" Frederick deliberately tried to frighten the Russian court into taking no part in European affairs because he was himself increasingly fearful of such participation and of irregular Russian troops as well, which explains the questions he put to Lübras about the cossacks and the Kalmyks.[14]

From Berlin Lübras made his way to Copenhagen, where the king of Denmark told him, "The Holy Roman empire is in a bad state, and if the king of Prussia persists in his present attitude, it will mean not only the imminent downfall of many princes of the empire, but also all neighboring states are in danger of attack unless immediate steps are taken to ensure their defence. The king of Prussia is absorbing one after the other, so that it will soon be the turn of the stronger powers, a fate Russia has every reason to expect."

Lübras replied that as long as his majesty himself recognized the need to restore the general peace, particularly in the North, that in itself would go a long way to effect it. "I will do everything in my power to help," the king answered, "but most important is the constant accord of Russia and Denmark, on which the true interests of both states depend. Everything in fact depends on the empress." As they parted the king repeated that it was his most earnest desire to remain on the best of terms with the empress, and with tears in his eyes looked up to heaven and added, "He who tells her otherwise is her enemy."

Lübras did not reach Stockholm until October 25. By November he was reporting that the French party's strength was increasing rapidly and that its numbers were growing daily since the arrival of the crown princess from Prussia. The French ambassador, Lanmarie, was suborning people actively in Stockholm and the provinces with sums of newly received money so as to have his faction organized in readiness for the opening of the Riksdag. Soon afterwards Lübras further reported that the Prussian ambassador proposed a defensive alliance between Prussia and Sweden, but that the king instructed the Russian court to be informed in advance. The crown prince assured Lübras that he would do all he could to ensure that no course of action would be taken contrary to the will of the empress, and that this would be his abiding principle.

Lübras pointed out to the senators of the patriotic (that is, Russian) party that by maintaining constant friendly relations with Russia, Sweden would have no reason to fear attack from any quarter, and consequently had no reason to enter into any other defensive alliance. But if as a result of continued German unrest the king of Prussia rendered himself liable to attack from any other country, Sweden would be compelled to join forces with the allies. The patriotic senators were naturally in complete agreement with Lübras's views, but when he made similar representations to the crown prince he was told that according to assurances from the Prussian court the main purpose of this alliance was to support him on the Swedish throne, and would be binding only on the conclusion of the present war in Germany. In Lübras's opinion, "it was suggested only to humor him."

In the circumstances, the members of the Russian party demanded that Russia conclude a treaty of alliance with Sweden as quickly as possible, as a warning to France and Prussia. The main difficulty was that without a subsidy Sweden was not in a position to conclude a treaty with anybody, while Russia was in no condition to pay one.

In mid-December news came from Lübras that with the assistance of the French and Prussian parties messengers went to the provinces and persuaded the deputies elected to the next Riksdag to introduce autocracy.[15] It was suggested that Sweden's impoverished state stemmed mainly from republican institutions, and that the inescapable consequence of these was discord. The soldiers and peasants were particularly attracted to this idea, as were many of the lower and middle classes, whose attitudes were normally shared by the clergy as well. The crown prince, under pressure from his wife and proponents of autocracy, would welcome this notion; he already obtained the rank of colonel of the guards without any difficulty. The lesser gentry wanted autocracy, while the rich alone were against it. But in the first place there were very few of them, and even they wanted to see the powers of the king strengthened to match those enjoyed by Gustav Adolf,[16] provided that declaration of war, conclusion of peace and imposition of taxes remained the prerogative of the estates.

Recognizing in this proposed change a grave threat to Russian interests, Lübras suggested that conditions be included in the treaty of alliance guaranteeing the inviolability of the present constitution in Sweden. To avert Swedish objections, he proposed that, for its part, Russia demand similar guarantees regarding the maintenance of the present mode of government in Russia.

POLAND

As far as Polish affairs were concerned, during 1742 and 1743 Elizabeth's court was inundated with complaints from Russians living in Poland about their persecution at the hands of the Catholics. Keyserling complained to the ministers and to the king himself on several occasions, but in vain.[17] At the end of 1743 he made "lively representations" to the king to the effect that the conscience of his Russian subjects was cruelly aggrieved by the abuse of their faith in a manner unprecedented in Christendom. Such un-Christian conduct sorely offended the empress, who considered it her duty to intervene on behalf of her co-religionists, particularly since this was her right under the terms of the peace treaty, which stated that Russians who became Polish subjects by the union of Lithuania and Poland were entitled to adhere to their faith.[18] Moreover this ruling also was endorsed by the king and the Sejms. The king replied that he was distressed to hear that such misconduct and insolence against his Orthodox subjects still occurred. "On the basis of your earlier complaints," said the king, "I wrote to both the Polish and Lithuanian chancellors instructing them to see that such persecution cease. Malice toward people of differing faiths necessarily involves the persecution of the innocent, without taking any account of the general good, or of laws or treaties. There are many such zealots in Poland, and the more the local laws tolerate the abuse of freedom, the bolder they are in their wilful behavior. I shall write again to the crown chancellor, asking him to intervene on behalf of the Orthodox inhabitants."

A decree was in fact sent to the chancellor, but this chancellor was a Catholic bishop. Keyserling wrote to the Polish magnates with the threat that the empress would not leave her co-religionists undefended, and would use whatever means necessary to counter the abuse they were suffering. He reminded the ministers that there existed an agreement of 1599 between the Orthodox and Protestants, mutually guaranteeing the freedom of the other's creed.[19] The crown chancellor replied that it was the Orthodox people who were in the wrong in addressing their complaint not to the Polish government but to the Russian court. Keyserling objected that the complaints of people of the Greek faith were heard at all the assemblies of the Sejm, but no one did anything to see that these complaints were investigated and the complainants satisfied.

The time for the assembly of the Sejm drew near and in March 1744 Crown Chancellor Zaluski[20] wrote to Keyserling that the king desired above all the closest links between Poland and Russia. He intended to win the support of the republic's elected deputies for this alliance. The king further hoped that the proposed increase in the number of troops, to be put before the Sejm, not only would be acceptable to the empress but that she personally would cooperate in working out this proposal, for its adoption would enable the republic to collaborate with Russia in the pursuit of their common interests.

Keyserling wrote to his court that an increase of troops was something all nations demanded and desired, and that it was out of the question to oppose it publicly. But how it was to be financed was another issue. This was a matter of considerable dispute at the previous Sejm. Nearly every day new proposals were advanced, only to be rejected. Time passed, and the Sejm broke up without reaching any decision. Anyone attempting to oppose directly the general desire for the increase of troops would earn universal hatred. Therefore if Prussia sought to block this increase, it was possible only by bribing the Sejm deputies to prevent agreement concerning the financing of operations. If this method proved impossible, the alternative was to dissolve the Sejm under some other pretext.

It long was well known that Potocki,[21] provincial governor of Bielz, was completely devoted to the Prussians, and it had to be expected that he would act in their interest at the next assembly of the Sejm. This was also thought to be true of old Tarlo,[22] the governor of Sandomir, although this still needed confirmation. There were perhaps even more supporters of Prussia in Poland, but they were not among the senators and upper classes as much as the lesser gentry and the army, so they could not exert any significant influence on the course of events.

Keyserling informed the royal ministry that the empress had no intention whatsoever of preventing the increase in troops, which she considered a matter for the king and the republic to decide. This announcement was received with considerable relief and pleasure.

In May Keyserling moved with the court from Dresden to Warsaw. Here the ambassador was met by complaints from Orthodox believers. On Trinity Sunday in Drohiczyn, at the instigation of the prefect Uszynski, students attacked an Orthodox procession. They pelted the clergy with mud, assaulted laymen with staves, tore down their banners and smashed the icons. Another related that in the province of Nowogródek two churches were taken from the Orthodox community and handed over to the Uniates.[23] Keyserling once more submitted a memorandum to the king, calling for the adoption of the most stringent measures to stop such abuse. The king placed the matter in the hands of the crown chancellor, who passed on to Keyserling an order for the rector of the Drohiczyn Jesuit college, forbidding the persecution of Orthodox believers. The king declared that if curtailment of this religious persecution lay within his power, it would have been implemented long ago. Keyserling could not speak highly enough of the friendly disposition toward Russia shown by the Polish king, the ministers and the Polish court dignitaries.

Then at the end of July attention was shifted from these Polish-Russian matters by the king of Prussia's activities. Keyserling sent back word that the Prussian ambassador Wallenrod arrived in Warsaw demanding the free passage of Prussian troops though Saxony and Bohemia. This was not all. Keyserling reported Franco-Prussian intentions to sow discord in Poland. The Lithuanian hetman

Sapieha, previously in the pay of Sweden and Prussia, received a letter from the elder of Czehryn, Jablonowski, urging him to join in forming a confederation, assuring him that the king of Prussia would give them every support. Sapieha's estates would be protected, but if he suffered any loss he would receive compensation. Sapieha showed this letter to the king, who decorated him for his good intent.

The French minister Chavigny wrote to Count Poniatowski that the time was now ripe as never before to strike a blow for freedom. These suggestions stemmed from the fact that in the event of an Austrian attack on Lorraine, France intended to renege on its obligations of 1738 regarding Stanislaw Leszczynski.[24] Keyserling wrote that the attention of the Poles was focussed exclusively on the movements of Prussian troops, which was the sole topic of conversation. No matter how much Count Wallenrod tried to assure the Poles of his court's friendly intentions, they received his blandishments with mistrust which grew daily. On a visit to the chief hetman Wallenrod declared that such was the extent of his king's devotion to the Polish nation, and so great was his respect for the republic, that if its integrity, its welfare or its interests were in any way threatened or violated, he would be prepared to come to its assistance and defense in every way he could. "Peaceful and friendly assurances from neighboring states," replied the hetman, "cannot but be pleasing to a republic which itself is an ardent lover of peace. But the assurances of the king of Prussia cannot be trusted. Three Prussian embassies assured the queen of Hungary of their country's friendly intentions, but with the fourth embassy, consisting of a large army, came the king of Prussia himself and annexed Silesia."

Soon afterwards Keyserling himself heard news from Wallenrod which he personally found curious. On August 24 the Prussian ambassador approached him at court and told him that he received certain instructions from his sovereign, in which the king wrote that since Keyserling did not serve Prussia's interests he wrote to his ambassador at the court of Petersburg proposing that the empress be asked that the chancellor's brother, Mikhail Petrovich Bestuzhev-Riumin, be appointed to the Polish-Saxon court, and Keyserling be transferred to the court of the Holy Roman empire. This decision, he claimed, already was taken in Petersburg. "Your excellency would do me a very great favor," wrote Keyserling to the chancellor, "if you would indicate the degree of credit I should give to these words."

It turned out that the news was true. M. P. Bestuzhev-Riumin was indeed appointed to the Polish-Saxon court, but Keyserling was to attend the Sejm at Grodno along with him, and afterwards proceed to Frankfurt, to the court of the Holy Roman empire.

Bestuzhev arrived in Grodno on September 23, on the eve of the opening of the Sejm. In his opening exchange Count Brühl, inviting Russia to join the alliance between Saxony, England, Holland and Hungary, expressed his certainty that the empress, as one of the leading crowned heads in Europe and in accordance with her well-known nobility and fairness, could not be indifferent to the danger threatening every part of Europe; for the aims of France and Prussia were extensive, and their consequences were perhaps more far reaching than it was now possible to foresee or subsequently would be possible to eradicate. The victorious forces of Peter the Great once before delivered northern Europe from conquest, and brought it peace and stability. Brühl expressed the hope that the blessed forces of the empress duly would circumscribe the long-term aims of those seeking mastery of Europe, and wanted to arrogate the exclusive right to determine the fate of other peoples and states.

Brühl concluded the conversation by quoting Cardinal Richelieu[25] "There is nothing more damaging to a state than to stand by callously and do nothing when some other monarch takes it upon himself to conquer the lands of a neighboring country, for such conquest might serve as a bridge to further expansion. Therefore the allies of the offended ruler should do everything in their power to give him support. Going to war on his behalf, they would also be standing up for themselves, but once the enemy stands at the gates it is too late to ask for protection."

With regard to the Sejm, Bestuzhev reported that the Prussian minister Wallenrod and the resident Goerman received twenty thousand chervontsy from Berlin, and were attempting by generous distribution to demonstrate to the Poles their court's benign disposition. The Prussian money was apportioned among the provincial deputies, in order to render the Sejm ineffective.

Bestuzhev had to see to it that no mention of Courland was made at the Sejm.[26] This was a difficult matter. The easiest course was to free Biron and let him go to Courland, as King August requested the empress, but Bestuzhev was obliged to inform the king that for reasons of state Biron and his descendants could not be set at liberty to travel beyond the borders of Russia. The empress proposed as duke the prince of Hesse-Homburg. The king sent word to Bestuzhev that it would be better were the empress to advance the cause of someone else; in the opinion of nearly all the Polish nobility, this candidate was out of the question; during the last revolution in Poland the prince of Hesse-Homburg won more enemies than friends.[27] Bestuzhev and Keyserling then proposed another candidate, Prince August of Holstein, and this suggestion was accepted with pleasure.

But Prussia continued to distract attention from Courland. In October Bestuzhev and Keyserling reported that Wallenrod offered the Polish crown to Tarlo, governor of Sandomir. Should he decline it, he promised to make Stanislaw Leszczynski king, as long as Tarlo joined the confederation and renounced allegiance to King August. A series of nocturnal meetings began between Tarlo and Wallenrod. The king ordered Brühl to tell Tarlo that he was surprised to hear of these, and that he felt sure that they could in no way be furthering the welfare and stability of the state, since honorable and permissible matters had no fear of daylight. Did the Sejm not achieve its desired end, the king would feel compelled to bring the behavior of the governor to the attention of the Senate and the Chamber of Deputies. Alarmed at this, Tarlo begged for an audience with the king, and gave him an account of what passed between him and the Prussian ambassador. He promised he would not allow his loyalty to be compromised by tempting offers from foreigners.

It was anticipated that the French envoy, S. Séverine, would bring the money to be used to instigate a confederation at Wolin. Bestuzhev and Keyserling wrote that in this instance the French were bound to act in agreement with the king of Prussia. "What emerges from all of this," the two ambassadors wrote, "is that France and Prussia are aiming to set up a puppet king in Poland in whose name every previous treaty with France, Sweden and Prussia would be reinstituted, maintaining a stranglehold over European affairs. Those who discern the damaging consequences of French and Prussian aims, and who have displayed their support for the interests of your majesty, are asking that we make it clear in your majesty's name that Russia holds no intention of standing idly by and watching the formation of a confederation or the growth of unrest in Poland, but will attempt to cut these off at source; nor will Russia allow its neighbor to be engulfed by the fire ravaging the rest of Europe."

The ambassadors drew to the attention of their government a genealogical table, published in Breslau, according to which George of Podiebrad and Vladislav were usurpers of the Hungarian and Bohemian thrones, whereas the lawful line was represented by Elector Johann of Brandenburg, from whom the present king of Prussia was descended.[28]

At the end of October the Sejm was overtaken by an extraordinary event. Deputy Wilczewski informed the whole diplomatic corps that the Prussian ambassador paid him large sums of money to disrupt the Sejm, a thousand efimki, and promise of a further three thousand chervontsy. Thereupon Wilczewski took from his pocket the money he received and threw it onto the floor of the chamber. Following Wilczewski's example, other deputies made similar declarations. But Wallenrod, without waiting for any announcement from the Polish ministry, demanded satisfaction.

Since the approaches made to Tarlo proved unsuccessful, Wallenrod addressed his proposal about the Polish crown to Court Tailor Potocki.[29] Brühl assured Bestuzhev and Keyserling that he read for himself the promises the king of Prussia made to Potocki. The ambassadors reported that the number of Prussian and French supporters was growing daily. The nobility, and the lesser gentry in particular, were bickering among themselves more than before, so the fire was already smoldering beneath the ashes. The ambassadors recommended the immediate mobilization of troops on the borders at Kiev and Smolensk, with an ultimatum that Russia would not permit the violation of peace in Poland. Decisive measures, it seemed, were vital, for Wilczewski's disclosure about his bribery did not help. Nine provincial deputies, suborned by Prussian money, prevented agreement between the lower house and the Senate, so the Sejm broke up prematurely. Those in the pay of the French and Prussians were told that unless they effected the disruption of the Sejm, their names would be made public.

After this M. P. Bestuzhev-Riumin considered it necessary to write from Warsaw to Mikhail Larionovich Vorontsov. "The Prussian ambassador here, von Wallenrod, and Ambassador Goerman on his return from Grodno, informed the Poles that Mardefeld wrote from Moscow claiming to have verbal assurances from reliable sources that the declaration made was simply a matter of form, aimed at somehow pacifying the Polish and Saxon courts, so that they would disregard it and fear nothing. Similar declarations, some friendly, others threatening, in the past were used to good effect on the Poles. What strong influence the Prussian court wields, to the corresponding diminution of our own previous superiority in Poland, is evident from the manner in which they broke up the Sejm in Grodno. Moreover we will no longer have this influence harming and jeopardizing Russian interests, if the Prussian court's campaigns in Bohemia meet with greater success, or were it to succeed in concluding this wretched war on its own terms.

"In this event doubtless Prussia very easily will annex not only Danzig and the diocese of Warmia, but the whole of Polish Prussia as well. Even though our fundamental interests would compel us in such circumstances to take action on Poland's behalf, it would actually be too late, for Prussia meanwhile will have time to amass even greater strength, making it much harder to prevent the pursuit of policies so very dangerous to Russia.

"Russia then will be in a position of the most extreme danger. France and Prussia, constantly seeking ways of reducing Russia's power in order to keep us out of European affairs, will find it very easy to prevail upon Sweden and Poland to attack us. This they will do by promising Sweden the restoration of Livonia and all the provinces we conquered, and by guaranteeing the Poles, a feckless nation in any case, Smolensk and Kiev. Meanwhile the Prussians themselves will attack us centrally through Courland and, together with the others, try to force us to withdraw to our previous boundaries.

"Then there are the Turks and the Tatars, at this moment negotiating with French and Prussian emissaries. A vitally important and thorough consideration, not only of our immediate national security, but also of the actual course of action best fitted to serve the glory and interests of Russia, has provided me with the opportunity of informing your excellency, her imperial majesty's loyal subject, a real son of the fatherland and my kind patron, of my true opinion, which I have set out above. I have stated these views, as far as I am able, according to the dictates of my conscience and prompted by my unswerving and zealous loyalty to the illustrious honor, glory and service of her majesty. It is well known that during Peter the Great's time Prussia depended greatly on us and had then no influence in Poland, but now Prussia presents a great threat to Russia particularly because of its strength.

"Presently the Prussian court is seeking to lull us into a false sense of security, lest we pursue our natural interests or take advantage of a favorable conjuncture of circumstances. It is felt that her majesty is in a position to curtail for some considerable time Prussian and French interference in European affairs, with the attendant shedding of innocent blood. Thus would she restore the balance of power in Europe (which still favors Russia) and be able to frustrate their dangerous plans at one blow. Upon establishment of general tranquillity in Europe we shall be assured of everlasting fame, and our sovereign gain substantial advantage.

"The unprecedented number of foreign ambassadors at our court serves to show how keenly nearly every power is striving to win our friendship. Consequently in the present circumstances it is up to us not only to preserve our natural allies, but also to restore on a sound and lasting basis the balance of power in Europe which, as I have indicated, was upset by France and Prussia, and establish our national safety. The abiding principle of any properly devised foreign policy should be that no neighbor be allowed to become stronger than us, for in so becoming that neighbor is bound to pose a threat; in other words, the stronger it becomes, the more defenseless and clearly the more vulnerable we are."

AUSTRIA

To restore European equilibrium Austria must be supported against Prussia. The most important prerequisite was to end the Russian empress's hostility towards the queen of Hungary caused by the Botta affair.

January and February of 1744 passed in a series of fruitless demands to Lanczynski's embassy in Vienna for an immediate and precise resolution of the affair. Earlier answers were repeated: a court was set up; that in diplomatic negotiations one could bend and twist one way or the other, but a court of law was a different matter, being compelled to act in accordance with the law, which cannot be bent or twisted. In March Lanczynski responded on orders from

Petersburg that the transfer of the Botta affair to the courts was deemed unseemly and unnecessary, that the empress was awaiting satisfaction according to natural law, which demanded a clear and corresponding redress according to the gravity of Botta's offence. In such difficult circumstances, the Vienna court appealed for Saxon mediation. King August III accordingly offered his good offices to bring the Botta affair to a close, but Lanczynski was obliged to answer that foreign powers played no part in the affair from the start, and had none to play now. There was no need for any mediation; all that was required was due satisfaction, and the empress would not dictate how the queen was to try Botta. Lanczynski added that one consequence of the stubbornness of the Viennese court would be his recall from Vienna.

Botta was declared under house arrest. The ministers treated Lanczynski kindly, but refused to discuss the Botta affair. In June Ulefeldt invited Lanczynski to be present at Botta's interrogation. The ambassador replied that, since Botta never gave any question a straight answer, he could not be a witness to such *equivocating,* nor could he take any part in the legal proceedings because the empress made an outright declaration she would not interfere, but demanded satisfaction on the basis of indubitable proof of the marquis's guilt.

A short time afterwards Ulefeldt informed Lanczynski that the commission of inquiry into the Botta affair completed its investigations. It imposed no sentence, but submitted a written opinion, a copy of which was sent to the empress. Meanwhile the queen, bringing the affair once more into the diplomatic arena, ordered Botta detained in a prison in Graz for six months or longer, if the empress so desired. If such satisfaction was unacceptable to the Russian court, it could apply to Vienna for records of the appropriate legal enactments relating to the trial, together with transcripts of the criminals' cross-examinations. In this case Botta would be brought back from Graz, and a retrial ordered. Lanczynski replied that sending Botta to Graz did not constitute satisfaction, and that he, Lanczynski, was ordered to return to Petersburg. Ulefeldt was astounded and asked him to wait until they heard how the empress reacted to the queen's imprisonment of Botta at Graz. Lanczynski agreed to wait, on the basis that Botta's transfer to Graz represented at least a step towards satisfying the empress.

Vienna was anxious to settle the Botta affair as expediently as possible, because the new initiatives by the king of Prussia placed Maria Theresa in a dangerous position once more. "Matters here suddenly have entered a period of very great danger," Lanczynski wrote at the beginning of August, "news is expected hourly of large-scale invasion of Prussian troops into Saxony and Bohemia. It is being said quite plainly here, almost publicly, that unless your majesty makes a move to help Vienna, both Austria and Saxony will be completely ruined and crushed by Prussia. The king of Prussia has published a statement saying that he has nothing against the queen, and it is not his interests that are at stake, but that he is taking upon himself the defense of the emperor, and wants to act as a mediator between the warring parties.

"It is known here for certain that a pact has been concluded between the emperor, the king of Prussia, the elector palatine and the prince of Hesse-Cassel, according to which the king of Prussia is bound to deliver Bohemia to the emperor in return for the emperor's promise to concede to him three Bohemian regions. The king of Poland, in his capacity as elector of Saxony, will be next in line; the king of Prussia is to take over Lusatia on the basis that it formerly belonged to Silesia. This will be followed by the acquisition under some pretext of Hanoverian territory. He then will gather up one neighbor after the other and abuse them all. Now, for example, without waiting either for permission or for an approved itinerary from the Saxon court, he simply sent a description of the route Prussian troops will take through Saxon territory."

At the same time Lanczynski informed the ministers that he was leaving Vienna for Dresden because of the Botta affair. The initial reaction was "astonishment and a shrug of the shoulders." Then the ministers said, "Your departure will cause our enemies great delight, and our friends despair. It is sad that our allies, who share with us natural and common interests, so palpably desert us, particularly in face of the imminent Prussian invasion. For the third time, we are obliged to call on God to help us and to defend ourselves as best we can. What more could the queen do than to send Count Rosenberg as ambassador with the most extensive instructions to provide the empress with complete assurance?" The ministers were given to believe that the ambassador would remain in Vienna. "But giving humble consideration to the fact that in the last orders I received it was clearly and repeatedly laid down without any conditions that I should leave, and not knowing what would be sent to your majesty from the queen's ministers, I could pay no heed to their utterances," Lanczynski wrote, "It is not my place to interfere in decisions which your majesty already has been pleased to take."

Lanczynski left Vienna for Dresden on August 31. Meanwhile Rosenberg reached Moscow on August 22, and handed the chancellors the following memorandum. "Of all the unpleasant difficulties her majesty encountered since succeeding to the throne, none has been so hurtful to her as the unexpected news that her ambassador to the court of her imperial majesty stands accused of a base and reprehensible crime. Her royal majesty immediately observed that her numerous enemies, some openly hostile and others only friendly for appearances' sake, exploit this situation to provoke discord and coolness between the empress and the queen.

"Knowing that her imperial majesty, a sovereign worthy of honor and gifted with ineffable and great qualities (not like those who are in the habit of flouting scornfully all manner of solemnly sworn treaties, obligations, oaths, guarantees and everything else which a human society can only term sacred), and as a Christian God-fearing ruler, the worthy daughter and heiress of Peter the Great and Catherine, will recall very easily that great friendship at the conclusion of the victorious Finnish war, which her sovereign father had with Holy Roman Emperor Leopold [I], and that solemn obligation undertaken in 1726 by Catherine, on her own part and on the part of her heirs, to the Austrian succession, which she endorsed with her own sacred and imperial word;[30] knowing all this, our enemies fear that the empress will defend nobly the queen of Hungary, who has placed herself in her imperial majesty's hands, entrusted by Empress Catherine to her heirs and successors.

"My gracious sovereign is by no means ashamed to admit that she is bound by the laws of those lands which she possesses, and consequently cannot act as other rulers do. Nevertheless, in profound respect for her imperial majesty, and having learned that Saxon mediation is unacceptable, the queen has expedited, as far as the formalities prescribed by law permit, the imprisonment of the accused, after a lengthy detention, in the fortress of Graz, which is where state prisoners customarily are kept. The queen is pleased to direct that the period of his confinement be determined according to the illustrious mercy of her imperial majesty."

On August 29 Rosenberg informed the chancellor that he since heard from the queen that she, having no other hope than the empress, was entirely in her hands and at her disposal, as was the safety of her house. After this announcement the chancellor and vice-chancellor tried to avoid seeing Rosenberg, and to decline under various pretexts his requests for an early reply to his note, and for an audience with the empress. This state of affairs continued two months. It was not until October 22 that Elizabeth initialled a draft reply to Rosenberg, which stated that for purposes of complete satisfaction the queen's government must recognize the errors made in its published statements concerning the Botta affair, the contents of which were far from compatible with those made by Rosenberg, for the government's pronouncements portrayed the affair as being of no significance, and vindicated Botta.

Rosenberg gladly agreed to these conditions, and issued this declaration. "The pronouncements referred to were not in any way intended for the consideration of the Russian court, much less for the attention of her imperial majesty's royal person, but were dictated by the need to refute the unauthorized disclosures of our enemies, and were the consequence of our unfamiliarity with the full circumstances of the matter at that time.

"But now that the queen has judged the crime of Marquis Botta to be base and reprehensible, these pronouncements are naturally to be deemed completely invalidated, expunged and consigned forever to oblivion.

"As proof of the validity of the foregoing, I hereby give in her majesty's name the firmest assurances that my sovereign is pleased to order that a notice be published immediately in the terms herewith presented, and sent to all her ministers. In witness whereof I, being the queen's authorized ambassador, do affix hereunto my signature and personal seal. Given in Moscow, this twenty-third day of October (third day of November) 1744. Philip Joseph Orsini, Count Rosenberg."

When subsequently Rosenberg put it to Bestuzhev and Vorontsov that Botta's crimes hardly surpassed those of Chétardie, he was told that Botta's were incomparably more serious. Chétardie's crime consisted solely of attempts to overthrow a ministry and bribe a few individuals, whereas Botta acted against the empress. He sowed dissent, and encouraged malevolents in their enterprises. Although the empress deigned to be satisfied with this declaration, she would have been much more satisfied had it been made nine months earlier. Rosenberg was granted an audience with the empress, and in reply to his speech heard the empress declare that "in consequence of the queen's express emissary and of his declaration, she considered the matter closed once and for all. Not wishing to take her revenge on Botta, she left his release to the discretion of the queen."

This most difficult issue at last was settled. It now became easier to start talking in terms of the need to help the queen of Hungary against the king of Prussia. There were new hopes that Brümmer, Lestocq and Mardefeld could be expelled like Chétardie. As before, the most powerful weapon against them was the continued monitoring of their foreign correspondence. Bestuzhev wrote to Vorontsov on September 1, "Although your excellency and I wished that her imperial majesty's permission be sought to cease the scrutiny of ministerial letters, I now find it necessary in the present circumstances to scrutinize those of Barons Merdefeld [sic][31] and Neuhaus. This is because they both frequently reveal their colors; particularly the latter, as you will see from the enclosed translation of one of his letters, especially in the passage written in code, which the skill of Mr. Golbach deciphered."

This dispatch from Neuhaus, dated July 13, was intercepted and read, "Yesterday, at the end of the day's treatment [Kurtag], the princess of Zerbst handed me a letter to your imperial majesty, adding that not only as a vassal did she pay all due fealty to your majesty, but that she also had the highest personal esteem for your majesty's royal house, to which she would win over her daughter and her entourage, together with her future spouse, who were in any case well disposed."

Mardefeld also *betrayed himself* concerning the princess of Zerbst, her daughter and future son-in-law. He wrote to Berlin on September 14 "I must give the princess of Zerbst credit for her sincere espousal of the queen's interests. She very much wants to return to Germany, but I cannot see how in all decency she could leave Russia before her daughter's marriage." Frederick II's campaign in Bohemia was successful, and he took Prague. Congratulating the king on his triumph, Mardefeld wrote, "The grand duke said to me 'My hearty congratulations!' The young grand duchess said repeatedly, 'Thank God!' The princess's mother could not find enough appropriate words to express her great joy. Many others also congratulated me, but more reacted badly to the news."

"About two weeks ago," wrote Mardefeld at the end of October, "the princess of Zerbst asked me to prevent the arrival of her husband, because she knew very well that the empress was not going to let him have Courland. I answered that I was confident of your majesty's desire to see the prince made duke of Courland, particularly since you have no designs on the principality for your own house, but that I saw two big difficulties: first, the empress recommended the prince of Homburg to all interested powers and, second, she had no wish to forfeit the revenue."

BIRON'S PLEA

Elizabeth did not want to hand Courland over to the prince of Zerbst. Instead she designated it for the prince of Homburg or of Holstein. All these claimants were equally unacceptable to Bestuzhev, who supported the candidature of his old patron Biron, still living in honorable exile in Yaroslavl. He wrote to Bestuzhev in December. "Hearing that your excellency was leaving Moscow, I could not refrain from writing to assure you of my everlasting respect, to wish you a safe journey, and to thank you for the affection, kindness and sympathy you have shown me. May you be rewarded in heaven! Do not be angry at me for relying constantly during my protracted and cruel poverty on your sorely tried diligence. O Lord, thou seest into my heart! If I knew that there was any evil in my intentions or actions, on account of which I am condemned to a life of poverty, I would be prepared to endure it. But to this day I do not know of any crime I have committed, unless it be that I dealt honestly with everybody. God knows that you and I and my brothers were the victims of savage people. The crime of which we stood accused was our desire to see the present sovereign and the grand duke enthroned. For this I was sent into exile.

"What have I done wrong then, and of what does my crime consist? Her imperial majesty is kindness and generosity itself, but I have been living in this impoverished state for three years. Your excellency has known me through twenty-six years of varying circumstances; have I ever stolen anything from anybody or offended anyone? Everything I had, I received from the sovereign. I acquired Courland not by deceit or cunning, but by divine providence and the kindness of the king, who had every right to grant it to me. Russia played no part in this, either by speaking to the king on my behalf, or by promoting my cause in the kingdom, or by providing me with any financial backing.[32]

"Now my family and I are in such dire straits that the taste of dry bread brings tears to my eyes. My wife is in a terrible physical condition, and her body is covered in tumors. I also suffer frequent fits which are more painful than the most agonizing death. My family is in such terrible need, that it would not be surprising if my despair drove me to suicide. We are house-bound because we have nothing to wear, so that we are almost rotting alive. We are constantly surrounded by guards, so that we cannot step across the threshold without being followed. But where could I flee in any case, and for what reason? Your excellency, have pity and petition for me to be sent from here to Narva."

When she heard that Biron was ill, Elizabeth sent Dr. Schmidt to Yaroslavl. Thanking her, Biron wrote to the empress, "When I see how my children growing up without education, forgetting what they knew, I am so sorely grieved that the very stones would have pity. If God were to grant them the happiness of sacrificing their lives to the service of your majesty, how joyfully I would give them my blessing! Most gracious sovereign empress! Hear at last our prayers, our sighs and our tears. I would never dare throw myself at your feet if I knew that I committed any crime. But I call on God as my witness that I have always acted honestly and loyally. While I have been in the abyss, I have never bowed before any threats or promises, or violated my obligations to your majesty."[33]

NOTES

INTRODUCTION

1. For a discussion of Soloviev's significance in Russian historical scholarship see A.G. Mazour, *Modern Russian Historiography* (Princeton, 1958), pp. 98-106.

2. On Pogodin and the period generally, see N. Riasanovsky, *Nicholas I and Official Nationality in Russia, 1825-1855* (Berkeley, 1967), and A.E. Presniakov, *Emperor Nicholas I of Russia. The Apogee of Autocracy* (Gulf Breeze, Fla., Academic International Press, 1974).

3. Mazour, p. 105.

4. See M. S. Anderson, *Europe in the Eighteenth Century, 1713-1783* (London, 1961).

5. See Chapter I, Notes 4 and 10.

6. See Chapter I, Note 4.

7. Peasant unrest culminated in the following reign with the peasant war (1773-1775) led by Pugachev. For a detailed study of peasant rebellions in early modern Russia, see Paul Avrich, *Russian Rebels 1600-1800* (New York, 1972).

8. T. Talbot Rice, *Elizabeth, Empress of Russia* (London, 1970), p. 48.

9. The *Memoirs of Catherine the Great*, ed. D. Maroger, trans. M. Budberg (London, 1955), p. 60.

10. V.O. Kliuchevskii, *Sochineniia* (Works) (Moscow, 1958), Vol. IV, p. 342. The best popular biographical work in English on Elizabeth probably remains that of R. Nisbet Bain, *The Daughter of Peter the Great* (London, 1899). See also Philip Longworth, *The Three Empresses* (London, 1972) and A. Lentin, *Russia in the Eighteenth Century* (London, 1973). The authoritative work, based on archival sources and treating social as well as political topics, is E.V. Anisimov, *Empress Elizabeth. Her Reign and her Russia, 1714-1761*, translated John T. Alexander (Gulf Breeze, Fla., Academic International Press, 1994).

11. Evidence of this is the fact that Elizabeth apparently remained blissfully ignorant of England's separation from the European continent by the English Channel.

12. See Anderson, p. 185.

CHAPTER I

1. The manifesto of November 25, 1741 declared Elizabeth's intention to rule on the successful overthrow of the Brunswick family and the infant emperor, Ivan Antonovich, the grand-nephew of Anna Ivanovna.

2. Catherine I (1725-1727) was Peter the Great's second wife, Marfa Skavronskaia. Her successor, Peter II (1727-1730), was the son of Alexis Petrovich. Elizabeth and Natalia were respectively the daughter of Peter the Great and the daughter of Alexis, Peter's son, who died in 1718.

3. Anna Leopoldovna of Mecklenburg was Anna Ivanovna's niece. She was married to Anton Ulrich of Brunswick, and their son was the ill-fated infant emperor, Ivan VI (reigned 1740-1741).

4. Heinrich Johann (Andrei Ivanovich) Ostermann (1686-1741). German by birth, he served under Peter I and, as leader of the cabinet during the reign of Anna Ivanovna (1730-1740), was the main force behind Russia's foreign policy. Burckhardt Christoph Münnich (1683-1767), also of German origin, was in overall command of the army at this time, and after Anna's death the most powerful figure in the brief regency of Anna Leopoldovna, princess of Brunswick. G. I. Golovkin (1660-1734) was Peter the Great's chancellor. A close friend since their childhood, he was from 1718 president of the College of Foreign Affairs, and assisted Peter with important legislative acts such as the Table of Ranks (1722). He was a member of the Supreme Privy Council from 1726, and then of Anna's cabinet after her accession in 1730.

5. Joachim Jacques Trotti, Marquis de la Chétardie (1705-1758), entered military service at an early age, attained the rank of colonel in 1734, and was named ambassador to Russia in 1739. He played a significant part in helping Elizabeth to the throne, though he was somewhat prone to exaggerate his role in the events leading up to the coup. In his farewell audience in 1742 he was given presents to the value of over a million rubles and was awarded the Order of St. Anne. Elizabeth tried to obtain his reappointment, and he returned in 1743 as minister plenipotentiary, but his credentials were not recognized by the Russian ministry since the document did not accord Elizabeth the imperial title. Chétardie nevertheless was made welcome by Elizabeth in his private capacity, though later he was to earn her displeasure by his intrigues against Bestuzhev. Finally her patience was exhausted, so she stripped him of his Russian decorations and had him escorted to the frontier in June 1744, at the same time writing to Louis XV explaining the reasons for the expulsion. Chétardie was banished for a while to his estates, but in 1745 was given a command in the Army of Italy. In 1749 he was appointed ambassador to the Sardinian court. Returning to military duties, he was appointed commandant of Hanau, where he died. Regarding speculation as to the nature of the relationship between Chétardie and the young Elizabeth, his biographer tactfully remarks, "It is claimed that Elizabeth's relationship with Chétardie extended much further than friendship, but these are allegations without proof, and a historian must guard against accepting them lightly." *Biographie Universelle,* Vol. 2 (Brussels, 1843-1847), p. 334.

6. This was Karl Peter Ulrich, son of Elizabeth's sister, Anna Petrovna, and of Karl Friedrich, duke of Holstein-Gottorp. He was to rule briefly as Peter III in 1762.

7. Korf, a Baltic German, was a senior chamberlain and diplomatist who subsequently became president of the Academy of Sciences.

8. Mikhail Ilarionovich Vorontsov (1714-1767) became a chamberlain at the court of Princess Elizabeth in 1728. During her adversity he helped Elizabeth with his pen and the money borrowed from his rich sister-in-law, the wife of his brother Roman. He was among the prominent supporters of the coup of 1741, accompanying Elizabeth to the barracks of the Preobrazhensky Regiment. He and Lestocq were among those who arrested Anna Leopoldovna. When Elizabeth became established on the throne she promoted Vorontsov to the rank of senior chamberlain and a lieutenancy in the newly formed Life Guards Regiment, as well as a generous award of lands. On January 3, 1742 he married the empress's cousin Anna Karlovna Skavronskaia. In 1744 he was made a count of the Russian empire and was named vice-chancellor. In 1748 he almost fell into disgrace because of alleged complicity in Lestocq's conspiracy, but managed to retain the empress's favor. When Bestuzhev was disgraced in 1748, Vorontsov moved into his position. As chancellor Vorontsov inherited Peter the Great's foreign policy of alliance with Austria against Turkey, which also entailed prolongation of hostilities towards Prussia, but under Peter III there was a reversal of alliances and a pact almost was concluded with Prussia. After the coup of 1762 Vorontsov refused to swear allegiance to Catherine II and was placed under house arrest. When he heard of the death of Peter III he considered himself released from his oath of allegiance and continued to serve Catherine II as chancellor, though now he had to share responsibility for foreign affairs with Nikita Ivanovich Panin. He also was hostile towards the current favorite Grigory Orlov. Marked coolness towards him on the part of the empress forced him into retirement in 1763.

9. Alexis Mikhailovich Cherkassky (1680-1742) was Peter the Great's agent for the construction of St. Petersburg. He was a senator during Anna's reign and formulated Russia's pro-British foreign policy. He was appointed chancellor in 1740. Although a friend of Biron, he survived his downfall to remain in government until his death of apoplexy in November 1742.

10. A. P. Bestuzhev-Riumin (1693-1766). A specialist in foreign affairs, he became chancellor in 1744. He was arrested by Münnich in 1741 for his support of Biron and banished to his estates.

11. Hermann (Armand) Lestocq (1692-1767) was born in Celle, the son of a Huguenot émigré who became court surgeon to Duke Georg Wilhelm of Brunswick-Lüneburg. He learned the barber-surgeon's trade from his father, then went to Paris and became an army medical officer. He was recruited into the service of Peter the Great in 1713. During Peter's travels abroad in 1716-1717 he was assigned to Catherine's suite. In 1719 he was

exiled to Kazan, but after Peter's death Catherine I appointed him personal physician to her daughter Elizabeth. In 1727 he married Beate Barbara Stenbock, née Rudenheim, and after her death in 1733, Alida Voss, née Müller. During the reign of Anna, despite the empress's hostility to Elizabeth, he maintained connections at court, acting also as a liaison between Elizabeth and the French and Swedish ambassadors, both of whom favored the triumph of the "national" party. He played an important part in the coup of 1741, being one of those sent to arrest the regent Anna Leopoldovna. With the triumph of Elizabeth he was appointed to the rank of senior state councillor, second in the Table of Ranks, and as director of the Medical Chancellery, with a salary of seven thousand rubles, together with a bonus of three to four thousand for each personal attendance on Elizabeth, a considerable improvement on his official salary during previous reigns, which ranged from 144 to 396 rubles. In any case he delegated much of the medical side of his duties to his deputy P.Z. Kondikoy. Eventually his intrigues against Bestuzhev brought about his downfall; he was further compromised by his third marriage, to Maria Aurora Mengden, Elizabeth's lady-in-waiting, whose family was deeply involved in court intrigues. In 1748 he was arrested for his alleged part in trying to dislodge the Holstein-Gottorp interest. From 1748 to 1750 he and his wife were detained in the St. Peter and Paul fortress. In 1750 they were exiled to Uglich and in 1750 further afield to Ustiug. After Elizabeth's death, in 1752 he was permitted to return to St. Petersburg and resume his former rank. He died five years later. There were no children from any of his three marriages.

12. Ernst Johann Biron (Bühren), duke of Courland (1690-1772). A German whose name became a by-word for oppression and misrule during Anna Ivanovna's reign. On her death he became regent for three weeks until his replacement by Anna Leopoldovna and Münnich.

13. Grigory Petrovich Chernyshev (1672-1745) served in top military and civil posts under Peter the Great and Catherine I. Under Anna he was a senator and governor-general of Moscow from 1731 to 1735; Elizabeth made him a count of the Russian empire.

14. Alexander Borisovich Kurakin (1697-1749), diplomat.

15. The brothers Alexander and Peter Ivanovich Shuvalov were among the members of Princess Elizabeth's court and among her most prominent supporters in the coup of 1741. In 1746 Peter was raised to the rank of count of the Russian empire, and also strengthened his position by marrying Mavra Yegorievna Shepeleva, the empress's confidante. Alexander (1710-1771) reached the rank of general-field marshal and served for many years as chief of the Secret Chancellery.

16. Alexis Grigorievich Razumovsky (1709-1771) was Elizabeth's closest favorite and perhaps even her husband.

17. M.P. Bestuzhev-Riumin (1688-1760) was the brother of Chancellor A.P. Bestuzhev-Riumin. He was resident minister in London (1720), Sweden

(1721-1726), where he returned as ambassador (1731-1741), Poland (1726-1730, 1744) and France (1756-1760). He played a central role in the formation of the 1724 defensive treaty with Sweden which greatly strengthened Russian security on the Baltic. He generally pursued a pro-Prussian and pro-English policy at the expense of the Austrian and Ottoman empires.

18. The Dolgoruky and Golitsyn families formed the power behind the throne of Peter II and were banished on Anna Ivanovna's accession in 1730.

19. Alexander Danilovich Menshikov (1673-1729) was Peter I's closest associate and after the tsar's death virtually ruled Russia during the reign of Catherine I. Varvara Mikhailovna Arseneva (died 1730) was Menshikov's half sister and daughter of Mikhail Afanasievich Arsenev. She became a lady-in-waiting to Peter the Great's second wife Catherine, and on the occasion of her cousin Maria's betrothal to Peter II in 1727 she was promoted to chief lady-in-waiting with an annual salary of two thousand rubles and the right to walk in procession half a pace behind wives of the generalitet, the military officers of the four highest ranks. On June 29, 1727 she received the Order of St. Catherine. This was stripped from her at the time of Menshikov's disgrace, and she was forced to take the veil at the Dormition convent in Alexandrov.

20. Artemy Petrovich Volynsky (1689-1722) was governor of Astrakhan from 1719 to 1742 and in this capacity played a major part in preparations for Peter the Great's Persian campaign (1722-1723). From 1725 to 1730 he was governor of Kazan, and became a cabinet minister in 1738. Soon he became the chief liaison between Empress Anna and the Cabinet, and one of the few native Russians to attain high position during the ascendancy of Biron. He formed a circle of friends who met at his house for discussions on history and plans for political reform. He also wrote several tracts, most of which were destroyed on the eve of his arrest. Through the intrigues of Biron and Ostermann he was seized and tortured by the Secret Chancellery. Convicted on a number of spurious charges, he was beheaded following the severing of his tongue and right hand.

21. Soloviev's text reads *v tsarstvovanii Ioanna III* (in the reign of Ivan III), but this is obviously a misprint, or otherwise a slip of the pen on the author's part.

22. "The oracle" was Ostermann's nickname at court.

23. *The Rock of Faith* (Kamen' very) is the principal written work of Stefan Yavorsky (1658-1722). It was published five years posthumously, with three editions appearing during the reign of Peter II (1727-1730). Although a vigorous anti-Protestant apologetic for traditional Orthodoxy, it used dialectical methods learned from Polish Jesuits, and therefore was considered heretical by numerous Russian churchmen. See Paul D. Steeves, "Yavorsky, Stefan," *Modern Encyclopedia of Russian and Soviet History*, 56 Vols. (Gulf Breeze, Fla., Academic International Press, 1976-1993) (hereafter MERSH), Vol. 45, pp. 24-30; Chapter III, below, of the present volume, and Volume 35 of this series, pp. 180-185.

24. Andrei Ivanovich Ushakov (1642-1747) served in Peter the Great's Preobrazhensky Chancellery (security police), and became head of Anna's Privy Chancellery, the chief office of terror for which her reign earned a special notoriety. Its sinister activities, and Ushakov's unsavory role in them, continued into Elizabeth's reign. He was replaced by Alexander Shuvalov.

25. See Note 20, above.

26. Reinhold Gustavus Löwenwolde (1693-1758). He entered Russian service during Peter's reign and attained the rank of chamberlain during Catherine's. He wielded considerable influence during the regency of Anna Leopoldovna. See also pp. 11, 12, below.

27. Yakov Petrovich Shakhovskoy (1705-1775) was chief of police under Anna. He survived Elizabeth's accession to become chief procurator of the Holy Synod (1741-1753) when he became chief of the commissary. In 1760 he succeeded N. Yu. Trubetskoy as procurator general of the Senate. On Elizabeth's death in December 1761, Peter III removed him from office, but he was recalled to service by Catherine II in 1762.

CHAPTER II

1. A body created in 1726 by Catherine I to deal with "matters of exceptional significance." It attempted to establish an advisory form of rule in Russia in 1730, but was abolished by Anna Ivanovna with the support of the Guards very shortly afterwards.

2. Semen Andreevich Saltykov (1672-1742) served under Peter the Great, attaining the rank of general-in-chief. He administered Moscow in the 1730s.

3. Alexander Lvovich Naryshkin (1694-1746) was a first cousin of Peter the Great's mother, Tsaritsa Natalia. Prince M.M. Golitsyn (1681-1764), formerly a close companion of Peter I, was admiral of the Russian fleet from 1725. He was appointed governor general of Astrakhan in 1740, and was Russian ambassador in Persia 1745-1748. He was commander-in-chief of the Russian navy from 1746 until his retirement in 1761. On A.P. Bestuzhev-Riumin and A.I. Ushakov, see above, Chapter I, Notes 10 and 24.

4. Nikita Yurievich Trubetskoy (1699-1767) was appointed procurator general by Empress Anna in 1740, and held the post for twenty years. An active supporter of Elizabeth's coup, he played an important part in organizing her government. He remained one of the most prominent officials throughout her reign, and among the best paid. See the entertaining essay on him by John T. Alexander, MERSH, Vol. 40, pp. 1-5.

5. The Brevern-de la Harpe were a russified Silesian family. Hermann Brevern was vice-president of the College of Justice from 1717.

6. Ochakov was a Turkish stronghold on the Black Sea captured by the Russians in 1737 during the Russo-Turkish war of 1735-1739. It was ceded to Russia by the Treaty of Jassy in 1792.

7. Andrei Yushkevich (1690-1745) was of Ukrainian origin. He received his early education in Polish schools, and went on to the Kiev Spiritual Academy, where he stayed on as an instructor. He entered the monastic life in 1731, taking the name of Ambrose. He became superior of the Holy Spirit monastery in Wilno, where he ran into trouble over his zeal for Orthodoxy. In 1734 he was appointed abbot of the St. Simon monastery in Moscow, later of the Hypatian monastery of Kostroma. In February 1736 he was named bishop of Vologda, but from 1739 he lived in St. Petersburg, where he took part in the work of the Holy Synod. In 1740 he was appointed archbishop of Novgorod. Although an absentee prelate, he devoted considerable care to the administration of his eparchy, where he founded a seminary to which he donated his considerable library. He wrote a number of theological treatises which were never published, though several of his sermons, including that delivered at Elizabeth's coronation, extensively quoted below, were printed and widely read.

8. See Note 6 above. Biron and Münnich were largely responsible for the war which Ostermann was obliged to conclude with French mediation by the humiliating Treaty of Belgrade in 1739.

9. The Savior (Zaikonospassk) monastery in Moscow was founded in the Kitay quarter by Boris Godunov in 1600. St. Nicholas street (Nikolskaia), behind which the monastery stood, was a traditional center for the icon trade, hence its name. It is the burial place of such monks and scholars as Gavril Buzhinsky, Simeon Polotsky, and Ioaniky Likhudy, who founded the Slavono-Greek-Latin Academy within its walls. See below, Chapter III, Note 10.

10. Kitay-gorod (literally "Bastion town") was a trading suburb situated under the eastern Kremlin wall.

11. See p. 15, above.

12. The Ecclesiastical Statute (Dukhovnyi Reglament) was drawn up in 1720 by Feofan Prokopovich. See A.V. Muller, *The Spiritual Regulation of Peter the Great* (Seattle, 1975); also James Cracraft, *The Church Reform of Peter the Great* (Stanford, 1971). See Chapter V, Note 14, below.

13. At French instigation Sweden declared war on Russia in 1741. Its course and conclusion Soloviev considers in detail below.

14. Feast day of saint after whom a person is named.

15. In this case apparently Mining and Manufacture were placed under a single college, whereas in Peter I's time there were separate colleges.

CHAPTER III

1. *Zemliannyi gorod,* a populous residential quarter of Moscow.

2. It was at this village that sovereigns on the way to their coronation in Moscow traditionally spent several days fasting and praying in preparation for the solemn event.

3. Soloviev, it will be remembered, was writing well before the Revolution. This part of his *History of Russia* first appeared in 1871-1872.

4. Ambrose deliberately uses the archaic word *sigklit* in place of *Senat.* The speech as a whole uses Church Slavonic rather than modern Russian syntax.

5. Peter II (reigned 1727-1730) became emperor at the age of eleven, but died of smallpox three years later.

6. An extravagant reference, in keeping with the elevated tone of the address, to the future Peter III, who reigned briefly in 1762.

7. See Chapter I, Note 23.

8. *..v knigakh tsarskikh pervykh..* The reference appears to be to 1 Samuel 13: 19-23: "Now there was no smith to be found throughout all the land of Israel; for the Philistines said: 'Lest the Hebrews make themselves swords or spears....'" The Slavonic Bible has four Books of Kings, corresponding with the Books of Samuel and Kings in the Western Bible.

9. The cathedral of the Annunciation in the Kremlin served as the ruling family's private chapel, and dates from the reign of Ivan III, in 1484, at the time when the Moscow Kremlin acquired much of its present appearance. The cathedral of Archangel Michael was commissioned early in his reign by Vasily III (1505-33), and was designed by an Italian architect, Aleviso Novi. It became the burial place of the ruling family.

10. The Slavonic-Greek-Latin Academy was founded in 1687 as the first school of higher education in Moscow. It became the center of higher education and a powerful influence in educational and religious affairs. Its supervisory role in the fields of scholarship and Orthodox doctrine in Russia became so absolute that Soloviev described the academy as "a terrifying inquisition." It was housed in the Zaikonospassk monastery (see above Chapter II, Note 9) until its transfer in 1814 to the Trinity-St. Sergius monastery.

11. The Red Porch was the triumphal gateway erected at the expense of the Moscow merchants in honor of the coronation.

12. The Dormition cathedral was completely rebuilt between 1475 and 1479 as the first stage of Ivan III's ambitious reconstruction of the Moscow Kremlin. It was modeled by the Italian architect, Aristotle Fioravanti, on the Vladimir cathedral of the same name. The Palace of Facets dates from 1487, the work of the Italians Marco Ruffo and Piero Solari. It derives its name from its faceted façade, and served mainly for formal court ceremonies and receptions.

13. Homburg was the smallest of the Hessian principalities and Ludwig, like so many other minor German princes, supplemented his revenues by service to foreign rulers. Apparently during the reign of Anna he served on the Crimean front (see Volume 35 of this series, pp. 3-15). He also played a part in the Russian intervention in Poland following the double election of 1733, though Soloviev reckoned this intervention to have been

counterproductive. See below, p. 201. Elizabeth also tried to promote his candidacy for the ducal throne of Courland. See below, p. 81.

14. Namely as director of Russia's foreign policy. Mikhail Petrovich Bestuzhev-Riumin (1688-1760) was the brother of Chancellor A. P. Bestuzhev-Riumin. He was resident minister in London (1720), Sweden (1721-1726), where he returned as ambassador (1731-1741), Poland (1726-1730, 1744), Prussia (1730-1731) and France (1756-1760). He played a central role in the formation of the 1724 defensive treaty with Sweden which greatly strengthened Russian security in the Baltic. He generally pursued a pro-Prussian and pro-English policy at the expense of the Austrian and Ottoman empires. Concerning Nikita Yurievich Trubetskoy, see Chapter II, Note 4, above. Alexander Lvovich Naryshkin (1694-1764) was a first cousin of Peter the Great's mother, Tsaritsa Natalia. He had an illustrious diplomatic career, mostly in European capitals.

15. The use of ovens was proscribed in Moscow's wooden city dwellings to avert the ever-present risk of fire, which frequently ravaged Moscow in the past. In 1737, for example, over one half of Moscow burned to the ground.

16. "Make not my father's house an house of merchandise." John 2:16.

17. "Lest while ye gather up the tares ye root up also the wheat with them, let them both grow together until the harvest." Matthew 13: 29-30.

18. Emperor Charles VI died in 1740, leaving as his rightful heir his daughter Maria Theresa. Normally the succession in Germany was strictly in the male line, but Charles issued the Pragmatic Sanction, overriding the Salic Law. Some princes of the Holy Roman empire disputed the validity of the Pragmatic Sanction and supported Elector Charles Albert of Bavaria, who styled himself Charles VII.

19. Frederick II invaded Silesia in December 1740 without declaring war on Austria. This action precipitated the War of the Austrian Succession.

20. Hanover was linked to England through a common ruler and was an ally of Austria.

21. Peter Lacy (1678-1751), an Irishman born in Limerick, entered Russian service during the reign of Peter the Great and rapidly earned himself a reputation for courage as a soldier of great distinction. See Patrick O'Meara, "Irishmen in Eighteenth-Century Russian Service," *Irish Slavonic Studies,* Vol. 5 (1984), pp. 13-25; also MERSH, Vol. 19, pp. 1-4.

22. Ulrich-Friedrich-Woldemar Löwendahl (1700-1755) was a French marshal of German descent who at various times was also in Austrian, Polish and Russian service. He participated in the successful Russian campaigns of 1741-1743 in Finland against the Swedes. He entered French service in 1744.

23. The term here refers to those of German and other Northern European descent in the service of the Russian court.

24. Edward Finch (1697-1771) was the fifth son of Daniel Finch, sixth earl of Winchelsea and second earl of Nottingham. He was educated at the

University of Cambridge, which he represented in successive parliaments from 1727 to 1768, and was cofounder of the Members' Prizes for Latin prose composition. Finch was sent in 1723 as ambassador extraordinary to the imperial diet at Regensburg, and served as ambassador to Poland for the years 1724 and 1725. He later served for ten years in Sweden (1729-1739), before being posted to St. Petersburg, where he served for three years. On his return to England in 1742 he was appointed to various honorific posts at the royal court. In 1764 he assumed the additional surname of Hatton, under the terms of a bequest from his aunt Elizabeth Hatton.

25. Count R. F. Lynar was a lover of Anna Leopoldovna, and therefore supported the Brunswick house against Elizabeth, whom he wished to see consigned to a convent.

26. Count Axel von Mardefeld (1691-1748) was a member of the diplomatic corps at the court of Empress Anna, when he formed a personal alliance with Biron and Münnich. After Elizabeth's accession, he became a close associate of Lestocq and the French ambassador, Chétardie. Bestuzhev, as chancellor, succeeded in having Elizabeth request Frederick II to order Mardefeld's recall to Berlin in October 1745.

27. The Treaty of Nystadt (1721) concluded Peter I's Great Northern War with Sweden, and represented a turning point in Russian history. Under its terms Sweden surrendered Livland (Livonia), Estland (Estonia), Ingria and part of Karelia.

28. This presumably refers to Count Löwenhaupt's support for the proclamation of Elizabeth's succession on November 25, 1741, in which the Swedish ambassador to Petersburg, E.M. Nolcken, was said by Chétardie to have played an active role. Soloviev dismisses the notion of Swedish involvement in the coup, as will be seen below.

29. Ulrike Eleonora was the youngest sister of Karl XII, whom she succeeded on his death in November 1718. In 1719 a new Swedish constitution was drawn up, and the following year Queen Ulrike managed to bring about the election of her husband as King Fredrik I of Sweden. She abdicated in 1720 and died in November 1741.

30. Jean-Jacques Amelot de Chaillou (1689-1749) was appointed intendant of La Rochelle in 1720, was elected to the Académie Française in 1727 and served as minister of foreign affairs from 1737 to 1744.

31. See Note 21, above.

32. In other words the Ottoman (Turkish) empire.

33. The archbishopric of Bremen and the bishopric of Verden (southwest Holstein) became Swedish territory in the Holy Roman empire after the Peace of Westphalia (1648).

34. In 1735 the expiring treaty of alliance between Russia and Sweden was renewed for a further twelve years.

35. Erik Matthias von Nolcken (1694-1755) served as Swedish envoy to Petersburg from 1738 to 1741.

36. General James Francis Keith, a Scot who entered Russian service in 1728. After a distinguished career, he left Russia for Prussia in 1747.

37. Soloviev is particularly hostile to the cossacks throughout his history, as is apparent here from his ironic tone.

38. One account of this stratagem stresses Lacy's good fortune in having this disused road pointed out to him, and emphasizes the surprise of the incredulous Swedish generals on being so unexpectedly outmaneuvered. As a result of their capitulation, all of Finland was left subject to the Russian empire. See M. O'Callaghan, *History of the Irish Brigade in the Service of France* (London, 1870), Vol. 9, p. 485; see also O'Meara, "Irishmen in Eighteenth-Century Russian Service," p. 18.

39. From Elizabeth's point of view this proposal was impracticable since the duke of Holstein, Peter Fedorovich, already was declared heir to the throne of Russia. But still his right to the Swedish throne was clear since he was the great-nephew of Charles XII and great-grandson of Charles XI of Sweden.

40. Adolf Friedrich (1710-1771) was a son of the duke of Holstein-Gottorp. He became prince-bishop of the secularized diocese of Lübeck in 1721. As described in the following pages, he was designated crown prince of Sweden in 1743 and succeeded to the throne in 1751. He was not very respected, being completely under the domination of his wife Luise Ulrike, sister of Frederick II of Prussia and the principal supporter of the aristocratic Hats party. Eventually his signature on state acts was replaced by a seal which often was used without consulting him. The last years of his reign were hailed by the aristocrats as the "era of liberty," and it remained to his son Gustav III (reigned 1771-1792) to restore royal authority.

CHAPTER IV

1. Antioch Dmitrievich Cantemir (1708-1744), poet and diplomat, served as ambassador also to England. He was ambassador in Paris from 1738 until his death. He befriended Montesquieu and translated his *Persian Letters*. A leading neoclassicist and the author of many odes, his celebrated *Satires* were published posthumously in London in 1750, the first Russian edition following in 1762. He is regarded as one of the initiators of a distinctively national Russian literature.

2. The Bashkirs are a Turkic-speaking Muslim people living to the south of the Ural mountains, who were colonized by Russia during the seventeenth and eighteenth centuries.

3. See above, p. 4.

4. See Chapter II, Note 8.

5. André Hercule de Fleury (1653-1743) was the son of a provincial tax collector. Entering the priesthood, he became in 1679 almoner to Maria Theresa, wife of Louis XIV, and in 1698 bishop of Fréjus. In 1715 he was

appointed tutor to the king's great-grandson, who soon succeeded as King Louis XV. On the death of the regent Orleans in 1723 Fleury suggested the duke of Bourbon as first minister, but was present at all meetings between the king and Bourbon. When the latter tried to alter this practice, Fleury withdrew from court until the king insisted on his recall. In July 1726 Fleury took matters into his hands by banishing Bourbon and the king's mistress Madame du Prie. He refused the title of first minister, but was elevated during the same year to the cardinalate, which according to protocol gave him precedence over peers of the realm. His frugal administration for a while ensured a budget surplus instead of the by now customary deficits. He stabilized the currency and built a network of superb roads. On the other hand, since he effected economies in military and naval affairs, the country was ill-prepared for war, as became apparent when he was forced in 1733 to throw French support behind the candidacy of Don Carlos to the duchy of Parma and the renewed pretensions of Stanislaw Leszczynski to the Polish throne. The dispatch of a French expeditionary force to Danzig merely assured humiliation for France. Fleury, forced by his foreign minister Chauvelin into a closer alliance with Spain, sent two armies against Austria into the Rhineland and Northern Italy, gaining favorable terms at the Treaty of Vienna (1738). France joined with other powers in guaranteeing the Pragmatic Sanction, but when Charles VI died in 1740 Fleury found an excuse to repudiate this undertaking. French intervention in Bohemia proving disastrous, Fleury wrote an abject letter in confidence to the Austrian general Königsegg, who immediately published it. Fleury was forced to disavow his own letter and died a few days after the French evacuation of Prague, on January 29, 1743, less than five months short of his ninetieth birthday. Fleury's departure from the scene is thought to have hailed the "rule of mistresses" at the French court.

6. Semeon Grigorievich Naryshkin (died 1747), diplomat, second cousin of Tsaritsa Natalia (mother of Peter the Great). Ivan Andreevich Shcherbatov (1696-1761) was Peter II's ambassador to Madrid, then Anna Ivanovna's envoy to Constantinople and London. He became vice-president of the College of Commerce, president of the College of Justice, and a senator.

7. John Carteret (1690-1763), son of George, first Baron Carteret, studied modern languages at Oxford, and was noted as one of the few Englishmen at that time fluent in German. He succeeded his father as Baron Carteret in 1695, and took his seat in the House of Lords in 1711. He supported the Hanoverian interest in 1715, and between 1719 and 1721 served with distinction as ambassador to Sweden. On his return to London he was appointed secretary of state of the southern department. Walpole, who resented his ability to converse with the king in his native German, arranged for him to be appointed lord lieutenant of Ireland, where he remained from 1724 to 1730. On his return to London he found Walpole firmly entrenched as prime minister, and took no further part in political affairs until Walpole's resignation in 1742. He was sympathetic to the cause

of Maria Theresa. George II, welcoming his views, appointed him secretary of state for foreign affairs. In this capacity Carteret accompanied the king on his visit to Germany in 1743. There he successfully promoted an agreement between Maria Theresa and Frederick II, but his policies were denounced in England as being too subservient to the interests of Hanover, and he was forced to resign in 1744. In the same year he inherited through his mother the earldom of Granville, though he still preferred to be known by his baronial title. In 1751 he was appointed president of the council, a post he held for the remainder of his life, but he played very little active part in political affairs, and in 1761 he declined Newcastle's offer to become prime minister in preference to William Pitt the Elder. Indeed, Pitt later declared that whatever he knew of foreign affairs he learned from Carteret.

8. The rumor was based on the news that Elizabeth promised her Ukrainian lover Alexis Razumovsky to let him take her on a conducted tour of his native land.

9. Lestocq was born in Hanover, where his Huguenot physician father settled after the revocation of the Edict of Nantes (1685). See Chapter I, Note 11, above. George II (reigned 1727-1760) was of course elector of Hanover as well as king of Great Britain.

10. Sweden's peace negotiations with Russia became closely tied to the question of succession to the Swedish throne, the aged King Fredrik being childless and the queen having died in November 1741. The main contenders were Elizabeth's candidate, Adolf Friedrich of Holstein-Gottorp, a kinsman of Karl XII's brother-in-law, and the Danish crown prince Frederik. Swedish agreement to the election of Elizabeth's candidate was a condition of the Treaty of Åbo (1743). Adolf Friedrich married, not an English princess, but the gifted and ambitious Luise Ulrike, sister of Frederick II of Prussia.

11. Peter married his son Alexis to Princess Charlotte of Brunswick-Wolfenbüttel. She died in 1715, three years before her husband, who was hounded to death by his father in 1718. The son of Alexis and Charlotte reigned as Peter II (1727-1730). The Habsburgs were allied to the house of Brunswick through the marriage of the future emperor Charles VI to Princess Elisabeth Christina in 1708.

12. Ludovic Lanczynski was Russian ambassador in Vienna.

13. Empress Catherine I.

14. Following the invasion of Silesia in December 1740 by Frederick II of Prussia, Maria Theresa appealed to her Russian ally for military assistance, but the Petersburg government was still in the hands of Princess Anna, Ostermann and Münnich. Sweden's declaration of war on Russia and Elizabeth's accession to the throne did not help Maria Theresa's cause, despite Bestuzhev's support.

15. The anti-Prussian allies hoped for Russian support for Maria Theresa against Frederick II, but Sweden's declaration of war on Russia thwarted

their plans. Duke Anton Ulrich of Brunswick (1714-1776) was the husband of Anna Leopoldovna, the regent deposed by Elizabeth, and father of the ill-fated Ivan VI (died 1764).

16. Charles VII (reigned 1742-1745) succeeded his father Maximilian Emmanuel as elector of Bavaria in 1726. He was elected Holy Roman emperor in opposition to Maria Theresa's husband Duke Francis of Tuscany. His Bavarian lands were overrun by Austrian troops. He was restored by Frederick II in 1744, but died January 20, 1745.

17. By the Peace of Breslau of June 11, 1742 Maria Theresa ceded to Prussia most of Silesia, which in any case was overrun by the Prussians the previous year. Silesia was held briefly by Austria in 1757, and by the French 1807-1813, but apart from these interludes it remained a Prussian possession from 1741 to 1945.

18. Under the terms of the Treaty of Nystadt (1721) with Sweden, Russia acquired Vyborg and Karelia, and hence control of Lake Ladoga, but returned the rest of Finland to Sweden.

19. Count Anton Corfiz Ulefeldt (1699-1760) was the emperor's ambassador to the Hague in 1733, and from 1739, following the Treaty of Belgrade, to Constantinople. From February 1742 he directed foreign affairs.

20. Namely Silesia. See Note 14, above.

21. See Chapter III, Note 26, above.

22. Brakel was chancellor of the duchy of Courland and Russia's ambassador.

23. She was, in fact, Elizabeth's cousin. M. I. Vorontsov (1714-1767) was a leading figure in the planning and directing of Elizabeth's coup. He was rewarded by a most advantageous marriage and an illustrious diplomatic career. See also Chapter I, Note 8, above.

24. The king resided in the Saxon capital of Dresden rather than in Poland, which he ruled through his agents. The two states were united since 1697 and remained so until the death of Poland's last Saxon king, August III, in 1763. He presided over increasing anarchy in Poland where the powerful Czartoryski and Potocki families acted independently of the state by forming private armies and negotiating directly with foreign courts.

25. Biron was duke of Courland until his disgrace. Although legally Courland was a fief of the Polish crown, it was to all intents and purposes under Russian suzerainty since 1718. It was one of a chain of minor German client-states along the Baltic littoral (the others being Mecklenburg and Holstein) linked by marriage to the house of Romanov.

26. Count Hermann Karl von Keyserling (or Keyserlingk, 1696-1764) was Russia's ambassador to Poland-Saxony three times, from 1733 to 1744, 1749-1752, and 1763-1765. He entered Russian service in 1730, and in 1733 was made president of the St. Petersburg Academy of Sciences. He went on to represent the Russian government at various foreign courts. In Poland he became known as a zealous defender of the Orthodox subjects of that country.

27. See Chapter III, Note 13, above.

28. Maurice of Saxony (1696-1750) was the illegitimate son of August II of Saxony. He was elected duke of Courland in 1726, much to the annoyance of the Polish nobility, but was ousted by Russian troops under Menshikov. He subsequently became an outstanding general in the French army of Louis XV. Soloviev refers to him as Elizabeth's "old suitor," though there is no evidence that they were ever betrothed, or were lovers.

29. The Sapieha clan was an ancient Polish noble family. The Sapieha referred to here is Peter, who in the mid-1720s was a favorite of Catherine I, widow of Peter the Great. The term "elder" (starosta) denotes a provincial administrator in the grand duchy of Lithuania appointed by the grand duke from the local nobility. The elder had judicial, civil and military powers. The Radziwills were another of Poland's great houses.

30. Count Heinrich von Brühl (1700-1763) entered the service of August the Strong in 1730, and in 1733 became president of the Chamber. From 1746 he was the prime minister and favorite of August III, whom he dominated completely. During the Seven Years War he fled with the king to Warsaw, and died soon after his return.

31. The Potocki was one of Poland's leading houses. It was generally anti-Russian, while the dominant faction, the Czartoryski, was broadly pro-Russian. The grand hetman was officially responsible for the country's defense.

32. King August III of Poland was also Elector Friedrich August of Saxony, which at that time was heavily involved in the War of Austrian Succession.

33. See Note 24, above.

34. Adam Tarlo led the Confederation of Dzikow in the cause of Polish independence and suffered defeat by Prussian and Russian troops in October 1743.

35. "Confederation" here means an armed uprising of various members of the *szlachta* (nobility) united by a common cause or grievance, usually in support of the *status quo*. The Polish *szlachta* was proportionately much larger than the Russian *dvorianstvo*, accounting in the eighteenth century for about eight percent of the population. It was headed by a handful of wealthy and illustrious families, below whom was a numerous "middle gentry," neither especially wealthy nor well educated. Members of the "middle" gentry in particular readily sold their sword to any attractive confederation.

36. Livland is the German name for Livonia, the Baltic state between Courland to the south, and Estonia (Estland) to the north. The territory now forms part of Latvia and Lithuania.

37. Fillip Orlik was hetman of Ukraine.

38. A. A. Veshniakov succeeded Ivan Nepliuev as Russian ambassador to Constantinople in September 1735.

39. Miralem was Turkey's ambassador to Russia.

40. The Lezghi, a Dagestani people, were superb horsemen, notorious as slave and cattle raiders on Georgia's northeast borders.

41. Nadir Shah was an inveterate military adventurer, one of whose conquests was India.

42. Vasily Fedorovich Bratishchev served in Persia from 1736 to 1745, first as interpreter then as envoy.

43. The Kabardians are a central Caucasus people.

44. The campaign against Russia in the event did not take place. Nadir Shah was murdered in 1747.

CHAPTER V

1. Anton Magnusovich Divier (1682-1745) was the son of a Portuguese Jew who converted to Christianity and moved to Holland. Being orphaned and destitute in his teens he took service as a cabin boy on a Dutch vessel. He was serving on a ship commanded by Peter the Great on his visit to Holland in 1697, and was recruited by the tsar into Russian service, very quickly mastering the Russian language. He became an aide and later adjutant general with the equivalent rank of colonel, and was the only member of Peter's entourage whose influence rivalled that of Menshikov. In an attempt to enhance his social standing following numerous snubs by boyar families, he pressed his suit for the hand of Menshikov's sister Anna, who was rather plain and getting on in years. Menshikov physically assaulted him, so Divier carried his complaint to the ruler, who ordered that the marriage take place forthwith. When the capital was moved to St. Petersburg in 1710 Divier established his family there, and was appointed chief of police in 1718. He also ingratiated himself with Peter's second wife Catherine, who protected him from Menshikov both during the latter years of Peter's rule and during her own reign. In 1725 he was awarded the order of St. Alexander Nevsky and was made a hereditary count. In 1727 he was sent to Courland to look after Russian interests, and was largely instrumental in annulling the election of Maurice of Saxony (See Chapter IV, Note 28, above). When it became plain that Catherine I was ailing, the question of the succession became urgent. Menshikov was enjoying his triumph just as Divier returned to St. Petersburg from Mitau. Divier naturally threw in his lot with the anti-Menshikov faction. He was arrested, tortured and then sent into exile in the wilderness eight hundred versts from Yakutsk and nine thousand versts from St. Petersburg. His wife, Menshikov's own sister, was exiled to one of the few remaining family estates near Yama. The fall of Menshikov and the accession of Anna apparently did nothing to alleviate Divier's plight, but when his fellow exile Skorniakov was appointed commander at Okhotsk, Divier was summoned

there to help put things in order after the maladministration of Skorniakov's predecessor. In June 1742 a decree from Elizabeth arrived in Okhotsk ending his exile. Arrived back in St. Petersburg he was restored to the rank of adjutant general, given back his order of St. Alexander Nevsky and reinstated in his former position of police chief; but fifteen years of privation and exile took their toll. He died June 24, 1745 and was buried in the cemetery of the Alexander Nevsky monastery.

2. Shubin was a lover of Elizabeth's while she was still in her teens. Empress Anna ordered his tongue to be excised and banished him to Siberia.

3. Kronstadt, on the island of Kotlin, off Petersburg in the Gulf of Finland, was Russia's main naval base and dockyard.

4. It was part of Peter's policy to give Russia good and solid institutions, and to make it thereby a "regulated state." The Chief Magistracy was established in 1721 to supervise the activity of local town councils.

5. A member of the Khovansky clan which was a powerful political force at the end of the eighteenth century during the regency of Sophia. Vasily Petrovich (1694-1747) was an equerry and chamberlain at the court of Empress Anna. Under Elizabeth he was a privy councillor and president of the magistracy.

6. Jacques Savary (1622-1690), author of *Le parfait négociant*, a celebrated guide to business first published in Paris in 1675. It went through numerous editions throughout the eighteenth century, and was translated into many languages, including English under the title The *Universal Dictionary of Trade and Commerce*, (London, 1751-1755). Sergei Volchkov's translation appeared in 1747 under the title *Ekstrakt Savarieva leksikona o komertsii*, and a fuller translation by Vasily Levshin was published in 1787, well over a century after its original French publication!

7. Astrakhan is situated on the Volga river delta near the Caspian Sea, almost 2,500 kilometers southeast of Petersburg. At this time it would have been remembered still as the center of Peter the Great's ruthless suppression in 1706-1708 of the exiled Moscow garrison, the rebellious *streltsy,* who defiantly set up a cossack-style government there. For Mylnikov this five-year appointment, amounting to internal exile, must have seemed a very mixed blessing.

8. Meaning Spitzbergen.

9. The original reads "Shcherbot." The quotation marks are Soloviev's.

10. The Mordvinians, a Finnic-speaking people of western Russia, were christianized later in the century.

11. The languages spoken by the Mordvinians were in fact Erzya and Moksha.

12. Kazan, Astrakhan and the Crimea were successor states to the Golden Horde. Kazan and Astrakhan were conquered by Russia during the reign of Ivan IV. The Crimean khanate continued to exist until 1783.

13. The schism split the Russian church in two in the 1660s. The so-called Old Believers refused to recognize the changes in ritual and emendations to the service books instituted by Patriarch Nikon. See Volume 21 of this series.

14. The Ecclesiastical Statute (Dukhovnyi Reglament) of 1721 laid down the fundamental principles by which the Russian Orthodox Church was to be governed. It remained in force until 1918. It abolished the Russian patriarchate and replaced it by the Holy Synod, through which Peter the Great ruled and reformed the church. For details, see James Cracraft, *The Church Reform of Peter the Great* (London, 1971).

15. See Chapter I, Note 23 and Chapter III, Note 9, above.

16. *Wahres Christentum* was written between 1606 and 1609 by Johann Arndt (1555-1621).

17. Cherkassky's "past sins" were the important political services he rendered Anna Ivanovna, in return for which he became her chancellor, and his support of Biron after her death. He was a man of unlimited wealth and limited intellect.

18. Elizabeth was betrothed to Prince Karl August of Holstein-Gottorp, but he died of smallpox before their wedding could take place.

19. The reference is to the disgraced Ostermann, who played a prominent part in the treaty negotiations, and was awarded the title of baron, becoming a count in 1730 at the time of Empress Anna's coronation. See Chapter I, Note 4, above.

20. A reference to the Treaty of Belgrade (1739), denying Russian ships access to the Black Sea and the Sea of Azov. See also Chapter II, Note 6, above. Wallachia was a Danubian principality under Turkish suzerainty whose independence Russia had aimed at securing in the event of victory over the Turks.

21. Persia retook Georgia from the Turks under the terms of the Treaty of Gandja in 1735 between Empress Anna and Nadir Shah. Russia was happy to have a strong Persian presence in Transcaucasia to counterbalance the Turks.

22. The "peaceful predecessor" was the administration dominated in the 1730s by Arvid Horn, who was anxious to avoid a war with Russia, which he knew his country would have little chance of winning. With his fall from power in July 1741 the Swedish opposition party, with the active and generous support of the French, succeeded in plunging the country into a war of revenge against Russia.

23. Presumably this was meant to be interpreted as a threat to elect the crown prince of Denmark or the prince of Birkenfeld.

24. A reference to the continuing antagonism between Austria and Prussia. It erupted into a new struggle in 1744, and was ended by the Treaty of Dresden in the following year.

25. A small province north of Vyborg.

26. It will be recalled that Ivan Cherkasov was appointed Elizabeth's secretary in the privy chancellery at the start of the reign. See pp. 5-6, above.

27. On Ushakov see above, Chapter I, Note 24; on Golitsyn, Chapter II, Note 3.

28. Field Marshal Peter Lacy was 65 at this point.

29. This was the War of Polish Succession (1733-1735) which was ended formally by the Third Treaty of Vienna in 1738. August III, elector of Saxony, the nominee of Austria and Russia, succeeded his father, August II, in 1733, defeating France's candidate for the Polish throne, Stanislaw Leszczynski.

30. See Chapter III, Note 21, above. It was for his part in the War of the Polish Succession that Lacy won his field marshal's baton.

31. Wielbark ("Vilborg" in the Russian text) is a small town 180 kilometers southeast of Danzig, and the theater of the "unimportant battle" in the War of Polish Succession (1733-1735) to which Yakov refers.

32. Mitava (Mitau), a town in Lithuania, fifty miles southwest of Riga.

CHAPTER VI

1. Reval is an Estonian port due south of Helsingfors on the Gulf of Finland. Nowadays it is known as Tallinn, and is the capital of Estonia.

2. Karlskrona is situated on the south coast of Sweden.

3. Karl XII of Sweden (reigned 1697-1718) repeatedly put off the question of his marriage until after the conclusion of the Great Northern War. Consequently when he was killed campaigning in Norway the succession to the throne was unsettled. The Riksdag therefore elected Charles's sister Ulrike Eleonora as queen, with a highly restrictive constitution, leaving the bulk of power in the hands of the land marshal, head of the aristocratic bureaucracy. Frederick, born 1676, son of Landgrave Charles of Hesse-Cassel (reigned 1670-1730), was recognized as consort. During her reign peace was concluded with Hanover at the price of cession of Bremen and Verden, with Denmark and the return of conquered territory on condition that Denmark keep Holstein, while Prussia retained much of Eastern Pomerania in exchange for a cash indemnity. In 1720 the queen abdicated in favor of her husband, who reigned as Fredrik I (1720-1751). For much of the earlier part of the reign power was in the hands of the land marshal Arvid Horn, who concluded the Treaty of Nystad with Russia and until his overthrow at the end of 1738 pursued a prudent policy of peace and retrenchment. He was replaced by the Hats, led by Count Karl Gyllenborg, who led Sweden into war with Russia in 1744. As narrated here, the war went badly for Sweden, but Elizabeth's government by the Treaty of Åbo gave up the bulk of its conquered territory in exchange for recognition of the Russian-backed candidate Adolf Frederick as heir to the throne. Adolf

Fredrik came to Sweden in 1744 and married Luise Ulrike, sister of Frederick II of Prussia. This and the conclusion of a defensive alliance with Prussia and France in 1747 led to a diminution of Russian influence, though for the last decade of Fredrik's reign the country remained at peace. See also Note 6, below.

4. On Cantemir see Chapter IV, Note 1, above.

5. See Chapter IV, Note 5, above.

6. Friedrich of Hesse-Cassel (1676-1751) married the sister of Karl XII of Sweden, Ulrike Eleonora, who abdicated in his favor in 1720. He succeeded to his Hessian principality on the death of his father in 1730. His Hessian successor Wilhelm VIII (reigned 1751-1760) was an ally of Great Britain in the Seven Years War in support of Prussia. The pro-British policy continued under Landgrave Friedrich II (reigned 1760-1785), who sent military help against the American colonists by the dispatch of nineteen thousand soldiers. See also Note 3, above.

7. Philbert Orry, comte de Vignory (1689-1747), served in various intendancies from 1725 to 1731, when he was appointed controller general of finances in succession to Le Peletier. He faithfully carried out Cardinal Fleury's policies of retrenchment. He reinstituted the dixième in 1731 and 1741 in order to prevent a raising of the taille; he taxed the clergy and balanced the budget. An extreme mercantilist, he established royal monopolies in the manufacture of textiles and paper, and appointed many more factory inspectors. He built the Crozat canal and imposed forced labor on all peasants from the age of sixteen to sixty in order to upgrade the road system. He encouraged trade with French dependencies in Canada and India, and added a wing to the Versailles palace. Eventually he fell out of favor with the king's mistress Madame Pompadour, and was dismissed in 1745. His integrity and haughty demeanor made him many enemies.

8. In 1743 the security police, instigated by Lestocq who hated Austria, alleged the existence of a plot to restore Ivan VI in which the Austrian ambassador, Marquis Botta, was implicated. Although the torture chamber failed to elicit any convincing evidence of guilt, several highly-placed personalities, including two of Petersburg's foremost beauties, Natalia Lopukhina and Countess Anna Bestuzheva-Riumina, wife of the well-known diplomat and sister-in-law of the vice-chancellor, were flogged publicly and had their tongues branded. Lopukhina was sent to Siberia with her husband Stepan who died there in 1748. Subsequently she was released, along with her son Ivan, by Peter III in 1762. See M.T. Florinsky, *Russia. A History and an Interpretation* (New York, 1953), Vol. 1, p. 453 .

9. *Kammerjunker* (chamberlain) was a low rank at the imperial court, granted to young men from aristocratic families.

10. Ivan VI was the son of Prince Anton Ulrich of Brunswick-Bevern-Lüneburg and Anna Leopoldovna of Mecklenburg. He was born in August 1740 and was named heir to the Russian throne under the regency of Biron.

Deposed by Elizabeth in November 1741, he was kept in prison until his murder in 1764.

11. Saltykov as a relative of Empress Anna did not at this time figure in Elizabeth's court, but was living quietly in Ukraine. He survived these insinuations to be appointed commander-in-chief in 1759 during the Seven Years War.

12. Here rendered as "Lewold."

13. Peter and Catherine were married in 1712, three years after Elizabeth's birth.

14. The marshal of the court.

15. Pavel Yaguzhinsky was Peter the Great's procurator general from 1722, and as such the most powerful official in Russia.

16. Julie Mengden was the favorite and lady-in-waiting of Anna Leopoldovna.

17. Evdokia Fedorovna Lopukhina was Peter the Great's first wife. They were married in 1689. She was confined to a convent in 1698 and died in 1731. Catherine Ivanovna (1692-1733), duchess of Mecklenburg, was the mother of Anna Leopoldovna and eldest daughter of Peter the Great's older half-brother Ivan V (reigned 1682-1696). Praskovia was the third daughter of Ivan V.

18. Elizabeth never liked Natalia Lopukhina. She was affronted both by her remarkable beauty and her disrespect, which were particularly evident during Anna's reign. She disliked Anna Bestuzheva almost as much. This antipathy was mutual. Small wonder that Sir Cyril Wych summed up this "dangerous conspiracy" as "the ill-considered discourses of a couple of spiteful and passionate women and two or three young debauchees." While Soloviev discreetly passes over the details, the barbaric cruelty of the sentences, aimed primarily at the physical mutilation of the women involved, shows that Elizabeth herself was equally capable of spiteful and passionate acts.

19. It is surely a remarkable comment on the lot of the serfs in the mid-eighteenth century that while guilty of nothing they were compelled to suffer exile with convicted state "criminals" as their servants and, further, that while these "criminals" were obliged to "make do" with 50 copecks subsistence per day at worst, these servant serfs "were paid" ten copecks a day. It is also worth noting that Soloviev himself refrained from making any kind of observation on this wretched state of affairs.

20. See Chapter IV, pp. 72-76, above.

21. Lord Carteret was clearly well versed in Scandinavian history, formerly having served as ambassador to Sweden. The Union of Kalmar was an attempt to unite the three kingdoms of Norway, Sweden and Denmark in 1397. Its existence, more often than not extremely precarious, was terminated in 1523, when Gustav Vasa seized the Swedish throne. See Chapter IV, Note 7, above.

22. Baron Gustav Johan Gyllenstierna (1709-1764) was the first secretary of the Swedish foreign office. At the 1740-1741 parliamentary session when the Hats were seeking a pretext to attack the Caps, some Hat spies apprehended Gyllenstierna as he was leaving a meeting with Bestuzhev. The Hat party was conservative and drew its support mainly from the nobility and senior officers; it sought revenge on Russia. The Cap party supported the traditions of Arvid Horn and represented chiefly the lower estates; it wanted to avoid war with Russia. Gyllenstierna was arrested and the matter was made as much of as possible since he had close relatives among leading Caps and it was hoped to compromise them. In the ensuing investigation into alleged treason, Gyllenstierna was forced to admit that he was bribed by Bestuzhev and betrayed certain secrets. But it was clear from his vague and contradictory information that he did not have the confidence of the leaders, and that in any case had not much information to pass to them. He was sentenced to death but the estates commuted the sentence to life imprisonment. In any event he was released in 1743 and ended his days on the Livonian estate given to him by Empress Elizabeth.

23. See above, Chapter IV, Note 16.

24. The prolonged absence is explained by the fact that M. P. Bestuzhev started his diplomatic career at Copenhagen when only eighteen, and since had represented Russia in London, The Hague, Hamburg, Hanover, Berlin and Stockholm, returning to Russia only on Elizabeth's accession.

25. In this notation the imperial ambassador is referred to incorrectly as "Neuhausen."

26. See Chapter IV, Note 17.

CHAPTER VII

1. The passage refers to bondsmen who bought their freedom or were granted it on any one of a number of grounds, for example through military service or accepting conversion to Christianity. Compulsory internal passports were introduced by Peter the Great in 1724, designed to restrict rather than facilitate peasant movement.

2. *Raznochinets* was a term applied to those who were not members of any of the standard social categories.

3. See Chapter V, pp. 91-92, above.

4. See above, Note 2.

5. The leader here is referred to ironically as "ataman," a title generally given to a cossack commander.

6. The sect described so graphically below were the *khlysty*, or flagellants, who first appeared in the late seventeenth century. The meeting Soloviev describes was typical.

7. The Old Believers' church, which emerged from the Schism of 1666 opposed to the reforms of Nikon, was mainly concerned with the preservation of traditions and outward display, such as making the sign of the cross with two rather than three fingers, a two-fold alleluia, processionalizing clockwise, and other practices. In the 1670s and 1680s they fiercely resisted the "heresy" of the reformed church, some to the extent of committing mass suicide by fire. More than twenty thousand died in this way. The persecution of the Old Believers continued in the eighteenth century. From 1716 their tax assessment was doubled and from 1722 they were compelled to wear special dress. As previously, they sought refuge in the forests of North and East Russia. Their lot did not improve under Elizabeth, but in 1762 Peter III decreed that Old Believers who had escaped abroad from Elizabeth's persecution might return.

8. D.F. Khovanskaia (1723-49) was a niece of V.P. Khovansky. See Chapter V, Note 5, above.

9. Metropolitan Dmitry Tuptalo ("Rostovsky") epitomized Roman Catholic influence in the Ukrainian church in the seventeenth century. Feofilakt Lopatinsky was a member of the Synod in the reigns of Peter the Great and Catherine I. He died in 1741.

10. On the Zaikonospassk monastery, see Chapter II, Note 9, above.

11. A town in Vladimir province founded in 1152 by Prince Yury Vladimirovich of Suzdal. Many of its ancient churches and monasteries have survived.

12. *Vechnaia pamiat'* (Eternal memory) is sung at the conclusion of the *panikhida,* a funeral or memorial service.

13. Khlynov, also known as Viatka, was the chief town of Viatka province.

14. The so-called "Elizabeth Bible" eventually was published in 1751.

15. The prince of Anhalt-Zerbst was an independent minor prince but in Prussian service in the capacity of governor of Stettin.

16. The War of the Austrian Succession (1740-1748) came at a difficult time for England which had been at war with Spain since 1739 over Jenkins's ear. With France escalating this conflict, England felt able to support Austria in its difficulties with Prussia only to the extent of a £300,000 subsidy. In the campaign of 1743 an Anglo-German "Pragmatic Army" formed at Ostend, advanced along the Rhine, and defeated the French under Marshal Noailles at Dettingen on the Main river on June 27. The conflict next involved Italy where France came to the aid of the Spaniards under the terms of the Treaty of Fontainebleau in October 1743, and finally officially declared war on England, Austria and Sardinia in the spring of 1744. The Saxon ambassador in Petersburg hoped to strengthen the anti-French forces with Russian auxiliaries.

17. The Russian Orthodox Church was traditionally more hostile to the Roman Catholic church than to Protestantism for a variety of historical

reasons. These are most clearly encapsulated in the doctrine of Moscow as the "Third Rome" (1511) which championed Moscow's supreme authority as sole repository of the true faith following the fall of Constantinople and Rome respectively into the hands of infidels and heretics. In any case, it was easy enough to rekindle old Russian fears of Catholic revanchism as with the Polish occupation of Moscow during the Time of Troubles early in the seventeenth century.

18. See Chapter V, Note 18, above.

19. The reference is to the War of the Austrian Succession which was a disaster for the Holy Roman emperor Charles VII (reigned 1742-1745). See Chapter IV, Note 15, above.

20. See Chapter IV, Note 17, above.

21. At the fortress of Dünamünde.

22. In other words, the overthrow of Elizabeth and the restoration of Ivan VI.

23. Simeon Teodorsky (born 1699) was the Ukrainian son of a Jewish convert. He received a Jesuit education and ranked among the most learned Russian Orthodox theologians of his time. It was under his aegis that the work of translating the Bible into Russian was completed. V. E. Adadurov was the first Russian to become a member of the Academy of Sciences (1733). His main achievement was to produce a Russian grammar (1731). He became curator of Moscow University in 1759.

24. *Mémoires de l'impératrice Catherine II et précédés d'une preface par A. Herzen* (Memoirs of Empress Catherine II, also preceded with a preface by A. Herzen) (London, 1859), pp. 10-13. (Soloviev's note). As the young Catherine herself already noted, Elizabeth and her mother did not get on. Elizabeth was irritated by the princess of Zerbst's unwarranted interference in matters of state, and strongly suspected her of being Frederick II's spy, which indeed she was. She eventually overreached herself, was exposed by the watchful Bestuzhev, and expelled from Russia in 1745. The reason for the scene described here is that she was mentioned by Chétardie in his now decoded letters as someone who shared his frustration and resentment at Bestuzhev's direction of Russia's foreign policy. Elizabeth clearly used the opportunity of their visit to the Trinity monastery at Zagorsk to confront the princess of Zerbst with irrefutable evidence of her undesirable opinions and associations. This is why, in the next section, Soloviev archly describes the painful episode of Chétardie's expulsion as "another not entirely unconnected scene."

25. Vorontsov did indeed become vice-chancellor, but not at Bestuzhev's expense. See p. 182, below.

26. They were in fact second cousins.

27. James O'Hara, second Baron Tyrawley (1690-1773), served in the War of Spanish Succession under Marlborough, and was severely wounded at Malplaquet in 1709. Later he served in Minorca, and was awarded the

baronage of Kilmaine by George II in 1723. In 1728 he was appointed ambassador extraordinary to the king of Portugal, where he remained as regular ambassador until 1741, meanwhile succeeding his father to the Irish baronage of Tyrawley. From November 1743 to February 1745 he was ambassador extraordinary to St. Petersburg, after which he returned to England and resumed his military career. In 1752 he returned to Portugal as ambassador and was also governor of Minorca until the Gibraltar expedition of 1756. In 1758 an attempt was made to censure him for his expenditures at Gibraltar, but he exonerated himself with a brilliant display of wit before a committee of the House of Commons. When a Spanish invasion of Portugal threatened in 1762 he was appointed plenipotentiary and general of the British forces but soon afterwards, to his disgust, was retired on account of age. A large mass of his official dispatches from his military and diplomatic assignments, including his posting to Russia, is deposited in the British Museum library.

28. Bestuzhev need not have worried. His promotion to the office of chancellor was a clear indication of the confidence Elizabeth had in his anti-French policy. At the end of the year he was given the requested Livonian estates and received Ostermann's erstwhile residence in Petersburg into the bargain.

CHAPTER VIII

1. Heinrich Gross (died 1765) was a native of Württemberg who, together with his brother Christian Friedrich entered Russian service during the reign of Anna. Christian was implicated in the Chétardie affair and committed suicide while under investigation. Heinrich continued to serve under Cantemir at the Paris embassy and stayed on as *chargé d'affaires* after the ambassador's death. Gross also, in 1758, translated into German Chétardie's *Lettres Moscovites,* together with Cantemir's rebuttal. He then went on to serve as minister plenipotentiary in London, where he died.

2. This reference is rather puzzling, since Carteret was of course foreign minister (1742-1744), not an ambassador. Indeed, his only ambassadorial assignment was to Sweden (1719-1721). He did, however, accompany George II to Germany in 1742 and used his linguistic talents in dealing personally with European rulers and statesmen. See Chapter IV, Note 7, above.

3. In the 1743 campaigns of the War of the Austrian Succession Habsburg success continued with the defeat of a French army at Dettingen on the Main in June. Habsburg forces then crossed the Rhine on July 1. Worried by the Austrians' success and fearful of a strengthening of Maria Theresa's position, Frederick concluded a new secret alliance with Louis XV. Whereupon, in August 1744 the king of Prussia marched through Saxony and invaded Bohemia, taking Prague on September 16.

4. See above, Chapter IV, Note 14.

5. Respectively Frederick I (1657-1713) king from 1701, who ruled from 1688 as Elector Frederick III of Brandenburg, and Frederick William I (born 1688, reigned 1713-1740). Both Bestuzhevs were educated in Berlin in the early years of Peter the Great's reign.

6. See Chapter IV, Note 17, above.

7. See Chapter V, Note 20, above.

8. Frederick II's reign commenced in 1740.

9. Namely the War of the Austrian Succession (December 1740).

10. Frederick's duplicity rapidly became legendary. For example he justified his aggressive occupation of Austrian Silesia, and his spurious claim to the former duchies of Liegnitz, Brieg, Groß-Jägersdorf, and Wohlau by reference to a testamentary union between the duke of Liegnitz and the elector of Brandenburg dating back to 1537! Bestuzhev took a very dim view of the terms of the treaties of Breslau (June 1742) and Berlin (July 1742) which ceded Silesia to Prussia and ended the First Silesian War. As he remarked in the correspondence quoted here, Frederick's word simply could not be trusted.

11. Bestuzhev's prediction was farsighted and proved absolutely correct. Luise Ulrike, sister of Frederick II, was an extremely forceful character who had no difficulty in directing Sweden's foreign policy with an eye to Prussian interests over the head of her feeble husband after he succeeded as Fredrik I in 1751.

12. See above, Chapter IV, Note 23.

13. Karl Gyllenborg (1679-1746) was the first Chancery president (kanslipresident) of the Hats government which ruled Sweden from 1739 to 1756. He served as Karl XII's ambassador in London.

14. The Kalmyks were originally a semi-nomadic Mongol-speaking Buddhist people who moved west from Turkestan in the seventeenth century to occupy the area of the Lower Volga. Like the cossacks, they had a deserved and established reputation as fierce fighters.

15. In the 1738-1739 *Riksdag* (parliament) the Hats brought about a fundamental change in parliamentary procedure. Under the prevailing constitutional practice members of the council could be convicted of failing in their duty to the estates and expelled. Their successors then were proposed by a committee of the three upper estates, and appointed by the king and his councillors. This complicated system permitted a form of parliamentary action which the Hats now implemented for the first time. It resulted in the ascendancy of the estates at the expense of the council, based on seventeenth-century traditions. The system of parliamentary government which resulted from this change was a significant phenomenon in Sweden's Age of Liberty, and it had certain common features with the older English form. The Swedish peasants, traditionally royalist in outlook, were attracted to the Danish absolutism represented by the candidacy for the Swedish

throne of the Danish crown prince Frederik. Yet it was Elizabeth's candidate, Adolf Friedrich of Holstein-Gottorp, who prevailed in the struggle over the Swedish succession. See Ingvar Andersson, A *History of Sweden* (London, 1970), pp. 260-262

16. Gustav II Adolf, king of Sweden 1594-1632, was a formidable ruler and military commander whose armies during the Thirty Years' War took Karelia and Ingria from Russia, Livonia from Poland, and Memel and Pillau from Prussia. In 1631 Gustav overran northern Germany, winning a resounding victory at the battle of Breitenfeld in Saxony. He died in action while securing another victory over Wallenstein's troops at the battle of Lützen in 1632.

17. On Keyserling, see Chapter IV, Note 26, above.

18. Poland and Lithuania were united by the Union of Lublin of 1569. From 1573 religious toleration was accepted as the law of the land.

19. Agreement on mutual toleration by Orthodox and Protestant inhabitants of the western borderlands came about largely as a defensive measure against the militant Catholicism of Sigismund III of Poland. The search for a measure of common action against Sigismund's policies dates from a meeting of leaders from both Protestant and Orthodox communities in Lithuania in 1595.

20. Andrzej Stanislaw Kostka Zaluski (1695-1758), bishop of Chmielno, 1739, bishop of Cracow, 1746. In 1733 he supported the candidacy of Stanislaw Leszczynski, and was an outspoken advocate of political reform. At the Sejm of 1744 he proposed establishment of an overall economic commission. He also encouraged mining and manufacturing on his episcopal lands.

21. Antoni Michal Potocki (1702-1766), *wojewoda bielski.*

22. On Adam Tarlo see above, Chapter IV, Note 34.

23. The Uniates were Catholics of the Slavo-Byzantine rite. They originated with the recognition in 1594 by the Orthodox bishops in Poland of the Pope's authority. The Orthodox liturgy and Church Slavonic as the liturgical language were retained.

24. Stanislaw Leszczynski (1677-1766). An attempt by his son-in-law Louis XV of France to secure for him the throne of Poland was defeated by Ostermann with Austria's help in 1733, by the election of August III of Saxony. See also above, Chapter V, Note 29.

25. Armand du Plessis, cardinal de Richelieu (1585-1642), was the celebrated *premier ministre* of Louis XIII from 1624, who died in office, predeceasing his royal master by a few months

26. On Courland, see Chapter IV, Notes 25 and 28, above.

27. See Chapter III, Note 13, above.

28. In 1457 George of Podiebrad was elected to the Bohemian throne from various foreign sovereigns by the diet of Bohemia, making the claim

of usurpation hard to sustain. It is true that Podiebrad secured the recognition of Ladislas (Vladislav), the posthumous son of Albert V, king of Bohemia and Hungary, as a means of extending Bohemia's alliances and the kingdom's prestige in Europe. But the young king died of tuberculosis in Prague in 1457. See also Note 10, above.

29. Given by Soloviev as *forshneidr* (Vorschneider), evidently one of the honorary court household offices.

30. This is a somewhat sanguine view of Austro-Russian relations. Peter and Leopold always regarded one another with mutual suspicion, and it was only at the conclusion of Peter's reign that signs of a rapprochement with Vienna were discernible. It is true that as an insurance against Turkey Catherine I, having lost French support in Constantinople, concluded an alliance with Austria on very favorable terms in 1726.

31. A scatological pun on Mardefeld's name.

32. Biron was elected duke of Courland in 1737 by a submissive Mitau diet acting under Russian pressure, the election being duly ratified by King August III of Poland. See Florinsky, Vol. I, pp. 447-448.

33. In 1742 Elizabeth permitted Biron to reside on the Volga at Yaroslavl. In 1762 Peter III allowed him to return to Petersburg, and a year later Catherine II restored him to the throne of Courland. In 1769 he abdicated in favor of his son Peter, the last ruling duke of Courland. Ernst Johann Biron died in 1772.

INDEX

THE EDITOR AND TRANSLATOR

Patrick J. O'Meara holds degrees from the universities of Keele, Oxford and Dublin. He was appointed to a lectureship in Russian at the University of Dublin in 1974, was elected a Fellow of Trinity College, Dublin in 1985, and was appointed head of the Russian Department in 1987. He has done research work in Moscow, Washington D.C. (Kennan Institute for Advanced Russian Studies), and Canberra (Australian National University Humanities Research Centre). His main publications have been on the Decembrist movement, notably *K.F. Ryleev. A Political Biography of the Decembrist Poet* (Princeton, 1984), which was translated into Russian and published by Progress. Currently he is completing a major work on the Decembrist Pavel Pestel. For many years he has acted as treasurer of the UK-based Study Group on Eighteenth-Century Russia. The current volume is a reflection of his interest both in the activity of the Study Group and in this period of Russian History.

FROM ACADEMIC INTERNATIONAL PRESS*

THE RUSSIAN SERIES Volumes in Print

*Request catalogs